The Psychological Study

of Literature:

Limitations, Possibilities, and Accomplishments

The Psychological

Limitations, Possibilities,

Study of Literature

and Accomplishments

Martin S. Lindauer

Nelson-Hall Chicago

The stanza from "Under which lyre," which appears on page 105, from *Collected Shorter Poems 1927-1957* by W. H. Auden, is reprinted by permission of the publishers, Random House (U.S.A. and Canada) and Faber and Faber (British Commonwealth).

Library of Congress Cataloging in Publication Data

Lindauer, Martin S.
    The psychological study of literature.

    Bibliography: p.
    1. Literature—Psychology. I. Title.
    [DNLM: 1. Literature. 2. Psychoanalytic inter-
pretation. WM460 L742p]
PN49.L49   801'.92   73-80499
ISBN 0-911012-74-5

Manufactured in the United States of America

To my parents,
Helen and Ben

Contents

This book examines the relationship between psychology and literature—including the literary material itself, the reader, and the author—from a scientific point of view. There are avenues to literature other than the psychological: historical, philosophical, sociological, and of course literary. Within psychology, the orientation toward literature may be nonscientific: anecdotal, illustrative, interpretive, clinical, and psychoanalytic. However, to the extent that these approaches are nonscientific, expository, and discursive, they will not be covered except insofar as they support the thesis that a psychological study of literature is possible, meaningful, and useful. The main focus will be the scientific analysis of literature: the systematic and objective collection of empirical data; the reliance on facts which can be measured, counted, and statistically described and analyzed so as to be publicly communicated; and the concentration on statements which have the potential for being confirmed or rejected.

The objective study of literary materials has been largely ignored or derided by those in psychology, literature, and aesthetics generally. Most psychologists see the psychology of literature as dominated by speculation, mainly in the form of psychoanalysis, while most aestheticians and literary critics think that the scientific analysis of literature is spiritually bounded by the scientism of rat runners and deadened by the weight of massive actuarial tables of statistics.

This book intends to show the inadequacy of these evaluations by psychologists and aestheticians. Part I covers the present neglected state of the objective approach to literature, along with some of the reasons for this lack of adequate consideration. The arguments that favor an objective study of literature are reviewed here also. Part II summarizes concrete examples of psychological research with literary materials and concludes with suggestions for future research. In order to substantiate and illustrate the themes of this book, and to offer as representative and complete a coverage of the field as possible, all available references are included.[1]

This book does not make any attempt to develop a theory about the psychology of literature, its origins, or the audience. Neither does it discuss many issues of general aesthetic interest: differences and similarities between the arts and within an art form (for example, tragedy versus comedy); the role of form, content, and the medium of art expression; distinctions between the truth value of art, reality, imitation, and appearance; the relationship between art as language and as symbol; contrasts between normative and actual responses to art (that is, what one ought to feel versus what one does feel); and the difference between utilitarian and pure art. While empirical studies of these and similar problems would prove useful, they do not exist; objective treatments of these issues and substantial data upon which to build theory are lacking. At this primitive stage of empirical knowledge, speculations and generalizations about the motivation and personality of an author, creativity and its context, the attitudes of the reader, and similarly broad topics are limited by the unavailability or uncertainty of facts, which if known, would markedly affect the present state of knowledge.

To ignore the shortcomings and the paucity of reliable facts in the psychological approach to literature, when these facts could be obtained, limits the methods and conclusions of literature to speculation, opinion, personal convincingness, subjectivity, intuition, examples, and the logic of internal consistency. These types of analysis are acceptable and legitimate criteria and sources of knowledge, and they have achieved a measure of success in the bulk of writings that relate psychology to literature. But these routes to knowledge, when they could be supplemented and extended by empirical techniques, are inadequate.

For these reasons, this book does not attempt to cover the voluminous amount of psychological content to be found in literature and its literary, aesthetic, and philosophical discussions, although it makes some mention of the general relationship of literary analysis to psychology. Although theories of aesthetics and literature rely on and extensively refer to psychological dimensions, their speculations are premature if the facts that might prove useful are absent or in doubt. Thus the book will rely almost exclusively on psychological rather than either aesthetic or literary arguments. Another less defensible reason for the bias against speculative discussions is that, unfortunately, my psychological training and modest nonprofessional literary background prevent me from competently judging materials which arise from literary sources and analyses. This shortcoming is reciprocated by the lack of psychological sophistication of most literary critics.

The goal of this book is to provide rationale and evidence to support the validity of an empirical study of literature, hopefully resulting in a furthering of literary analysis, aesthetic theory, psychological research, and most broadly, interchange between science and the humanities. These activities have not been vigorously pursued within empirical psychology because they were not thought to be serious possibilities. The scientific neglect of literature (along with other aesthetic areas and topics in the humanities) has been responsible for the meager number and low quality of objective efforts in the study of literature. As S. Smith has wryly concluded: "All forms of art, including literature, have tended to be viewed as outside the realm of science."[2] The empirical study of literature has not had an extensive past or a promising future. To modify this static situation is the purpose of this book. The conclusions of the last section suggest specific research directions by means of which the scientific study of literature can be empirically stimulated.

The empirical framework is not designed to replace or usurp the traditional methods and status of literary, philosophic, and aesthetic analysis. The scientific approach is only one of several sources of and approaches to knowledge. It is relevant to only some selected aspects of literature, those which can be shown to lend themselves to empirical examination. Just as there is said to be an art of psychology (for example, in therapy), there is also a science of art.

The broader goal of this book is to encourage a reciprocity between the efforts of psychology and literature: "Being youthful, it would be becoming [for psychology] to learn a few basic truths from literature."[3] Yet the book recognizes that there are boundaries that will limit an interchange between the two fields: "Psychology will not supplant literature, nor will . . . the artist hinder the growth of psychology."[4] While I agree with Barron that psychologists have something to contribute to the "understanding, recognition, and encouragement of art and artists [and] of artistic interests and aesthetic values in general,"[5] the arts can also contribute to psychology. Of the two types of interchange, this book looks more to the contribution of literature to psychology than the reverse, although the two are essentially inseparable.

Notes

1. In keeping with this criterion of completeness, relevant articles noted after the manuscript was completed (about three-quarters of which fell between 1970–73) are appended as Additional References at the end of the book. Supporting the thesis of this book, that the empirical study of literary materials is possible, almost half of these recent contributions are objective investigations.

2. S. Smith, Review of *Psychoanalysis and literary process,* edited by F. C. Crews, *Contemporary Psychology* 16 (1971): 208.

3. G. W. Allport in R. N. Wilson, "Literature, society, and personality," *Journal of Aesthetics and Art Criticism* 10 (1952): 299.

4. Allport in *Psychology in action,* edited by F. McKinney (New York: Macmillan, 1967), p. 348.

5. F. Barron, *Artists in the making* (New York: Seminar Press, 1972). p. xv.

PART ONE

THE STATUS OF AN OBJECTIVE STUDY OF LITERATURE

The psychological study of aesthetics deals with the experience and response to objects of beauty, as well as with their creation and appreciation. The specific concern of aesthetics is with the arts, which (following Barnett's 1959 analysis) may be classified as the fine arts: visual arts, music, literature, architecture, and sculpture; the combined arts: dance, theater, and opera; the applied arts: ceramics and textile design; and the popular arts: motion pictures, popular music, magazine stories, and radio and television plays. Aesthetics and its various divisions are of interest to psychology because each is in some way concerned with human experience and behavior. Aesthetics is a source of knowledge about man, whether it be in dramatically illustrating, clarifying, and explaining psychological themes, generating research ideas, or providing a source of data for further analysis.

Therefore, it would seem that there should be a close rapport between the disciplines of psychology and aesthetics. However, despite the mutual bonds and the potential for close connections, aesthetics is only a minor topic of psychology. Furthermore, of the various fields of aesthetics, literature has received even less attention than the others, especially art and music. Given the possible interchange between the themes of literature and psychology and their potential contribution to each other's goals, the challenge of involvement has been largely met with indifference, if not by an outright denial of any relevance, and by a less than adequate exploration of the possibilities.

Psychology's relationship to aesthetics in general and to literature specifically is treated in chapter 1, which also reviews several reasons for the low status of the arts in scientific psychology. Two major factors that account for literature's minor place in psychology are separately discussed in different chapters because of their prominence. Chapter 2 outlines the psychoanalytical approach to literature and its limitations. Literature's low evaluation of psychology's role, despite its importance in literary analysis, is considered in chapter 3.

The ways in which literature supplements objective psychology are discussed more fully in chapter 5. The parallels and similarities between the arts and sciences are outlined in chapter 4, demonstrating that the orientation and techniques of empirical psychology are applicable to the materials of literature. Chapter 6 illustrates the ways in which the empirical analysis of literary materials has been accomplished in the social sciences exclusive of psychology.

1

Psychology's Neglect

of Aesthetics and Literature

Historical and contemporary psychology have paid little attention to aesthetic problems in general and the field of literature in particular. Evidence of this neglect and several reasons for it are reviewed in this chapter. These stem largely from psychology's development as a science, which supported a view of aesthetics and similar subjective topics as not susceptible to empirical attack. Another important reason for literature's neglect is its particular subtleties as a stimulus object, which seem to make it even more difficult to treat objectively than the other arts. Other reasons for psychology's indifference to aesthetics and literature, including a negative attitude toward psychoanalysis, and literature's own rejection of scientific psychological assistance, are reviewed in chapters 2 and 3.

Psychology as a science

A brief analysis of a few critical historical antecedents in the development of psychology may help account for scientific psychology's limited examination of aesthetics.

Contemporary psychology, as Boring has represented its development, had its major roots in physiology and in the philosophy of eighteenth century British empiricism and associationism. Their approach to the functioning of the body and the structure of the mind encouraged a reductionistic conceptualization of man: the complex was explained by simplifying its components into their smallest units; these were then added together in order to make the whole.

An atomistic model of psychology's methodology and subject matter was supported by psychology's emergence as an experimental science. Primary consideration was given to the development of a suitable methodology. Appropriate techniques were thought to have equal or greater importance than the sources of psychological knowledge. Indeed, psychologists felt that content and validity would almost automatically follow so long as the tools of science were correctly used. This preoccupation was noted by the historian Peters as well as by past luminaries such as William James and most recently by G. A. Miller in his text, *Psychology: The Science of Mental Life.*[1]

As a consequence of these "hard-headed" trends in its history, a rigorous brand of psychology has had little trouble joining with biology and mathematics, and becoming part of the natural, as well as the social and behavioral, sciences. In contrast, psychology's ties with the arts and humanities, particularly literature, have been historically tenuous. Although aesthetics was of major interest to Fechner, one of the first psychologists of the scientific era, his quantification of preferences for nonsense and similarly simple shapes, in an attempt to derive a formula for beauty, represents an approach and a point of view which remained in the reductionist tradition.[2]

The application of a more flexible framework to psychology, while still remaining objective and empirical, came from sources which differed from the mainstream of thought outlined above. From such roots as the philosophy of Kant and phenomenology, European psychologists emerged who termed their subject *Geisteswissenschaft* rather than *Naturwissenschaft* (description versus explanation); their aim was a *Verstehende* or understanding type of psychology.[3] It was not a dogmatically behavioristic point of view, but one open to subjective data and appreciative of knowledge gained by intuition. However, approaches to psychology which include impressionistic data and nonexperimental methodology have been anathema to the rigorous orientation of psychology, especially in the United States, and have only recently been represented in scientific psychology.

Probably the best philosophical discussion of these methodological issues is found in Giorgi's recent critique of psychology. He notes that psychology's historical development was influenced more by the introspective laboratory of Wundt than by the personality theories of Dilthey, Spranger, Stern, and McDougall, and led to the choice of only one of several possible models of science, that of the natural sciences. "Psychology should be far more interested in what happens among social sciences than [among] the natural sciences."[4] Giorgi argues that this decision to imitate and borrow from one particular approach to knowledge has limited and dehumanized psychology's study of man. More qualitative and less reductionistic methods, that is, the historical, cultural, and philosophical, have been ignored. The natural sciences model, continues Giorgi, has led to the priority of measurement over content: "Measurement precedes existence [for academic psychology, so that] a phenomenon *is* to the extent it is measurable."[5] This narrow orientation has led to the exclusion of interesting and relevant topics of human experience, including consciousness, reflection, and the person, because they cannot be successfully measured.

In order to overcome the tensions, disunity, and lack of direction which result from this schism between the content and method of psychology, and to investigate meaningful problems in a meaningful way, Giorgi suggests a humanistic-phenomenological approach. This approach places the study of the person first; the scientific means for accomplishing this will hopefully follow in a manner which is intrinsic and appropriate to this goal.

Although Giorgi's attempt to revise psychology's approach to its subject matter does not deal with literary materials as such, it appears sympathetic to their inclusion. That is, literature does refer in holistic terms to "uniquely human phenomena," which include the personal, subjective, and experiential. "[Literature deals] with human phenomena in a human sense and in a human way, articulating the phenomena of consciousness and behavior."[7]

However, Giorgi exceeds the research cannons of most scientific psychologists by his willingness to give up measurement and experimentation or to give them secondary importance if they do violence to the study of human experience. Another alternative posed by this book, in which new kinds of materials can be incorporated into psychology, is to adapt and modify—but still retain—the methods and techniques (including quantification) of traditional psychology.

The devaluing of a subjective point of view in psychology has led to a methodological purism that ignores and mistrusts the intuitive aspects of knowledge, an attitude which Bakan has brilliantly criticized for its triviality. One consequence has been the neglect of aesthetics (and as a corollary, literature) in psychological research. The antipathy with which the scientist views the artist, regarding the objective point of view as antagonistic to the subjective view, is illustrated in this quote from Wilson:

> It has been thought that brusque manner and awkward expression were the outward signs of scientific respectability, and that the morning coat of the humanities must be renounced for the academic shirtsleeves of the laboratory physicist. . . . Scientists [have] dissociated [the arts] from the empirical study of the springs of human behavior. The arts were [considered] superficial, tenuously clinging to the rim of ultracivilized society.[8]

In fact, argues Lowenthal, there exists a general mistrust between scholars in the humanities and their colleagues in the social sciences.[9] The lower status of the arts in the socie-

ty at large, in comparison to the prestige enjoyed by the
sciences, also matches the attitudes of the professionals involved.

The minor role of aesthetics

Given this conservative methodological context, it is
not surprising to find scientific psychologists reluctant to
study aesthetics. It is difficult to treat materials as data if one
believes that the scientific criteria of objectivity, rigor, accuracy of measurement, and adequacy of control and explanation cannot be satisfactorily or even appropriately
applied. Scientific psychology is consequently really unin-
terested in the arts and humanities.

Psychology's neglect of aesthetics, despite its distinctively human aspects, is apparent when the treatment of
aesthetics is compared against the broad array of topics that
describe the diversity of psychology. The omission of aesthetic topics is pervasive whatever output of psychology
one examines, whether texts, advanced handbooks, reviews,
or analyses of psychology's history and method.

Koch's major six volume review of the field, *Psychology:
A Study of a Science,* has no single chapter which deals with
the arts and humanities, although there are several chapters
which deal extensively with psychology in relation to the
social and behavioral sciences. Somewhat of an exception is
Zener and Gaffron's article on space perception in volume 4
of the Koch series, which refers to art at great length. In
psychology's treatment of its history and theories, a representative text such as Marx and Hillix's *Systems and Theories
in Psychology* is typical. They present a hierarchical arrange-
ment of disciplines which study man, among which is psychology; nowhere is there a reference to the arts or
humanities.[10] A typical text on research design, McGuigan's
Experimental Psychology, is an exception to the general trend in
that it includes music, art, and literature among those subjects thought to be related to psychology. However, these
topics are placed at the periphery of a core of ten other

disciplines (near metaphysical), apparently to indicate that the arts are far removed from those topics thought to be more closely related to psychology.[11]

REASONS FOR NEGLECTING AESTHETICS

In addition to those reasons for psychology's reluctance to study subjective phenomena that are rooted in its history, there are other motives for the neglect of aesthetics. Two related major factors are the multitude of areas into which the different arts can be classified (at least a dozen) and the wide range of disciplines which share a deep interest in aesthetics: psychology, sociology (and other social sciences), philosophy, and of course, the various arts. The resulting diversity of interests and purposes of aesthetics is confusing. This may account for Pratt's complaint that "aesthetics has no clearly defined boundaries or directions [and no themes or models to provide a] common bond or goal."[12]

Berlyne adds a number of other factors, specific to psychology, that have resulted in the neglect of aesthetics. These include an over-reliance on biology and behavioral data to the exclusion of the mental, symbolic, and nonverbal; the consideration of art as nonfunctional, nonadaptive, and unique; the neglect of early research in aesthetics which has thereby prevented the development of a firm foundation in contemporary work; and an overconcern with the normative (good-bad) dimensions of the arts to the exclusion of other aspects.[13] In another context, but still relevant, Berlyne also points out that psychology's narrow preoccupations have led to the neglect of the topics of laughter, humor, and play because, like aesthetics, these "forms of behavior . . . seem to be lacking in 'seriousness' and have, on the whole, not been taken very seriously by psychologists." As a consequence, Berlyne concludes that "current theories [of psychology] have difficulty in accommodating these phenomena, [from which] we must infer that these theories have grave shortcomings."[14]

Literature in the psychology of aesthetics

The psychology of literature has received even less attention than other topics of aesthetics, especially if the psychoanalytic approach to literature—a largely expository interpretation of literary prose which constitutes the bulk of psychological interest in literature—is excluded. Of the many who discuss the relationship between psychology and aesthetics in general terms, those who like Munro and Sparshott look to the scientific possibilities of cooperation between the two fields select their illustrations for discussions of aesthetic issues mainly from the context of art and to a lesser degree music. Most theories of aesthetics ignore literature or give it only slight attention.

Philosophy's neglect of literature in its discussions of aesthetics is acknowledged in a recent essay by B. H. Smith, and it is implicit in the scant coverage of literature in the Weitz reader in aesthetics, which offers small sections on poetry and tragedy only. Greenwood has recently presented an interesting defense of the relevance and usefulness of a philosophical analysis of literature. Many of the justifications for philosophy's involvement with literature are true for psychology: some philosophical works are also literature (for example, Nietzsche); some literary works embody philosophical themes (for example, Tolstoy's *War and Peace*); philosophical analysis of literature assists in its understanding; and philosophical analysis is similar to literary analysis. A concrete example of a logical analysis of the various interpretations of *Hamlet* is found in Weitz. The application of the phenomenological method of analysis is clearly represented by Hynes' review of a book on Joseph Conrad. An excellent introduction to the philosophical approach to literature, which although not empirical remains relevant to many psychological themes, is Ross' *Literature and Philosophy: An Analysis of the Philosophical Novel*.

The field of aesthetics' exclusive preoccupation with nonliterary materials—with the exception of the few writers noted above—has consequently implied that aesthetics means art and art means the visual arts. General discussions of aesthetics, beauty, and the arts are therefore actually oriented toward, ask questions about, and are illustrated by the specialized topic of visual art. Research in aesthetics, for the most part, also really means research in art, as does research in creativity, experimental aesthetics, and aesthetic education. For example, the classic quantitative treatment of aesthetics, Birkhoff's *Aesthetic Measure,* devotes only one chapter to literary materials and that to poetry only; the others refer to visual materials. This narrow definition and treatment of aesthetics, in which literature is ignored, has been surprisingly overlooked by critics of aesthetics, such as Bloom and E. Murray, who concentrate only on its deficiencies in the field of art.

In a rare reference to literary materials, found in one of the few reviews of aesthetics in a psychological journal, Pratt notes psychology's cursory treatment of literature. Not unexpectedly, his remark is placed in a footnote: "Far more attention is given to those arts in which form predominates, than to those in which words are the fleeting clues to meaning and ideas."[15] Many recent and comprehensive surveys of aesthetics, including those by Farnsworth, Langfeld, McWhinnie, and Valentine, also reflect the minor status of literature by their scant attention to the field.

For example, one of the most prolific reviewers (and workers) in the field is Child. His 1968 review makes passing mention of literature in an otherwise almost exclusive coverage of art, the artist, and the observer of art. His 1969 discussion of the psychology of literature takes up less than 10 percent of almost seventy pages. His most recent 1972 review also contains only a few pages on literature, mainly limited to psychoanalytic contributions, and a discussion of general aspects of language which may have some bearing on literature.

McCurdy's review of the psychology of literature

rightly notes that it is "ignored, yet a natural subject [of psychology]."[16] The most recent and extensive psychological theory of aesthetics, Berlyne's *Aesthetics and Psychobiology*, places no special stress on literature, paying the most attention to visual material. Psychology's lack of interest in literature also holds true for the older work on psychological aesthetics: fewer than 10 percent of some two thousand references listed by Chandler and Barnhart for the period 1864–1937 refer to literature, and half of those deal with poetry.

While there are some exceptions to the paucity of literary analysis in psychology, these are limited in various ways. Nixon's early review of literature in a psychological context is restricted to those studies which might aid and supplement the writer's practical skills. Holsti has the most extensive but still brief and scattered survey of empirical studies of literature. However, his purpose was to illustrate the advantages and possibilities of content analysis within a sociological context. An outstanding exception to the preoccupation with art is Vygotsky's *The Psychology of Art*, in which literary rather than art examples abound. However, his theory has not been sustained by active research efforts.

Evidently, despite Ogden and Richard's twenty or so definitions of beauty, most discussions of aesthetics have apparently not been able to apply such definitions to literature. Sartre's arguments in favor of the importance of the writer have obviously not been heeded. Unlike other contributors to aesthetics, notes Sartre, the writer uses language as a direct instrument of communication. He therefore should have more of a significant effect in directing and guiding our perceptions than the artist or musician, according to Sartre. Nevertheless, there exists an impoverished relationship between psychology and literature. While noting that they both talk about the same things, Malmud has expressed his dismay over the chasm that exists between the two.

REASONS FOR NEGLECTING LITERATURE

Humanistic psychologists, like Royce and Bugental, although they have not rejected the applicability of literature to psychology, have expressed their uneasiness about the relationship. Despite their sympathies to both art and science, they think most psychologists see the two as largely separate and distinct. Shoben makes this point by noting that scientists, unlike poets, cannot (and should not) evoke either the richness of human life or what is humanly felt. He argues that psychological statements cannot reflect the same sort of warmth as those written by a writer, nor can psychological theory indicate "an appreciation of the poignancy, the heartache, the gayety, and the dignity of human life." To ask this, Shoben continues, is to request too much, if not the wrong thing, of psychology: "It is the poet's job rather than the scientist's to describe events in such a way as to evoke a sense of participating in them, of experiencing rather than accounting for experience."[17]

Skaggs amplifies this discouraging view of literature's relevance to science by arguing that science is supposed to be removed from everyday experience and thus cannot portray or understand nature as the novelist does. One reason for this, asserts F. Wyatt, is that the available techniques of psychology cannot properly assess the unique case, especially when it is from the past. It is the unique case which so essentially characterizes the content of literature. Lana is even more pessimistic: "To say that literary analysis of social situations will eventually be reducible to the terms of psychology is useless, both for the current understanding of social activity and for the promise of future development."[18] At best, many psychologists have agreed with Osgood, writing about psycholinguistics in general, that while literature has a great potential, there has been little fulfillment of its promise.

The nature of literary materials.   A closer look at the basic nature of literature as a stimulus-object, in contrast to the

other arts, may help account for the disparity of psychological interests between these different fields of aesthetics.

Most of the arts depend upon a perceptual event whose
stimulus properties are relatively specific and concrete. The
visual and auditory sources of art and music, although still
extremely complex, are considerably easier to define, measure, and manipulate than the verbal material of literature.
It is therefore possible to describe the structure of nonliterary aesthetic events with relatively greater ease, to simulate
them, and ultimately, to relate them functionally to the
processes of creativity in the artist, to the concrete outcome
of their efforts, and to the observer's response of appreciation. The greater subtlety of the writer's craft is indicated
by comparing his relatively brief formal training, if any at
all, with the immense technology and extensive formal education necessary in art and music.

Literature as a stimulus, on the other hand, is manifested more indirectly and symbolically in language. The source
of the literary response greatly depends upon the evocation
of subtle and covert associations and images. These refer
less to denotable elements of perception, as do art and music, than to cognition and thought (although these, too, are
part of all the arts). For example, compare the difficulties in
measuring words with the relative ease of exactly specifying
forms, colors, and sounds. Eysenck has discussed this distinction between the arts and literature in terms which distinguish their empirical possibilities:

> [The arts] in contrast to [novels and drama are] of major
> interest to psychologists because they alone lend them-
> selves easily to measurement and, hence, to the formu-
> lation of laws and the accumulation of experimental
> evidence so desirable when exact statements of rela-
> tionships are required.

The consequence, according to Eysenck, is that literature has
a reduced potential for quantification:

> [A novel] deal[s] with content rather than with form.
> It is subjective rather than objective. It does not make
> exact statements in numerical form, but rather tries to
> convey impressions by means of words. These features
> ... render it somewhat suspect to the scientist.[19]

Pratt has argued for a distinction between the arts and literature along similar lines:

> The formal or the fine arts lend themselves to scientific
> analysis ... more readily than do the verbal arts [which
> are] a large domain of psychological experience difficult
> to get at except from the philosopher's sturdy old arm-
> chair.[20]

Put another way by MacDougall, the difficulty lies in literature's special use of language, a vehicle of communication
which even in ordinary conversation is a source of confusion. To this list of problems of language and quantification,
McCurdy adds that of the disruptive emotions aroused in
the reader, which contribute further difficulties to the un-
masking of the author's covert intentions.[21]

   In short, a major difference between the susceptibility
of the arts and literature to empirical investigation is the
relative ease with which one can study their causes and
effects. The arts are based on an immediate and spontaneous
visual or auditory perceptual experience, message, or impression; prose materials depend on less articulate, delayed,
and mediated cognitive judgments. These practicalities of
research have led to a neglect of the empirical study of
literature and a reluctance to treat literature within the
theoretical boundaries of general psychology.

The consequences.   There are several serious consequences
to psychology's inattention to literature. For one, literature

has rarely been tied to psychological theories, as has art, for example, with gestalt psychology.[22] Art within gestalt theory is represented by Arnheim's *Art and Visual Perception* and his *Entropy and Art.* Although language is treated in his *Visual Thinking,* it is in terms of the perceptual images evoked. An exception to gestalt psychology's almost exclusive concern with art is Koffka's discussion of the actor's techniques. Gibson's field theory of perception does discuss writing and language but does not use literary examples. There are theories of aesthetics which have been linked to attention and motivation rather than perception, like Peckham's, but these characteristically exclude literary examples. One minor exception to the neglect of literature in psychological theory is Moles', which includes a brief discussion of the relevance of information theory to poetry and the theater. Cooperation between a psychologist and a literary critic, as in Maier and Reninger's joint effort, *A Psychological Approach to Literary Criticism,* is rarely found.

Literature has also not been related to research topics of general experimental psychology, as have art and music. The reviews by Deutsch and Wallach, which emphasize the use of musical materials in the context of several lines of investigation, illustrate literature's omission. Further, literature has not been extensively used within an applied context, as Meier has indicated is the case with art (for example, in art therapy) and as R. A. Smith has noted in art education.

A final contrast between the limited place of literature in psychology and the broad relevance of art should illustrate the low status of literature. Literary materials have not usually been considered relevant to an understanding of civilization and its development, as this quote suggests has been the consideration of art: "Art has been, and still is, the essential instrument in the development of human consciousness. . . . Not a fortuitous activity, not secondary or superfluous, but absolutely essential if the human mind does not want to cripple itself. [Art enables men] to comprehend the nature of things."[23] Such claims for the rele-

vance of literature to psychological concerns are virtually
nonexistent.

Notes

1. W. James, *The principles of psychology* (New York: Dover,
1950), chap. 7.

2. M. S. Lindauer, "Toward a liberalization of aesthetics," *Journal of Aesthetics and Art Criticism* 31 (1973): 459–465.

3. B. B. Wolman, *Contemporary theories and systems in psychology* (New York: Harper, 1960), chaps. 10–12.

4. A. Giorgi, *Psychology as a human science: A phenomenologically based approach* (New York: Harper & Row, 1970), p. 21.

5. Ibid., p. 65.

6. Ibid., p. 185.

7. Ibid., p. 205.

8. R. N. Wilson, "Samuel Beckett: The social psychology
of emptiness," *Journal of Social Issues* 20 (1964): 62.

9. L. Lowenthal, "Literature and sociology," in *Relations of
literary study: Essays in interdisciplinary contributions,* edited by J.
Thorpe (New York: Modern Language Association, 1967),
pp. 89–110.

10. M. H. Marx & W. A. Hillix, *Systems and theories in
psychology* (New York: McGraw-Hill, 1963), table 3, p. 34.

11. F. J. McGuigan, *Experimental psychology: A methodological
approach,* 2nd ed. (Englewood Cliffs, N. J.: Prentice Hall,
1968), figure 1.1, p. 2.

12. C. C. Pratt, "Aesthetics," *Annual Review of Psychology* 12
(1961): 71.

13. D. E. Berlyne, "The psychology of aesthetic behavior." Talk given to the Department of Art Education, Pennsylvania State University, 1968, Penn State Papers in Art
Education, no. 5.

14. Berlyne, "Laughter, humor, and play," in *The handbook
of social psychology,* 2nd ed., edited by G. Lindzey & E. Aron-

son (Reading, Mass.: Addison-Wesley, 1969), vol. 3, pp. 795–796.

15. Pratt, 1961, p. 74.

16. H. G. McCurdy, "The psychology of literature," in *International encyclopedia of the social sciences,* edited by D. L. Sills (New York: Macmillan & Free Press, 1968), vol. 9, p. 425.

17. E. J. Shoben, "Psychological theory construction and the psychologist," *Journal of General Psychology* 52 (1955): 187.

18. R. E. Lana, *Assumptions of social psychology* (New York: Appleton-Century-Crofts, 1969), p. 158.

19. H. J. Eysenck, *Sense and nonsense in psychology,* rev. ed. (Baltimore: Pelican, 1958). Both quotes are from pp. 331–332.

20. Pratt, 1961, p. 85.

21. McCurdy, in Sills, 1968.

22. Pratt, Introduction to *The task of gestalt psychology* by W. Kohler (Princeton: Princeton University, 1969), pp. 3–29.

23. H. Read, *Icon and idea: The function of art in the development of human consciousness* (New York: Schocken, 1965), pp. 17–18.

2

The Dominance of Psychoanalysis

in the Psychology of Literature

A general review

The greatest psychological interest in literature has come from psychoanalysis, in both its classical and modern versions, and it is for many authors, such as Kris and Roback, synonymous with the phrase "psychology of literature." An examination of the titles and journals cited in Kiell's bibliography indicates that about 90 percent of approximately 4,500 psychological references to literature are psychoanalytic or psychiatric orientations. (The bulk of these are nonempirical—hence the brevity of this chapter's review.) According to Crews, "Psychoanalysis is the only psychology to have seriously altered our way of reading literature. [There are no] possible literary implications of physiological psychology, of perception and cognition psychology, or of learning theory [or] Gestalt psychology."

The reason for this, continues Crews in a similarly grand manner, is that "literature is written from and about motives and psychoanalysis is the only thoroughgoing theory of motives that mankind has devised."[1]

In addition to motives, adds Crews, Freudianism is also especially endowed to deal with such topics as emotional conflicts, latent themes, and subliminal effects, to expose the writer's innermost thoughts, and to explain how a literary work is received and judged. Similarly, Holland argues that psychoanalysis "is the only psychology I know that can talk about an inner experience with as much detail and precision as a New Critic can talk about a text.... Psychoanalytic psychology offers a more valid and comprehensive theory of inner states than any other."[2] Despite the extensive interest of psychoanalysis in literature, Roback and Baskin's review of the psychoanalytic publications has nevertheless complained that their role in literature is relatively minor:

It is one of the unaccountable curios that although [the psychoanalytic variants of] psychology and literature deal with the same subject-matter, viz., imagery, ideas, emotions, feelings, and so on, the psychology of literature has received but scant treatment ... there is no systematic textbook or treatise which covers the growing borderland.[3]

Freud's psychoanalytic approach to works of art, their creators, and the audience, as represented in several of his briefer works (for example, on the poet and daydreaming), depends on various unconscious mechanisms. These indirectly reveal substitutions and compensations for deep-seated problems of growth and personality. Freud's thesis considers the literary imagination similar to any other product of imagination, especially dreams. Creative products are a symbolic manifestation and gratification of unconscious wishes and fantasies. The readers of literature and the audience in general are said to respond unconsciously to the disguised content inherent in creative productions. They react to the repressed pleasures and satisfactions which art evokes and which also happen to be the author's means of working "his way back to reality."[4] In these dynamic terms, Freud has discussed the lives and works of many authors and artists: Shakespeare, Dostoevski, Ibsen, Leonardo da Vinci, Michelangelo, Heine, Goethe, Homer, and Balzac;

and he has also used Greek plays and characters (for example, Oedipus), fairy tales, legends, and myths for illustrative purposes. Ego psychology (a contemporary extension of classical Freudian psychology represented by such authors as Rapaport, Slochower, and Withim) differs from traditional psychoanalysis in placing greater emphasis on the more conscious forces in creativity.

Other contemporary depth psychology studies of literature, as sampled in *Literature and Psychology,* a journal which specializes in that approach, or in Mannheim and Mannheim's collection from that journal, appear to rely as much on Jung as Freud.[5] Even more than Freud, Jung uses myth and legend as sources for many of his key concepts, although contemporary works (for example, Joyce's *Ulysses*) are examined as well. Jung's approach is opposed to Freud's in that he views creativity as a more positive force. Rather than derived from and dependent upon other instinctive sources, and their conflicts and resolutions, as Freud saw it, creativity exists as a unique and autonomous force of its own.

These and other psychoanalytic views of the author's personality and creativity, comprehensively and intelligently summarized by Holland, have been well received by only a few psychologists such as McCurdy and Rosenzweig, but by many more literary critics like Auden, Edel, and Ransom, especially as such analyses reveal new meanings in an author's works.

Literature's evaluation

Despite the popularity of psychoanalysis, neither the Jungian nor Freudian views have been uncritically accepted within the mainstream of literary criticism. A summary of some typical reactions follows. Goldstein holds that most critics either deny psychoanalytic criticism or assign it a minor role mainly because of resistance arising from ignorance. Even those critics who assign psychoanalysis a major role, Goldstein continues, show a certain degree of provincialism and lack of openness to varied and interdisciplinary efforts. Of those who are psychoanalysis' most severe critics, Carmichael has objected to those oversimplifications of psychoanalysis that disparage a literary effort by interpreting it as something other than it is. Evaluating a work as merely fantasy, as unreal, or as disguised irrationality denies the possibility that literature also validly clarifies the world and enables it to be more realistically grasped. Rothenberg also sees psychoanalytic views as limited, forced, and rigid because of the omission of literary qualities.

> But an emphasis on the Oedipal conflict is virtually a psycho-literary cliché, and the conflict is often considered the be-all and end-all explanation for everything in a literary work. The reader and critic are seduced away from the rich subtleties and cognitive processes within the work.[6]

These critical comments are by S. Smith and Lucas, respectively:

> Criticism based on analytic principles is suspect because its aim is not to reveal the lofty nature of literature but to examine its very bowels. . . . There is more to life than infantile conflicts and more to a work of artistic creation than the sum of the author's conflicts.[7]

> The unconscious may be the dark abyss whence rise the inspirations of genius; but I do not see dramatists and the public descending to the bottom of it for an afternoon's entertainment.[8]

Other criticisms are more moderate and accommodating. Mazlish supports the Freudian contribution to any historical type of analysis. He notes that while psychoanalysis, in reducing a subject to psychology, does not explain or give causes, it can assist understanding. Edel admits to psychoanalysis' excesses, but he nevertheless defends its value in biographical analysis. Fraiberg also maintains that psychoanalysis complements ordinary literary analysis: it helps in the elucidation and apprehension of the literary experience. Roback and Baskin have also commented on the need to balance psychoanalytic with literary analysis, especially if the literary treatment can be separated from an analysis of the personality of the author:

> The psychology of literature is something apart from its producers and must be envisaged in relation to life [and to the interpretation of the literature itself].[9]

Eissler points out the necessity of making a distinction between the analysis of the work itself and an analysis from without (that is, in terms of the author's life). He makes another relevant distinction between psychoanalysis as explanation (for example, the Oedipus complex of Hamlet) and as a personal rather than literary aid to understanding. He also reminds us that while Freud used literature to illustrate and apply previously established clinical and theoretical assumptions, the psychoanalytic analysis of literature also was an impetus to new inquiries and thought. Psychoanalytic criticism is therefore open to modification and change.

The most extensive (and extreme) defense against the criticisms of literary psychoanalysis comes from Crews, who finds little justification for its detractors, denies most deficiencies, finds its speculations cautiously presented, and sees the problems that remain as minor. Discussions of psychoanalysis in all its variations are not confusing, asserts Crews, nor is their jargon an over-riding factor in their comprehension. Crews also denies that the writer is necessarily neurotic (these forces are sublimated, though), that everything is reduced to sex or the unconscious, or that form is ignored for the sake of content. In response to criticisms of methodology, Crews contends that psychoanalysis can be tested and verified (although only in part because of its complexities): "The confirmation and refinement of Freud's discoveries have been proceeding in a fairly orderly way for many years."[10]

Holland also finds objections to psychoanalysis to be based on "an extraordinary variety of misconceptions." In extending psychoanalysis to its effects on the audience and reader, Holland feels that the model offers hypotheses that can be tested by experiments that may either confirm or deny their validity. However, his theory remains based on subtle, complex, and arcane phenomena, for example, oral conflict, defense, fixation, and introjection, which even in nonliterary studies have proven difficult to test. For example, a potentially testable statement of Holland's, regarding the reader's reaction to literature, includes the proposition that there is a suspension of belief, which also involved "a partial, selective, ego-syntonic ego-regression, an extension of ego boundaries downward to the level of basic trust . . . a kind of fusion or introjection based on oral wishes to incorporate."[11]

Holland's proposed hypothesis testing also depends on instruments which are extremely difficult to use successfully, those of interviews and projective tests. Even Crews has labeled Holland's attempt to be scientific as "limited [because it does] not capture the literary enterprise," by which Crews means the capacity to be moved or personally involved. In fact, continues Crews, most efforts to put Freudian analysis on sounder logical and empirical bases have led to narrow and circumscribed "trivialization." The psychoanalytic contribution to literature is therefore a personal one, one which Crews feels is negotiated by the ego and thus cannot be a basis for evidence. Crews sees the search for evidence as indicating "shallowness," "folly," and "naivety." Perhaps these feelings are the basis for his disparaging evaluation of the scientific status of contemporary psychoanalysis:

Unfortunately, Freud's achievement is entangled in an embarrassingly careless scientific tradition. The slowness of psychoanalysis to purge itself of unsubstantiated folklore and outmoded concepts [and reifications and oversimplifications] cannot be denied. . . . The virtual hibernation of psychoanalysis during the current period of revolutionary gains in natural science is cause for dismay.[12]

Psychoanalysis, psychology, and literature

While social scientists have been moderate in their evaluation of psychoanalysis and have referred to its tenets to varying degrees,[13] academic (that is, nonclinical, nonanalytic) psychologists have generally viewed psychoanalytic efforts disdainfully or dismissed them altogether. Their essential criticism has been that psychoanalytic concepts are used too facilely, proving anything—and therefore nothing. This point is most sharply illustrated in a quote from Eysenck, one of psychoanalysis' most outspoken critics, in response to E. Jones' analysis of Shakespeare's personality in the characterization of Hamlet:

To make such a diagnosis of a person 300 years dead, of whose life practically nothing is known, on the strength of a few lines probably, but not certainly written by that person, on the basis of a story already existing at that time in several different forms, seems to be a somewhat exaggerated claim. Whether the reader feels that the explanation given by Jones is a likely one or not, he will agree that the whole process of arriving at this explanation is a literary rather than a scientific device, and while it undoubtedly is more colourful than the more sober scientific type of research, it can hardly aspire to the same degree of confidence in its conclusion.[14]

Eysenck concludes that this type of approach to literature indicates "the utter impossibility of subjecting these analogies to any rational test of truth or falsehood." Even a writer once as enthusiastic as Roback seems to have become less positive about the value of psychoanalysis. He notes its excesses and noncritical simplifications ("fanciful extrapolations") with distress; and he now feels that existential psychology is more relevant to an understanding of present-day literature.[15] Contemporary ego psychology, a psychoanalytic position with closer ties to general psychology, the topic of perception, and gestalt theory, just about ignores literary creativity, looking instead to artistic behavior in its arguments and illustrations. Ehrenzweig, for example, discusses jokes as the most suitable verbal materials that bear investigation. Even McCurdy, an early and staunch advocate of Freud, recently reached this relatively harsh conclusion:

> [There has been a] failure . . . to gather any particular forward momentum. No very significant developments have taken place . . . beyond the initial work of the master. Freud thought of psychoanalysis as a science, i.e., as a discipline capable of making discoveries. . . . Unfortunately, the application of psychoanalysis to Shakespeare has not meant making discoveries, nor has it led to studies that build progressively from one sure point to another with cumulative effect.

He sees the relevance of literature to psychoanalysis as quite limited:

> it has meant the use of Shakespeare to illustrate some view already held by the analyst or to serve as the starting point for his own quasi-dramatic efforts. There is nothing wrong, of course, with using literature to illustrate a point, nor is there anything wrong with allowing a great poet to set off a train of ideas in some-

one else. . . . But neither can give us a science . . .; nor does either give us the sort of literary criticism which sets the literary work in the lucency of its own unique virtues.

He concludes with this rather negative evaluation:

70 years of psychoanalytic examination of Shakespeare has yielded neither a systematically pursued distinctive method of approach, nor fundamentally novel results, except insofar as the grafting of the mythology of psychoanalysis onto the parent stock of literary criticism may have brought to flower some isolated illuminations or illusions, as the case may be, bearing on what Shakespeare meant, or how his creative mind worked, or what the connection was between the content of his plays and his life history.[16]

The strong identification between the psychology of literature and the psychoanalytic movement, a field whose status in contemporary psychology and literary criticism is largely suspect because of its methodological and conceptual shortcomings, is an indirect yet powerful reason for general psychology's cautious and skeptical attitude toward or even outright rejection of literature. Psychology's avoidance of the psychoanalytic orientation has also possibly contributed to a reluctance to study personality through literature. Many psychologists think it premature to take the ambiguous route to knowledge offered by literature, whether it be via the author, his characters, or plots, in the difficult search for an understanding of personality. The richness and diversity of the highly complex and subtle area of personality, regardless of its psychoanalytic overtones, is already considered by many as having a surfeit of both theory and data.[17] However, most literary critics' reactions to psychologizing are just to these variants of psychology, psychoanalytic theory and the topic of personality, conceptions and fields of research which actually hold only minor status in empirical studies. Hence, it may not be too surprising if literature's reactions to psychology are less than balanced.

Notes

1. F. C. Crews, "Literature and psychology," in *Relations of literary study: Essays on interdisciplinary contributions,* edited by J. Thorpe (New York: Modern Language Association, 1967). The quotes are from p. 73 and p. 74, respectively.

2. N. N. Holland, *The dynamics of literary response* (New York: Oxford, 1968), p. xv.

3. A. A. Roback & W. Baskin, "Psychology of post-Freudian literature," in *New outlooks in psychology,* edited by P. Powers & W. Baskin (New York: Philosophical Library, 1968), p. 406.

4. S. Freud, *A general introduction to psychoanalysis* (New York: Permabooks, 1953), p. 384.

5. A particularly clear secondary source is C. S. Hall & G. Lindzey, *Theories of personality* (New York: Wiley, 1957), chap. 3. Original sources by Jung are noted in the references.

6. A. Rothenberg, Review of *The sins of the father: Hawthorne's psychological themes,* by F. C. Crews, *Transaction* 6 (1969): 676.

7. S. Smith, Review of *Psychoanalysis and the literary process,* edited by F. C. Crews, *Contemporary Psychology* 16 (1971): 208, 210.

8. F. L. Lucas, *Literature and psychology,* 2nd ed. (Ann Arbor: University of Michigan, 1957), p. 38.

9. Roback & Baskin (1968), p. 420.

10. Crews, 1967, p. 77

11. Holland, 1968. The quotes are from p. xv and p. 104, respectively; see also pp. 315 ff.

12. Crews, "An aesthetic criticism," in *Psychoanalysis and literary process,* edited by F. C. Crews (Cambridge, Mass.:

Winthrop, 1970). The quotes are from pp. 18, 21, and 17, respectively.

13. See for example S. Koch, *Psychology: A study of science* (New York: McGraw-Hill, 1963), vol. 6.

14. H. J. Eysenck, *Sense and nonsense in psychology,* rev. ed. (Baltimore: Pelican, 1959), p. 339.

15. In Roback & Baskin, 1968, p. 425.

16. McCurdy, Review of *The design within: Psychoanalytic approaches to Shakespeare,* edited by M. D. Faber, *Contemporary Psychology* 16 (1971): 116.

17. Hall & Lindzey, 1959, chap. 7.

3

Psychology's Role in Literature

Literary arguments against scientific psychology are discussed in this chapter, along with counterarguments intended to show that outright rejection of a scientific viewpoint in literature is unwarranted; some meaningful compromise between literature's subjectivity and psychology's objectivity is possible. Psychology's past and present usefulness to literature will also be briefly discussed, although the main task of this book is to encourage psychology's involvement with literature, rather than the reverse.

Literature's rejection of psychology

Many literary critics have been pessimistic regarding any reciprocity with psychology. Objections are raised not only to psychoanalysis but also to the more objective psychological approaches. A scientific approach to literature, were it even considered possible, would be judged as trite, narrow, and irrelevant. Thus Krutch views general psychology as severely limited in its potential for an understanding of literature (if not of man as well). Stegner puts it this way:

It would be the wildest folly to think of reducing art to the laws and the orderliness that are the ideal and monumental strength of science. Only a philistine world would even attempt it. For art reduced to law and order is only a cliché.[1]

Stegner's critique of a scientific psychology of literature is worth considering at some length because of his temperateness, extensive treatment, and clarity. First he admits that science and art are similar in some creative ways:

> At their most creative edge, science and art both represent original questionings, pure research, and both rely upon a galvanizing and originating intuition.[2]

However, they are similar only up to a point. They differ not only in their proofs but in their approaches to the same problems:

> When a science and an art accost the same materials, the same apparent problems, it becomes very clear that they ask a different kind of question.

Further, the two do not use their findings in the same way:

> When scientific research has succeeded, moreover, and has reached the stage of public verification, it is open to exploitation as technology, whose function is the reproduction of useful goods, but when art has unveiled some truth and it has become everybody's property and the method of its unveiling is part of everybody's technique, its name is stereotype, and stereotype is not valuable in artistic matters, whatever it may be in an industrial world dedicated to mass production and interchangeable parts.

Nor does literature use accumulated prior knowledge in the way science does:

> Artistic insights tend to remain discrete; they do not

necessarily make the building blocks of future insights; the traditional accumulates less by accrual than by deviation and rebellion.

Stegner argues that art goes beyond science, in that it is not understood by analysis but by exposure; its results are not reducible to laws. To seek such orderliness in literature, he continues, is to miss the essence of a literary work, a goal that can only be pertinent, moreover, to each specific reader. Stegner asserts that although literature may not be truth in the verified and verifiable sense, it is not inferior to such information; it is a kind of exemplary knowledge which remains nevertheless interesting. Stegner then states more explicitly the type of knowledge which literature does contribute.

But if literature is not "knowledge" in the scientific sense, it is a clarified, selected, and purified model of life, complete with the values that life evolves and preserving even the distressingly awkward variables. It is built on a framework of symbolic conventions, but it is the farthest thing from arbitrary, even when it experiments or revolts.[3]

Stegner approvingly quotes Conrad on the personal goals of literature:

The power of the written word to make you hear, to make you feel ... to make you see. That ... is everything. If I succeed, you shall find there ... that glimpse of truth for which you have forgotten to ask.[4]

Stegner then indicates the dangers of applying an objective approach to literature:

And if we are ever tempted to write or read by the rules of the quantitative method, if we ever approach litera-

ture as if it were "subject matter," we would do well
to remind ourselves that the love and appreciation of
literature come by exposure, by a meeting, not through
paraphrase or explication.[5]

Martin has also unfavorably evaluated the outcome of objective psychology's attempts to understand creativity and
its conditions. "Experimental psychologists have succeeded
so far only in confirming rather obvious and sometimes
trivial facts."[6] He sees sociology and psychoanalysis, and
perhaps the concepts (but not the achievements) of gestalt
psychology, as more suitable alternatives to scientific psychology.

    Wellek and Warren also note, in an otherwise favorable
essay, several limitations to a more scientific approach to
literature. Literature is not a good source of psychological
information about the mind of the author, they point out,
because dramatization is a form of falsification. Dramatic
liberties result in artistic but not psychological truth. They
also criticize psychology (especially psychoanalysis) for the
genetic fallacy—substituting the origins of art for its explanation. Psychology's role in literature, conclude Wellek and
Warren, may in fact be superfluous:

> Great art continually violates standards of psychology
> [for it is] without universal validity [and its] psycho-
> logical insights . . . can be reached by other means than
> a theoretical knowledge of psychology. In the sense of
> a conscious and systematic theory of the mind and its
> working, psychology is unnecessary to art and not in
> itself of artistic value. . . . While it may play some sup-
> plementary role for some artists, psychology is only
> preparatory to the act of creation; and in the work itself,
> psychological truth is an artistic value only if it . . . is
> art.[7]

The limitations of psychology in literature have also been

affirmed by several authors. William Faulkner: "What does it matter what complexes I have. It is my work that counts. Judge that. I am unimportant. If I hadn't written me, someone else would have."[8] Arthur Miller feels that the author is not so much interested in facts, as is the scientist, but rather in what can be done with them: "A writer records facts in order to transcend them, to unearth their inner coherency."[9] The extensive interviews with Miller by a psychologist reveal an acceptance of the importance of psychological themes (for example, conflict) but a rejection of the fragmentation and labels which characterize contemporary psychology. Except for perhaps humanistic psychology and some neo-Freudians, Miller expresses serious qualms about the value of knowing any psychology, including an author's personality, in order to understand a work: "[An author does not] look at dramatic characters the way you look at people. They aren't really individuals."[10]

These literary views on the distinctiveness of psychology and literature create barriers to a meaningful exchange between the two fields. The barriers have also been raised by psychology, as noted in chapter 1. Empirical psychologists find literary statements of psychological content to be speculative, overgeneralized, unsystematic, and impossible to objectively confirm. The absence of mutual respect and communication between psychology and literature, and in general, between the sciences and the humanities, stems mainly from the differences in methods and procedures with which the two fields carry out their goals. One finds science, mathematics, and objectivity in psychology; and intuition, illustrative examples, and subjectivity in literature. These contrasts sustain what Snow has called the conflict between two cultures. While a reply to the objections of psychologists will take up the rest of the book, the complaints of literary critics will be treated only briefly.

In reply to literature's objections

Perhaps of greatest concern to literary critics' evaluation of psychology's role in literature is their fear that scientific analysis may take something away from the integrity of an author's artistic achievement. At its extreme, most often found in psychoanalysis, the psychologizing of literature interprets a work as nothing but psychology. In a discussion of this issue, Wilson recognizes that the analysis of literature can become a psychological exercise in which artistic expression is interpreted as nothing but a symptom of neurosis. However, Wilson also notes that an objective treatment of literature can be indifferent to whether art is but neurosis or an artistic expression of symptomology. Art need not be explained away "as only a reflection of personal idiosyncracies or obsessions." While a work may be based to some extent on the psychological troubles of its author, argues Wilson, these must be transcended if the literary message is to communicate any truth to its reader. There must be a basic objectivity and truth to an author's work:

> [A literary product] is also grounded in [an author's] psychological health. Otherwise, it could not penetrate so deeply the social reality of our time. The private nightmare, if it is there, is profoundly related to, and helps us understand, public events.

In more general terms, Wilson feels that the psychological analysis of literature is also useful because it can "throw one more bridge over the chasm between the humanities and the social sciences, at once illuminating both personality and literature."[11]

Richards also offers a balanced view of the dangers and the advantages of literary psychology; it need not excessively psychologize nor be neglectful of literary facts. On the one hand, he indicates his suspicions:

Poetry has suffered too much already from those who are merely looking for something to investigate and those who wish to exercise some cherished theory.

But then, he adds, there is an appropriate middle ground, although admittedly rarely explored:

It is possible to combine an interest and faith in psychological inquiries with a due appreciation of the complexity of poetry. [However, few psychologists] have been able to devote much attention to literature. Thus this field has been left rather too open to irresponsible incursions.[12]

PSYCHOLOGY'S GENERAL USEFULNESS TO LITERATURE

Early in this century, Downey listed four psychological programs that would be useful to literature. These are: (1) the standardization of tests to determine literary ability; (2) the use of different psychological points of view, such as the psychoanalytic, that make reference to the emotions, personality, and creativity of the author, in the understanding and analysis of literature; (3) the specific application of the results of experimental investigations, especially those concerned with the topics of imagery and language, to literary analysis; and (4) the development of means whereby the imagination of authors might be estimated and facilitated.[13]

Nixon's survey of psychology's role in literature, written early in this century like Downey's, placed his emphasis on more practical applications. He looked to psychological knowledge as increasing the writer's skills and as clarifying those factors which might increase the popularity (and sales) of an author's work (for example, the appeal of different titles and the attractiveness of certain characters).

Most recently, McCurdy has specified psychology's contribution to literature. He indicates that psychological concepts can be used by nonpsychologists in aesthetic analysis. In particular, he refers to creativity, imagination, imagery, and personality. He also argues for the inclusion of psychoanalytic theory into literary analysis. Unlike Downey and Nixon, McCurdy does not neglect literature's contribution to psychology, a balance that would make their relationship truly mutual.[14]

SPECIFIC APPLICATIONS OF PSYCHOLOGY TO LITERATURE

Psychology's place in literature, whether expressed in its content or in the reader's mental and emotional response, and its use in critical analysis and aesthetic theory are so pervasive and obvious as to be easily overlooked or taken for granted. There has been an interplay between literary critics and objective psychologists for some time. Louttit has indicated that Locke's conception of the association of ideas, an underlying theme of contemporary psychology, was explicitly utilized in a late eighteenth century critical work. Rands has shown that Thomas Brown's theory of associationism and perception, a forerunner to psychology's development, characterizes not only his own poetry but also different types of literature written in his day. McKenzie has demonstrated that literary critics of the eighteenth and nineteenth centuries generally referred to British empiricism, the major philosophical base for much of scientific psychology, as a means of understanding the effect of a work on the mind and emotions of an audience.

More recently, contemporary aesthetic theories of literature, such as Abrams' *The Mirror and the Lamp*, have speculated on what goes on in the author's mind and consciousness, especially those psychological processes concerned with literary creation and genius. For example, there is an interest in whether the writer passively mirrors reality or actively projects himself on reality, which is perhaps another way of posing the question of whether writing is an expression peculiar to its author or is representative of human nature in general. Other aesthetic questions of psychological relevance deal with whether an author illuminates as well as clarifies and whether a work can please at the same time it persuades. An interest in the reactions of the audience or reader is also part of general aesthetic theory but to a lesser degree than an interest in the author.

There are also methodological parallels between literary critics and psychologists. Critics like Gordon have argued that literary techniques, such as the use of examples, internal consistency, close reading, and reliance on reflection, match the procedures of scientific psychology. An attempt to explicitly duplicate literary and scientific analysis is found in Dudley's classification approach to literary materials. It was purposefully modeled on the categorization schemes of biology and physics, in which careful classification is a means of getting at the underlying structure of a phenomenon. In addition, Dudley used psychological concepts from the theories of Titchener and Watson, among other psychologists, to sort literary material with respect to such topics as imagery, emotion, and intuition. Richards' *Principles* also applied standard (of the 1920s) conceptions of general psychology, including behavioristic and gestalt theories, to literary analysis. In particular, he used theories about sensation, memory, imagery, and attitudes along with psychologically informed discussions of the role of pleasure, pain, and frustration in the context of literature.

G. O. Taylor has also written about the influence of psychology on the content of the novel. He showed that several nineteenth century authors, H. James, Howells, Crane, Norris, and Dreiser, paid more attention than earlier authors (for example, Stowe) to psychological analysis. The result was that more emphasis could be given to conscious experience, thereby liberating subsequent authors in their treatment of dynamic, irrational, unconscious, and conflicting forces. Similarly, E. Johnson traced the influence of William James' *Principles of Psychology,* in terms of his original treatment of experience, perception, consciousness, volition, the self, and the individual, on such modern authors as Joyce, Hemingway, Steinbeck, Wolfe, and Faulkner.

It is usually difficult to show specifically how an author relied on psychological knowledge and themes because of the subtle and implicit ways in which they are used in writing. An exception may be Gertrude Stein, whose training in psychology and its influence on her work have been remarked upon by the critics Creelman and Hoffman and the psychologist Skinner. Her psychological background was directly reflected in her treatment of the split personality and the phenomenon of automatic writing. A more general example of the explicit use of psychological hypotheses is the biographer's tracing of an individual's life, which D. H. Russell has argued is usually shown in the analysis of genetic, environmental, and personal-idiosyncratic influences. In another specific instance of science contributing to literature, Burnshaw has argued that Cannon's physiological work on the adapting and balancing mechanism of the internal organs and systems, together with other comparative and biological findings, can be used to understand some of the involuntary, innate, and chemical sources of creativity. Foster relied on gestalt psychology to elucidate several themes in different writers and poets; and Koffka used the theory in an analysis of how an actor communicates emotions to an audience. Bleich used the free association method, chosen because of its ability to indirectly manifest emotional meanings, to facilitate understanding of a work by Harold Pinter. R. N. Wilson probed the existential psychological themes of emptiness, hostility, hopelessness, and meaninglessness in the context of Beckett's works.

The most widely known illustration of psychological principles, Skinner's *Walden Two,* applied concepts of learning and reward to a utopian novel. Zoellner has related the techniques of Skinner's operant conditioning (for example, more doing than talking, immediate reinforcement, speed of learning paced to an individual's ability), along with some aspects of Pavlovian conditioning, to the teaching of writing, although not without controversy over their applicability.[15] Lucas strongly defended psychology's value to literary analysis, especially in understanding the reader's response:

> Our own century . . . has the chance, thanks to psychology, of judging the influence-value of literature rather better than before. Psychologists can . . . bring a good deal of new understanding.[16]

Of the various forms of writing which have attracted psychological attention, poetry has dominated. Discussions of poetry by Arnheim, Richards, and Tsanoff refer to several psychological dimensions: the emotions aroused by different forms and content; the physiognomic nature of verbal images, metaphors, and similes, and their relation to projective techniques; and the stages of creativity represented in a poem's revisions:

> A poem's first draft is an objective record of a spontaneous process. In it, the poet has . . . introspected while creating.[17]

Psychology may assist the writer in several practical ways. As elaborated by Nixon, it discloses useful facts and concepts, contains points of view about the human condition, and provides tools and techniques on the craft of writing—all of which may facilitate the processes of thinking, imagination, and creativity. Other psychological topics of potential benefit to the writer are those of imagery (including synesthesia) and language (including the meaning of words and the response to style). Further, psychology may offer useful practical information on those factors which increase the popularity, attractiveness, and sales of literary materials.

The one area of psychology which has had the most appeal to literature is that of personality as it contributes to an understanding of the writer and his work. (The preoccupation with personality is reciprocated by most psychologists who work with literature.) For the most part, the psychoanalytic approach to personality is used. Edel's treatment of the experiences and consciousness of Proust, Joyce, Eliot, Woolf, Stein, and H. James in *The Modern Psychological Novel,* and Lucas' discussion of the psychological meaning of Shakespeare's plays (among other works), the different periods and styles of literature, and of literature as a source of pleasure and influence are all fairly moderate applications of psychoanalysis to literature, tempered by a familiarity with contemporary academic psychology.

However, although a clinical orientation to personality persists, not all of the psychology relied upon by literary critics has been psychoanalytic. Other literary uses of psychology, discussed by David-Schwarz, Haimovici, and Teagarten, include a trait analysis of personality (the psychograph), which focuses on overt rather than unconscious features of behavior; an emphasis on the influence of body physique on personality and attitudes; an examination of the social values explicitly held by an author; and an analysis of the way personal introspection is relied on by different authors. Another closely related line of inquiry not necessarily psychoanalytic although still clinical is the examination of an author's works as an expression of his inner conflicts, that is, as a channel for a therapeutic release. This approach is most explicit in Albrecht's analysis of the motives of the author Green in his novels. This use of literature as a kind of projective test has proved useful in McCurdy and Dilthey's examination of the poetry of Keats, Lessing, and Goethe.

Other advantages of applying psychology to literature are implied in subsequent discussions of literature's advantages to psychology. To the extent that psychology can objectively demonstrate that a literary thesis is valid or useful, this information may become more extensively relied upon, amplified, and more broadly applied in literary works and criticisms.

Summary

In evaluating the arguments up to now, it seems apparent that many of the problems encountered by a scientific study of literature cannot be completely overcome or satisfactorily resolved. Literary materials require a level of analysis which involves greater difficulties than the more stimulus bound visual and auditory representations of aesthetics. Further, the study of literature is dominated by psychoanalysis, a point of view rejected to a large extent by academic psychologists and one which furthermore is concerned with personality, one of the most intractable of psychological topics. The two disciplines are therefore seen by many nonpsychoanalytic psychologists and literary critics as largely incompatible. At best, objective psychology is indifferent to literature. To the psychologist, literature offers a loose set of post hoc generalities or charming illustrations. Of the several factors responsible for this impasse, a major one stems from the methodological differences between literature and psychology in approaching their materials. Their purposes also differ: exposition and entertainment are the goals in literature, as opposed to explanation and prediction in scientific psychology. Their divergence is exaggerated by psychology's historical development as a natural and experimental science.

While some of the conflicts between literature and psychology can be overcome, others must simply be accepted as part of the distinction between science and art. Unresolvable problems can be balanced against other advantages and opportunities which literature provides psychology. These are illustrated in the studies reviewed in chapters 7 and 8. Because psychology and literature share a common interest in the experience and behavior of man, there are several parallels and similarities between the two fields which should sustain their mutual interest. A discussion of these follows. Generally, these common grounds are found in the types of questions they ask about man and the sources of information used for their answers, namely, observations of and introspections about human experience.

Notes

1. W. Stegner, "One way to spell man," *Saturday Review* 41 (1958): 44.

2. All subsequent quotes from Stegner, unless otherwise noted, are from p. 9.

3. Ibid., p. 43.

4. Ibid., p. 44.

5. Ibid.

6. F. D. Martin, "The imperatives of stylistic development: Psychological and formal," *Bucknell Review* 11 (1963): 56.

7. R. Wellek & A. Warren, *Theory of literature* (New York: Harcourt, Brace, 1942), p. 88.

8. In D. C. McClelland, *The roots of consciousness* (Princeton, N.J.: Van Nostrand, 1964), p. 94.

9. In H. Mindess, Review of *Psychology and Arthur Miller* by R. I. Evans, *Contemporary Psychology* 15 (1970): 428.

10. R. I. Evans, *Psychology and Arthur Miller* (New York: Dutton, 1969), p. 29.

11. R. N. Wilson, Review of *Dreams, life, and literature: A study of Franz Kafka,* by C. S. Hall & R. E. Lind, *Contemporary Psychology* 15 (1970): 597. All quotes are from this page.

12. I. A. Richards, *Practical criticism* (New York: Harcourt, Brace, 1950), p. 322.

13. J. E. Downey, "A program for a psychology of literature," *Journal of Applied Psychology* 2 (1918): 366–377.

14. H. G. McCurdy, "The psychology of literature" in *International encyclopedia of the social sciences,* edited by D. L. Sills (New York: Macmillan, 1968), vol. 9.

15. R. Zoellner, "Talk-write: A behavioral pedagogy for composition," *College English* 30 (1969): 267–320. Responses by others, mainly in disagreement, are in the same issue, pp. 645ff.

16. F. L. Lucas, *Literature and psychology,* 2nd ed. (Ann Arbor: University of Michigan, 1957), p. 22.

17. R. A. Tsanoff, "On the psychology of poetic imagination," *American Journal of Psychology* 25 (1914): 535.

4

Science, Art, and Method

Science and art

Barriers and antipathies have been noted between science and art stemming from each field's contrary functions and goals: reason, information seeking, and utilitarianism versus imagination, beauty seeking, and entertainment, respectively. Admittedly, there are many difficulties which, as Koch argues, have fed the antagonisms between the two cultures.[1] But there are also sufficient similarities and parallels between the humanities and science to encourage cooperation. There is even, according to Maslow, a humanistic biology. The arts, argues Koestler, may be on the same continuum as the sciences: the divergence between them may lie only in the particulars of their methods and the degree to which these methods differ in objectivity and verifiability. An interchange of their pluralistic points of view, an opportunity noted by C. P. Haskins, could lend flexibility and versatility to the objectives of both.

Toulmin has traced the influence of seventeenth century science on the arts, showing that its effects on literature were even greater than on music and architecture. Not only was there a close connection between literary and scientific prose (especially so in the case of Bacon), but there was also a profound effect of science on the content, outlook and style of literature. In fact, Toulmin speculated that the ideas, imagery, and techniques of Milton, Dryden, Swift, Donne, and others would have been different had there been no Kepler, Newton, and Galileo (although surprisingly he did not think this was necessarily true of Shakespeare). Presumably, science influences literature just as much today, although the influence is not as clearly seen as from the perspective of 300 years.

A basic source of communality between many of the sciences and the arts is that both begin with a concern and questioning about man and end with answers and achievements related to this common focus. The humanities' special preoccupation with ethics and values, subjective judgments about man which the sciences purposely avoid, can be a basis for a bridge between the two, a possibility pointed out by Keeney. An aesthetic undercurrent is also found in science. According to McMorris, for example, there is an aesthetic elegance in the order, simplicity, and efficiency of nature. A further connection between art and science is revealed in the language of metaphors, which can be models of how nature works. MacCormac and Dreistadt have shown that metaphors (and analogies) have played a major role in the discoveries and concepts of all the sciences.[2] There are Newton's falling apple and gravity, Rutherford's solar system and the atom, Darwin's living tree and evolution, Freud's iceberg and the unconscious, and many others. Metaphors about nature imply a useful "as if" quality. They also express nuances difficult to communicate and suggest phenomena that can be tested out more directly.

Another tie between the arts and science stems from a biological context as a response to stress. The arts reveal man's motivational and emotional adaptation to his environment, that is, as a need to play and to use symbols to relieve tensions. Finally, the combining of science and aesthetics is represented by such outstanding men as da Vinci and Goethe, a noted playwright, poet, and novelist who also developed a biological-psychological theory of color perception.[3]

A feature common to science and art is their problem-solving demands.[4] Consequently, both depend on creativity:

> Science, especially at theoretical levels, involves creative processes which no formalism can reduce to rule, processes in fact not dissimilar to those mediating the activity of poets, artists, historians, and other residents on the other side of the barricades.[5]

The two disciplines must also rely on subjective criteria. Science without a qualitative orientation, especially at the initiation and conclusion of its investigations, would be empty and purposeless:

> If one is engaged in research which appears to begin and end in quantitative or numerical terms, it is probably naive. Behind the quantities there must be a clearly defined qualitative problem. Good research begins with good questions, and ends with careful decisions; both are qualitative and both involve the exercise of common sense.[6]

The close relationship between the arts and science is also seen in the application of the scientific method to the arts. Both Beardsley and Toffler have supported the value of objective measurement. This provides factual statements about developments and trends in the arts, objective information that could support arguments on the importance and usefulness of the arts to society. Statistics based on empirical studies, rather than speculation, opinion, and authority, could be a basis for rational decisions and plans in the arts.

An affirmation of the shared features of science and art does not mean that scientific truth and artistic truth are the same, as this quote from Keats might imply: "Beauty is truth, truth beauty—that is all ye know on earth and all ye need to know." Nor can one accept the superiority of one discipline over the other, as Burt does when he suggests: "We know most about man from men of letters, not scientists."[7] A balanced view c⸲ the relationship between science and art is perhaps best expressed by Dewey: "Art is not nature, but nature transformed"[8] in that "science states meanings, art expresses them."[9] Further, Dewey continues, if one presumes an inability of the artist to communicate his perceptions and insights about nature to the scientist, this may be the fault of the observer of art, not the artist.[10] Oscar Wilde's aphorism, "Nature influences art more than art influences nature," suggests that the two are in some way related. Whatever the direction and extent of the relationship between art and nature may be, art may tell the scientist something useful about nature (and the reverse as well).

PSYCHOLOGICAL SCIENCE AND LITERATURE

The acceptance of the arts within the framework of science can open psychology's boundaries to all sorts of new or neglected aspects of conscious experience: the subjective, personal, self-expressive, intuitive, and phenomenological. A dependence on uniquely human sources of information exemplifies a humanistic approach to psychology that maintains a positive and optimistic theory of man and sees the individual as healthy, fulfilled, and rational. Ignoring this view of man, which according to Wilson is the result of psychology's neglect of the humanities, has led to the distortion of man. A sophisticated being, asserts Wilson, is made to seem something other than he is for the sake of obtaining manageable, workable, and clear-cut uniformities and variables; important properties and complexities of man, especially those found in the arts, are ignored because they do not prove amenable to easy classification.

An example of such [neglected] properties is artistic creation and aesthetic experience, a realm of activity

characteristic of man, and as vital to an understanding
of him as the activities involved in toilet training. . . .
Social science has long borne a pronounced animus
against the aesthetic and graceful.[11]

Literature's traditional humanistic concerns—human values, consciousness, and experience—serve as a corrective to
psychology's predominantly biological, comparative, and
oftentimes rigidly behavioristic model of man. The objective study of literature could be an antidote to a study of
psychology limited to strict scientific analysis and rules,
which Koch has termed "ameaning" or pseudoknowledge.[12]
Literature's contribution of a humanistic theme to psychology may offset what Bertalanffy and a wide variety of
other humanistic writers—whose works are collected in
readings by Bugental, Severin, and Sutich and Vich—have
called the triteness of its ideas and accomplishments. That
a humanistic psychology can be placed within a scientific
framework has been advocated by several psychologists:
Bühler, Hilgard and Atkinson, Kelly, and Matson. (Criticisms of this argument, which essentially hold that psychology does not need to be humanistic, or already is, are
discussed by Day and MacCorquodale.)

Literature and psychology have much in common: both
share a perplexity about man; and both begin their inquiries
with experience, use experience in their analyses, and ultimately relate their findings back to this source. Although
the two disciplines follow different routes in fulfilling their
specific interests, they both start with a collection of impressions and hunches. Creativity, whether literary or
scientific in origins and purpose, is based on facts, hypotheses, and theories that spring from observations of man
by man.

However, the search for psychological relevance in literature means more than obtaining illustrations that allow
one to stand in awe and wonder; or finding metaphors to
substitute for scientific statements. An appeal to literature

also means more than exhorting psychology to expand its boundaries. Nor does a humanistic approach to the psychology of literature disavow the empirical and objective approach of science, with its experimental procedures and statistical techniques. While much of literature may not be presently amenable to the type of controlled laboratory study which depends on the most exacting scientific methods and techniques, literature may still suggest derivative studies, or failing that, offer tentative answers for those questions not empirically answerable at this time. The holistic illustrations and statements of literature have the advantage of dealing with the more everyday and complex aspects of psychology in terms which most people usually believe psychology is all about. The immediacy and relevance of this literary information, in contrast to scientific abstractions, are challenging and difficult to study.

Nevertheless, if there is to be a rapprochement between psychology and literature, more than general parallels and similarities between scientific and aesthetic dimensions, appeals to humanistic criteria, and exhortations to be more meaningful need to be made. There must also be concrete specifications of the means whereby literature can be scientifically studied. That is, if the conceptual and informational ties between literature and empirical psychology are to increase, methods and techniques for the objective study of literature have to be available.

Method and literature

"It has often been said that aesthetics is a field of inquiry in search of a method."[13] Without the empirical tools with which to investigate literature, a serious impasse between psychology and literature will remain despite optimistic attempts to unite them. The application of method to literature is the essential means of bridging the gap between science and art. Without objective methods, it would be difficult to encourage, sustain, and further a vigorous interchange between the content and goals of psychology and literature. The appropriateness and utility of the fact-gathering capacity of scientific empiricism is reviewed in the survey of the techniques available for the objective study of literature which follows. However, before specific techniques can be discussed, it is first necessary to meet the objections of both psychologists and literary critics to the possibility and value of an objective methodology for literature.

OBJECTIONS TO SCIENTIFIC METHODOLOGY IN LITERATURE

The most scientifically rigorous branch of psychology is experimental psychology, which obtains its data directly from subjects under conditions which are strictly manipulated and controlled in a laboratory setting. Experimental psychology rejects data which are indirectly obtained from already existent historical sources because they are neither manipulable nor controllable. Literature especially exemplifies the shortcomings of post hoc sources of data since the investigator has no control over those variables that may or may not be responsible for the presumed causes and obtained effects. At best, only general and descriptive statements, rather than causal and functional relationships, are possible with literary materials. Literature is thus similar to anecdotal evidence, in that the specification of what is happening, why, and how, must necessarily remain unclear; and confounding and irrelevant factors play an unknown role. Underwood, a leading figure in experimental psychology, contends that analysis based on after-the-fact data does not "meet acceptable research standards."[14] The resistance of literary material to rigorous methodological investigation adds to literature's already tremendous complexity, its multiple determinants and levels of analysis, the subtlety of its implications, and the covertness of its intentions.

It is true that literary facts, unlike "harder" evidence—for example, that based on rats and rote learning, to name two of the most controlled laboratory sources of information—do not originate in the psychology laboratory and are of less rigor than facts so obtained. However, the painstaking and massive application of experimental procedures has not always successfully demonstrated its value, nor has it led to many triumphs or resulted in the establishment of more than a few laws at best. For example, the laboratory study of verbal learning has not yet proven relevant to an understanding of learning in the classroom, where it should presumably be most relevant. Nor does the highly controlled use of experimental techniques prevent serious error. For example, the experimenter's unconscious bias can unavoidably favor certain hypotheses and thereby influence his data collection. Nor does statistical sophistication solve conceptual dilemmas, as revealed by the controversy over the meaning and use of the highly developed psychometric scales of the IQ test. Bakan has asserted that experimentation has been overemphasized, as if physics were the only possible scientific model for psychology; psychology can now therefore, he insists, "kick the science habit."

Other empirical approaches, while also dependent on observation and experience but not experimental manipulation, have been relatively neglected in psychological research. Experimental "overkill," argues Tyler, has made good craftsmen but poor thinkers of psychologists. He maintains that while they know how to design experiments, use sophisticated techniques, build equipment, and obtain facts, the narrowness of their training has not educated them to look to and use sources of knowledge based on experiencing. Pereboom also cites many of the faults of the laboratory in acknowledging that there is more than one approach to science, and that all data, regardless of their origins, are probabilistic and conditional. In addition, Pereboom argues that control over individual differences, and isolation of context in order to create the manageable conditions of the lab, while necessary criteria of experimentation, lead nevertheless to biases in the data and defy the diversity which is the hallmark of man.

Pereboom also complains about the oversystematization of experiments, that is, the study of many variables and variations. This results in a data explosion (an "endless series of novel experiments with novel results"), difficulties in replication, the possibility of more than one explanation for each experiment, and the likelihood of confirming nearly any hypothesis. These shortcomings of experimentation not only result in its minimal generality, concludes Pereboom, but also foster triviality: there are "large quantities of very fashionable but fragile facts."[15]

Deese, his credentials buttressed by his own stature as an experimentalist, has also challenged simplistic views of the power of experimentation, questioning many of its accepted strengths. He has re-examined many of experimentation's presumed advantages with respect to causation, objectivity, control, and manipulation; its sampling and statistical procedures; the priority, correctness, and truth value of its facts, and the belief in their progressive accumulation toward better theory; and the underestimation of other methods, including correlation, interviews, and the study of the single case. Deese argues that the pervasiveness of experimentation in psychology is much weaker than claimed.

> Much ... is based on unarticulated intuition and assumption. ... The real basis for many of the generalizations that appear in textbooks and other places is intuition and speculation of the flimsiest sort built on the basis of a few rather limited and often highly specialized observations.[16]

In discussing the study of language, Deese generalizes that not all discoveries require a laboratory or statistics:

> Some facts about human behavior and thinking are so obvious that they scarcely need a laboratory [or statistical analysis] to demonstrate them, and they may be far more important than the facts that come out of the laboratory.[17]

The experimental model, Deese continues, is based on an outdated conception of science as classical physics and also on an outmoded view of philosophy as limited to the operationalism and logical positivism of the 1930s.[18] In addition, the experimental method has been too rigidly, blindly, superficially, and hence inappropriately applied to many topics of psychology (for example, social psychology, personality). This is perhaps why "so much empirical research [reduces important problems to the] trivial and pointless."[19] It is because of these errors of experimentation that many view psychology with distrust, suspicion, and a feeling of futility; it is consequently in a "state of crisis."[20]

In order to modify the idealized, rigid, and outdated orthodoxies of experimentation, maintains Deese, it is first necessary to recognize that theories and models, rather than data and method, are important to science. "Data alone do not make a science. Data only give science something to be about."[21] Inferences are thus critical to science, and these represent an art: inferences are essentially metaphorical or mythical statements filled with assumptions and faiths. Science therefore depends not only on facts and logic but on an intuitive appeal to personal and human experience. For Deese, science is akin to the arts in its dependence upon subjective qualities, though this dependence is unrecognized and even flatly denied by many. Science and art are therefore compatible with one another and with psychology. Psychology without art is a rigid type of knowledge, which rejects new and different topics and methods and consequently inhibits its own development as a science.

However, psychology as an art only, which some would have as an alternative to psychology as science, is not an acceptable solution to Deese. Antiscience is also antirational and anti-intellectual, and oversimplifies by mistakenly condemning all quantitative, systematic, and rigorous types of inquiry. Deese holds that the difficulty with a psychology totally free from scientific restraints is that its assertions are not subject to test except by intuition. While the way in which science and art are to be combined remains an open and unresolved issue, Deese nevertheless feels that the recognition of the relationship will lead to an openness to method which will further the tie. The techniques which develop should be dependent upon the nature of the problem rather than upon any single or general criterion of science or methodology. Deese rejects the notion that there is only one way of looking at things—either in terms of the way we look (method) or what we look at (subject matter). The consequence of redefining psychology's subject matter and method is to broaden it and free it from traditions that have unnecessarily bound it. However, Deese cautions that one should still remain committed to the tradition of evaluating strictly the new methods and sources of data that emerge.

Although Deese does not deal directly with aesthetics (his reference to "art" is really to the *practice* of psychology), he believes that the revival of interest in the mind, consciousness, and experience will be fruitful and beneficial to psychology. Also of interest to aesthetics, he argues that to ask whether art (or literature) is subject to empirical inquiry or can be used as data is to ask the wrong type of questions. Such questions presume that there is one type of data, methodology, or empirical practice which is proper. Instead, Deese feels that the data one uses and how one obtains them depend upon the purpose of the investigator, how he intends to use them, and their role in theory. If there are barriers that prevent psychology from using the arts and humanities, contends Deese, these are not based on any valid facts, philosophy of science, or some "natural order." Instead, these restrictions erroneously arise from a false attribution of status to certain subjects because of their method, the history of psychology, current fashions and prejudices, and the personality and intellectual style of researchers.

Unfortunately, Deese looks to the liberalization of psychology through its interdisciplinary efforts with the social and other sciences rather than with the arts and humanities. He also implicitly presumes that experimentation is inapplicable to the arts although the method hardly has been used in this field. Since rigorous empiricism in the arts is infrequent, it would be premature to abandon it for alternate methods or approaches.

The obvious difficulties in achieving scientific control over literary data should be recognized. A suitable balance between the rigor of scientific method and the scope of literary material has to be achieved. The solution may be reached through ingenious research designs and techniques. The intransigence of literary materials to objective study offers an opportunity to find new models of research which are still faithful to the criteria of empiricism. There can be a pluralism of methodology; whatever contributes to a knowledge of human nature, including the personal, natural, historical, subjective, and observational documents of literature, should be part of scientific psychology. An openness to the descriptive generality and phenomenological plausibility of literature might counter the dangers of experimental triviality.

Several recent works have encouraged and supported the use of innovative methodology, thereby providing the means by which unique research possibilities may be exploited and managed by nontraditional techniques. Discussions of liberalized methodologies are found in Allport's *The Use of Personal Documents in Psychological Science;* Bakan's *On Method;* Davidson and Costello's $N = 1$: *Experimental Studies of Single Cases;* Webb, Campbell, Schwartz, and Sechrest's *Unobtrusive Measures;* and Willems and Raush's *Naturalistic Viewpoints in Psychological Research.* The successful use of various quantitative research designs for subtle, controversial, and difficult types of social problems is found, for example, in Tufte's collection, *The Quantitative Analysis of Social Problems.* They indicate the possibilities for an objective study of literature. These studies reveal that the limitations of any one method, the possible misuse of statistics, and other problems inherent in complex but interesting areas can be overcome. The demonstrated applicability of computer technology to the various arts, examples of which are found in Reichardt's collection, gives promise of possibilities for further research.

Another indication of the validity of applying quantitative techniques to extremely personal and subtle data is their previous success in objectively treating protocols from projective tests, and more recently, in the analysis of the emotional content of speech, as in the work of Gleser et al.; dreams, as in Hall and Van de Castle's research; and the products of earlier civilizations, as reported in McClelland's *The Achieving Society*. While liberalized procedures allow new opportunities for error to occur, these may be countered by the use of multiple techniques to supplement and validate the data obtained by "soft" procedures. The gain in flexibility of method, allowing the imaginative use of novel materials, can offset the possible loss of accuracy risked in the use of atypical material.

Literature, along with other personal documents (for example, diaries), is data. Treated in an impersonal sense, to meet the objections of rigorous-minded scientists, it can be objectively categorized as a source of historical data; it is no more unusual than any other example of archival, episodic, and private material collected by someone other than an experimenter whose original purpose was not scholarship.

A second major source of criticism leveled at a quantitative approach to literature, originating in literary criticism and the humanities in general, is that reducing literature to cold and impersonal numbers debases its content. Literature treated as data loses its individuality and the reader's personal identity with it, essential characteristics of literary materials.

The charge that an empirical consideration of literature is crass and philistine may be answered in several ways. Statistical abuses can be recognized and minimized, mainly by integrating the results of objective analysis with impressionistic interpretations. It is not the intention of empiricism to usurp literary analysis. Instead, objective data can supplement, support, and extend subjective statements. Many of the arguments against the possibilities of investigating subtle materials and their defense appear in the context of the similarly difficult materials of dreams. This material is successfully handled in Hall and Van de Castle's monograph. McCurdy's *Personal World* also contains arguments for the value of combining objective with subjective analysis. The intuitive method, which he sees as an involvement of the self with data, is not outside of the boundaries of psychology; as a personal experience, it is authentic. Intuition should be and can be cultivated, continues McCurdy; its value may be especially appreciated for those phenomena which are presently outside of an objective approach, or it may be useful where the objective method fails.

Another argument that challenges literature's resistance to objective analysis is the acknowledgment that literary analysis is itself the application of a method; and that statistics, in the form of counting, have been relied upon by many literary critics in their examination of literary materials, although in a largely informal and unsystematic manner. Mathematics is most clearly represented in music and manifestly characterizes many aspects of poetry (for example, meter, rhyme scheme, stanza). Schoeck has also noted that mathematical concepts (along with biological references) are frequently found in literary metaphors. Even as staunch an advocate of the humanities as Norman Cousins has defended the applicability of computer techniques to literature. However, he also cautions that the generation of data has to be tempered by the interpretative wisdom and sensitivity of the poet, who provides the computer with better questions to be answered and better uses of its answers. Jennings' recent collection of readings from the computer-statistics field illustrates the applicability of quantitative concepts of literary criticism. These readings affirm the interdisciplinary value of science; they suggest the means whereby the humanities can broaden its specialized knowledge.

THE METHOD OF CONTENT ANALYSIS

Various methods, including the experimental as well as the correlational, have been employed in the objective study of readers' responses to literature. Among less traditional techniques, the connotative scales of meaning of Osgood, Suci, and Tannenbaum's semantic differential (for example, a concept can be rated as good-bad, hot-cold, fast-slow) have measured the reaction to drama and could be used for the arts in general. Other methods that could be used to study the literary response are panels and interviews, discussed by Lazarsfeld and Lasswell in the general context of social science research. Although these are ordinarily employed for other purposes (for example, marketing, voting behavior, and social issues), they could also be utilized for the study of readers' reactions to literature. However, the method most often applied to literary materials by the majority of social scientists, for an explication of its subject matter, is content analysis.

Content analysis is essentially a counting procedure in which the frequency of occurrence of certain events is placed within highly sophisticated categories. The nature of these categories and their number and subtlety vary with the purpose of the investigator and the type of material used. Holsti has contributed the most extensive survey of content analysis studies in the humanities and social sciences, disciplines that rely more extensively on historical data and the written word than does psychology. Although prose is difficult to quantify, Holsti contends that it cannot be ignored, since writing is the most pervasive form of evidence to be found in human affairs. Literary sources are included in Holsti's review because they are a form of verbal communication, but they receive far less coverage than ordinary written materials, such as newspapers and documents; their special province is to supplement more artificial sources of information.[22] While Holsti does not consider an author's intuitive statements, as such, as objective evidence, he feels that they nevertheless are facts and can be empirically used. An author's comments can be analyzed through inference and by taking context and other biographical and literary circumstances into account.[23] Since the results of more objective analyses also require intuitive thinking, subjective and objective approaches to data can supplement and interact with one another: quantitative results help discover, confirm, ad extend impressionistic analyses.

Cartwright's review of the content analysis of qualitative data in a social psychological context also deals more extensively with written material in general than with literature. He does, however, point out the relevance of literary content analysis in quantifying the reading ease of prose, comparing stylistic features, settling authorship disputes, and understanding literature's intentions and effects on an audience. The usefulness of the content analysis of literature has also been shown by Sorensen and Sorensen in the adjudication of literary infringement cases.

Determining the appropriate units of prose to be used in content analysis is the subject of much controversy; the choice varies with different purposes. The units include the number of lines spoken by different literary characters, which McCurdy has used as a measure of their importance;[24] Yule counted nouns and C. B. Williams relied on sentence length in determining authorship; J. B. Haskins devised an adjective-verb ratio as an index for action with which to compare short stories and nonliterary materials; Sedelow and Sedelow tallied the frequency of key words in *Hamlet* in order to illustrate that this technique could contribute to traditional scholarly analysis; and Raben used a computer analysis of line length and rhythm of poems to study poetic style, a poem's emotional and intellectual meaning, similarities between poets, and the development and changes in

poetic motifs over time. The procedures of content analysis
have been made easier, and more subtle and complex questions have been asked, through the availability of the computer. This tool has been widely promoted for humanistic
research by Bowles and Pierson et al.; Sebeok and Zeps have
written on its suitability for statistical surveys of literature.

Other content analysis studies have been less concerned with literary materials than with other types of
prose, for example, Webb and Roberts' treatment of love in
songs, although their techniques could be easily applied to
more literary forms. Baldwin applied his personal structure
analysis to the case study of a single personality ("Letters
from Jenny"). He tallied the frequency of use of certain
categories (for example, woman as unfavorable, disliked,
stupid). Together with impressionistic interpretations of the
same material, which served to check their reliability and
validity, quantitative analysis revealed the importance of
certain themes in an individual's personality. White's "Value-Analysis" examined the autobiographical novel of Richard Wright, *Black Boy.* He classified the prose along fifty
broad dimensions (for example, physical, social), each of
which was then subdivided into briefer themes (for example, hostility, self-approval). He then applied this objective
system to the emotions, personality, and cultural values
found in the textual material and presumably reflective of
the author. White realistically recognizes that the specific
categories of his value analysis would change as the content
of the materials changed. He also admits that one needs to
go beyond this type of analysis to other sources, especially
impressionistic surveys, in order to understand the context
of the quantitative findings. In a similar content analysis
procedure, Dollard and Mowrer developed the discomfort-
relief quotient, based on counts and ratios of different types
of words, as a means of quantifying tension in qualitative
data. Although they applied it to a case study, the procedure
would also be relevant for any autobiographical material
and other personal documents.

CRITIQUE

It may be well to conclude this review of the advantage, promise, and usefulness of content analysis with a recognition of its limitations, disadvantages, and abuses as an empirical tool, many of which have been readily admitted by its advocates. The usefulness and validity of content analysis depend greatly upon the ingenuity and resourcefulness of the researcher, who must establish meaningful categories into which to place frequency counts of prose. The counting procedure is merely clerical and it can be given too much prominence. A frequent error is counting different aspects of the materials for the sake of counting, without any particular goal in mind, in the hope that something worthwhile will show up:

> The temptation to count things for the sake of counting [as "fishing expeditions"], unless resisted, is almost certain to yield precise findings which are either meaningless or trivial, or both.

This sort of research reflects poorly on the method.

> The low esteem with which content analysis is held in some quarters derives largely from its frequent use . . . in research unguided by broader theoretical considerations and undisciplined by a research design.[25]

Maccoby also points out the atheoretical weakness of content analysis, while also noting its strength as a means of handling masses of all types of written data in order to abstract their regularities and generalities:

> [Content analysis] is not a substitute for theory development and hypothesis testing. . . . The method is not a substitute for deductive theorizing and experimentation. However, when used in its appropriate place and

in conjunction with other research methods, it can be a highly important and useful tool in behavioral communication research.[26]

Numerous other deficiencies, as well as the sheer drudgery of labor involved, have been catalogued by many critics, including Kadushin et al., Kracauer, Schutz, and Stephensen. Methodological errors occur in choosing content categories and labeling them; selecting the unit of analysis; insuring the adequacy of the coding procedure; checking the reliability of the counting technique; and determining the representativeness of the sample of material examined. More general conceptual problems include arriving at hypotheses after rather than before data collection (that is, post hoc interpretation, especially likely if one does not know in advance what to look for); obtaining data which are merely a shorthand replica of the original source and just as clumsy to analyze; building assumptions into so-called objective categories; losing nuances, context, subtleties, and meaning in frequency counts; an overconcern with technique to the neglect of hypotheses; a resistance to going beyond frequency counts to their qualitative elaboration; and making uncritical and unsophisticated generalizations from the results.

However, one must maintain a perspective in response to this long list of criticisms. There are problems with all types of inference, whatever the method or data, a point noted by Dibble. Further, the rigorous methods and more accessible data sources of psychology (that is, from animals, physiology, and behavior) are not free of error and misapplication. To admit the faults of content analysis is not to deny either the legitimacy of prose as a source of data or the possibility of overcoming or reducing the method's deficiencies. Content analysis is difficult; and it is made even more difficult when it is applied to the subtle materials of literature: "Interesting but elusive variables necessarily require investigations of often painstaking efforts."[27] Such efforts may be worth the pain if the outcome of literary analysis is as interesting as its original content.

This chapter has indicated that there are many conceptual and methodological bridges between science and art and between psychology and literature. In the next chapter, the various ways in which the content of literature can contribute to psychology will be discussed.

Notes

1. S. Koch, "Psychological science versus the science-humanism antimony: Intimations of a significant science of man," *American Psychologist* 16 (1961): 629–639.
2. R. Dreistadt, "An analysis of the use of analogies and metaphors in science," *Journal of Psychology* 68 (1968): 97–116.
3. Goethe's role in science is also noted in chapter 5.
4. H. Gardner, "Problem solving in the arts and sciences," *Journal of Art Education* 5 (1971): 93–113.
5. Koch, 1961, p. 631.
6. R. G. Taylor, Jr., "Qualitative vs. quantitative methods in scientific research," *Human Potential* 1 (1968): 85–86.
7. In A. Koestler, *The act of creation* (New York: Macmillan, 1964), p. 18.
8. J. Dewey, *Art as experience* (New York: Minton, Balch, 1934), p. 79.
9. Ibid., p. 84.
10. Ibid., pp. 104–105.
11. R. N. Wilson, "Literature, society, and personality," *Journal of Aesthetics and Art Criticism* 10 (1952): 97.
12. Koch, "Psychology cannot be a coherent science," *Psychology Today* 3 (1969): 14–68.
13. C. C. Pratt, "Aesthetics," *Annual Review of Aesthetics* 12 (1961): 87.
14. B. J. Underwood, *Psychological research* (New York: Appleton-Century-Crofts, 1957), p. 99.
15. A. C. Pereboom, "Some fundamental problems in ex-

perimental psychology: An overview," *Psychological Reports Monograph Supplement* 2-V28, 28 (1971): 439–455. Quotes are from p. 446 and p. 453, respectively.

16. J. Deese, *Psychology as science and art* (New York: Harcourt Brace Jovanovich, Inc., 1972), pp. 61–63.

17. Ibid., p. 23.

18. Ibid., p. 24.

19. Ibid.

20. Ibid., p. 1.

21. Ibid., p. 71.

22. O. R. Holsti, *Content analysis for the social sciences and humanities* (Reading, Mass.: Addison-Wesley, 1969), pp. i–ii.

23. Ibid., pp. 32–33.

24. H. G. McCurdy, "Literature as a resource in personality study: Theory and methods," *Journal of Aesthetics and Art Criticism* 8 (1949): 42–46.

25. Holsti, 1969, p. ii and p. 41, respectively.

26. N. Maccoby, Review of *The analysis of communication content,* edited by G. Gerbner et al., *Contemporary Psychology* 15 (1970): 598–599.

27. Holsti, 1969, p. iv.

5

Literature's Role in Psychology

There are many parallels between the origins, procedures, and goals of the arts and sciences in general and between psychology and literature in particular. These communalities are furthered by the application of an empirical methodology to the study of literature. Other conceptual bonds tie literature to psychology and psychology to literature although it is difficult to separate the two components of this relationship. Literature provides facts and their analyses (as interpretation, explanation, or hypothesis) and illustrates these facts and analyses. This chapter will review the various conceptual roles of literature.

Literature as illustration

Literature's illustrative role in psychology is probably its most recognized and accepted function. This is particularly evident in psychoanalysis. Literary examples and allusions are extensively used in psychological discussions of personality and psychotherapy. These psychodynamic interests are represented in several collections of literary extracts and short stories by Levitas, Rabkin, Shrodes et al., and Stone and Stone. Psychologists have relied on literary examples in a wide range of other contexts: Cohen in his discussion of subjective time, Ashmun in his treatment of emotions, Sperber in his analysis of illusions, and McCurdy in his conception of imagination and creativity.[1] (Other topics in which literature plays an illustrative role are found in the context of literature as fact, explanation, and hypothesis, discussed subsequently.)

Literature as illustration in the most didactic sense has been used in teaching courses, at both the college and high school level, in personality, motivation, general psychology, developmental psychology, social psychology, and psychiatry; and in the psychology curriculum as a whole.[2] Literature in these educational settings, however, typically has only an indirect bearing on scientific study, for which better proofs are required. Literary examples are treated as a peripheral source of information, acting as a kind of realistic supplementary case material, an intuitive test of hypotheses and assumptions about human nature, enhancing interest and awareness in order to facilitate learning, and demonstrating the humanistic, empathic, and ideographic (that is, single case) approaches to knowledge. "The aim of literature is to depict reality as it is lived. . . . When we encounter good literature . . . we are able to participate with the characters."[3]

Literature's role as illustration and its roles as fact, hypothesis, or explanation are difficult to disentangle because they are highly interwoven within the literary context. Since it is hard to separate content from its analysis, there is an ambiguity between what is offered as fact and what is presented as an interpretation of that fact; description and analysis in literature are inextricably bound together.

The difficulty of conceptually separating the different functions of literature can be demonstrated in Cantril and Bumstead's interesting collection of literary extracts which were used to illustrate a wide variety of general psychology topics from a transactional point of view. This perceptual theory has its philosophical and psychological roots in Dewey and functionalism and it draws on man's expectations and assumptions, derived from his past experiences, to explain how perception copes with environmental demands. The authors used literary examples to illustrate the usefulness of a particular psychological theory and to make psychology more attractive to its readers, but they also recognized the novelist's and poet's roles in adding to the facts of human experience:

> Hence a poem, a painting, or a prayer should be regarded as a psychological datum just as much as the establishment of a sensory threshold in the laboratory or the measurement of an I.Q.[4]

They also used literary illustrations as a basis for the subsequent uncovering of facts (as hypotheses) and as a source of explanation. Various functions of literature—illustration, data collection, hypothesis, and explanation—are interconnected with one another in the following set of comments; they followed a series of literary examples dealing with the nonhomeostatic nature of motivation (that is, its striving and unbalanced qualities):

> Man cares more for the process of attaining goals than for the goals themselves; the achievement of the one goal serves principally as a jumping-off place for the pursuit of the next; man wants continuous betterment as he anticipates the future; man will deliberately imperil his comfort; man's motivation is a struggle between opposing forces—the desire for preserving a safe, secure, predictable world and the dread of completely achieving it; and finally, man is always dissatisfied, what he wants is inexpressible and unattainable.[5]

Literature as fact

While some authors have not made clear distinctions between literature's different roles in psychology, others have been bold in separating these roles. Teagarten flatly asserts that literature contributes to the factual pool of psychology:

And what indeed is *literature* but a record of human behavior? And just that is also the definition given at the beginning of many a discourse on the subject matter of *psychology*. From this point of view, then, psychology, literature, and history, are certainly blood brothers, if not indeed identical triplets. . . . We interpret modern literature . . . as being an attempt to get at real facts which may throw light upon human behavior, and as an earnest endeavor not to lie, distort, or ignore vital elements.[6]

The factual possibilities of literature have been related to specific topics. Butler showed that descriptions of aging by a diverse group of authors—from Goethe to H. L. Mencken —reflected positive rather than negative evaluations of growing old during the so-called declining years. Less dramatically, Plank extracted the motives for space travel from literary works—including science fiction and children's literature—along with several nonliterary sources. Ross, B. N. Wyatt, and David-Schwarz, studying views of man's values in philosophical novels by such writers as Mann, Sartre, Camus, Updike, and Hartmann, have interpreted these views as valid descriptive statements (that is, man as rational-irrational, seeking order, needing justice, searching for identity, in conflict with idealism).

   Several writers have discussed the factual contribution of literature to various topics of psychology. Among them is Hall, who made this statement on perception:

Contrary to popular belief among many experimentally inclined psychologists and sociologists, the productions of artists and writers represent rich, unmined beds of hard data on how man perceives. To be able to distill and identify the essential variables of experience is the essence of the artist's craft.[7]

Hall has related information from literature to the perception of subjective space, that is, the preferred distances between people as it varies with changing relationships. Related to subjective distance, he has also examined the role of the senses in different societies as expressed in literature:

> If one examines literature for structure rather than content, it is possible to find things that will shed light on historical trends and shifts in sense modalities [as objects of interest]. Such shifts are highly relevant to the type of environment that man finds most congenial at different times for different cultures.[8]

Changing perceptions of the social environment have also been manifested, according to Barbu, in the themes, attitudes, and images of poetry, plays, and other aesthetic products of the past.

Literature has also provided useful facts for a theory of attention. Platt has discussed how the stimulus complexity of poetry—as well as music and art—affects attending. Poetry evokes an expectation, leading to a surprise which is fulfilling and pleasing as the expectation is resolved. Berlyne also refers to several aspects of poetry, such as sentence length and sounds, as well as the detective novel and fiction generally, in similar terms of arousal and its resolution: curiosity is aroused by creating expectations and frustrations, and then these are satisfied in surprising and unusual ways.[9]

Other stimulus characteristics of literature that have a factual relevance for cognitive processes include Lee's analysis of the structure of sentences (that is, syntax, verbs, tenses) in relation to an author's style and Downey's discussion of the importance of the imagery aroused by literary figures of speech. Among the various units of literary expression that might have psychological implications, imagery has been considered especially critical for an understanding of thinking, imagination, and creativity in the artist. Consequently, types of imagery in the works and autobiographies of various authors have been extensively reviewed and compared by Bartlett, Friedman, Lindauer, and McKellar.[10] Schorer examined a literary form related to imagery, the metaphor, in novels by Jane Austen, Emily Brontë, and George Eliot, in order to contrast the authors and their works and to provide general information on the nature of metaphorical language. Buch used figures of speech as the basis for an analysis of thinking and concept formation processes.

Not only does the literary work contribute to psychology's factual pool, but so does information about its reader. Wilson has indicated that knowledge of one's reading reflects personality;[11] and Waples has dealt with the broader topic of the social effects of reading. Literature may also, of course, affect an individual in a personal way. Psychologists as different as H. Murray in the area of personality, Wolman in clinical psychology, and D. O. Hebb in the field of neuropsychology have each defended the place of literature in their professional development and thinking.[12] Teagarten has also indicated that literature can debunk the readers' prejudices and stereotypes.

Another topic in which both psychology and literature share an interest is creativity (see also chapter 7); it too can provide a factual pool for psychology. Jacob has informally surveyed its relation to normal processes, and its distinctive functions in different types of creative people (for example, artists versus scientists). Hudson's *Contrary Imaginations* includes a discussion of the biographies of creative people (for example, the artist Turner, the poet Rilke, and the scientists Kepler and Darwin), which is intended to examine the diversity with which creative intelligence expresses itself.

Literature as analysis

Many feel that literature is a source of valid psychological explanations, hypotheses, and theories. Verplanck asserts that novelists and playwrights "do a remarkably good job of giving plausible accounts of behavior, often in terms that seem pertinent."[13] According to Berlyne:

The developments [in the study of aesthetic phenomena] offer no end of promising hypotheses for the theories and variables for the experimenter to manipulate. . . . A fuller understanding of artistic creation and appreciation must surely throw light on principles of psychology (and especially motivation) that underlie behavior in general but are otherwise less accessible to investigation.[14]

Bruner and Taguiri, writing about social perception and the recognition of emotions, also claim that poets and dramatists, although not psychologists, nevertheless have specialized knowledge about man; they can contribute this knowledge to psychology despite the difficulties involved.[15]

LITERATURE'S ANTICIPATION OF FACTS AND ANALYSIS

Literature's potentiality as either fact or analysis is supported by its past fulfillment of these roles. Literature has anticipated much of what has become part of contemporary psychology. Given an active role in the present, literature could anticipate facts and interpretations which contemporary psychology has not yet grasped, perhaps because they involve issues which are too difficult, broad, or complex. While it may be neither fact nor explanation, literature can provide hypotheses and it can act as an impetus for further inquiry.

[Literature can] inquire into the inner nature of the still unformulated types of knowledge and then [we can] learn whether the horizons and conceptions of science cannot be so extended as to include these ostensibly pre-scientific areas of knowledge.[16]

Topics and themes which have been of long-standing interest in literature, including sensory experiences, emotions of all sorts, imagination, fantasy, dreams, imagery, personality development, learning, leadership, social and interpersonal relations, and conflict, to name just a few, have become dominant interests of current scientific psychology.[17] This earlier interest explains the often heard claims that the Bible or Shakespeare anticipated a good deal of psychology.[18]

Writers have always been known for their apt descriptions and interpretations, especially of personal dynamics and social situations:

> It is scarcely accidental that some of the most worldly and discerning of novelists—for example, Henry James, Marcel Proust, Ford Madox Ford, Gustave Flaubert, Thomas Mann, E. M. Forster, Conrad Aiken, and F. Scott Fitzgerald—are continuously and even obsessively preoccupied with the concept of congruities, ironies, and tragedies of human experience.[19]

Further, Dreistadt has maintained that the intuitive prophecies of Jules Verne and H. G. Wells, and also to some extent the literature of classical Greece and the Renaissance, anticipated our knowledge of the exceptional abilities and perceptions of geniuses.[20]

There are a wide range of specific instances of authors anticipating later social psychological themes. A short story by Sherwood Anderson, *Seeds (The Triumph of an Egg)*, according to Cohen in *Humanistic Psychology*, antedated Lewin's conceptions of the personal life-space, with its boundaries, regions, and other qualities. E. T. Hall used material that dealt with the subjective environment from Shakespeare's *King Lear*, Thoreau's *Walden*, Butler's *The Way of All Flesh*, and the writings of Mark Twain, Kafka, and several French and Japanese authors to demonstrate the various ways in which the spatial environment is perceived. (The subjective environment refers to the psychological meaning of distances between people, and how these have varied and changed over time and between cultures.)

Dufort has indicated that novels about utopian societies are based on assumptions and techniques of behavior control antedating current psychology. Even Milne's *Winnie-the-Pooh* with its description of the logic, language, and fantasy of the child anticipated a host of concepts from the noted developmental psychologist Piaget: "egocentrism, time confusion, animism, [playful] symbolism, immanent justice, artificialism, realism, centering, adaptation, preoperational logic, conservatism, and collective monologue."[21] Although Milne based his writing on observation and intuition, and not systematic study, he apparently quite closely paralleled Piaget's theory of progressive growth periods and their changing characteristics.

McKinnon and Jastrow have found the brief personality portraits drawn by ancient Greek literary characterologies (for example, "The Flatterer," "Fool," "Virtuous Woman") as useful, universally accepted, and recognizable descriptions of personality types, thereby revealing the constancy of human nature across twenty centuries.[22] These characterologies have favored that view of man which emphasizes the dominance of a few traits and their pervasive manifestation in a variety of ways. Other literary characterologies have represented different conceptions and classifications of personality, that is, not the fixity of character or the dominance of one trait, but either the congruence of many traits or the uniqueness of traits.

Roback has extensively reviewed the accumulated contributions of literary characterology to personality theory from its earliest origins to its decline in the eighteenth century, when wit and style became more important than accuracy and universal agreement.[23] Along with other traditional methods, he includes it as one of several major and legitimate approaches to personality study.

The literary character sketches are a cross between direct observation and imagination united by the method of interpretation. . . . The *understanding* of the individual or of the type is of paramount importance here, and the grasping of essentials will determine the nature and the division of the types of classes.[24]

The observations, introspections, and intuitive interpretations of literary characters may have a special status compared with the results of other methods because of their historical consistency:

Literary men of all ages and countries have at one time or another ruminated on character and character differentiation, and ... the results of their excogitations might offer a foothold for further inquiry.[25]

Roback also uses proverbs and epigrams, which he distinguishes as follows:

Proverbs are more direct expressions of the common people, aphorisms and reflections are less spontaneous and issue from the more or less outstanding mind. They are more subtle, often more elaborate, more specific, and more artistically expressed, but do not necessarily come nearer the truth than the sayings circulating among the masses.[26]

Roback also deals with fables, statements from the Talmud, biographies, and fiction in general, although he does distinguish the novel from other forms:

Fiction [is like other forms] but the imaginative component is of greater proportion than that of direct observation, and, in addition, the type is particularized or individualized. In fact, the great characters in fiction are not to be found in everyday life. We can hope to discover only approximations to them. There are thousands of sharply drawn characters in fiction, yet they cannot be said all to represent different classes of people.[27]

Among those authors whose reliance on psychological analysis antedated objective psychological study, Proust has received attention from many, including Blondel, Bychowski, Heider, and Wakefield. They have discussed his work with reference to the psychology of imagery and memory, the subjective or psychological environment, and most broadly, to a conception of the interrelationship between art and literature. Swartz has noted that although Proust is a "sublime subjectivist," he anticipated the reinforcing effects of anxiety reduction, a critical concept of subjectivism's staunchest opponent, behaviorism. Swartz approvingly points out Proust's foresightedness (and that of authors in general):

> [There are] correspondences between early literary and late scientific statements. [The former are] anticipations of those to come . . . Proust . . . epitomizes the situation of countless other artists. The science [of psychology] is not so far along in its development that it cannot be enhanced by [these contributions].[28]

McClelland examined Gide's life and works for their expression of French national character and cultural values.[29] Dostoevski is also noted for his psychological expertise. His theories of motivation and of the social nature of man were reviewed by Simonov and Fernandez. Among more popular authors, Truzzi and Morris point out that Arthur Conan Doyle, in his character Sherlock Holmes, applied scientific method to problems in a social setting. Another author-as-psychologist who has received a good deal of interest is Coleridge. Kahn argues that he anticipated a long list of current psychological theories: psychoanalytic conceptions of dreams and madness, the James-Lange theory of emotions, and gestalt psychology. Keith noted that Vergil's modest psychology of feelings, emotions, attitudes, and behavior, as expressed in the descriptions of his characters, is accurate in contemporary terms. F. T. Russell has shown that the nature, types, characteristics, and goals of emotions in Browning's poetry are consistent with scientific views. Meyerson has found different personal concepts of man that anticipated objective psychological analysis in works written as early as the nineteenth century.

Mardershtein has argued that both the Russian classics and current Soviet writings anticipated Pavlov's conception of brain functions, as well as this early forerunner to behaviorism's treatment of sleep, dreams, and drugs. Similarly, Bringmann et al. point out references to conditioning therapy in the autobiography of Goethe, who evidently used it in a way congruent with current research and thinking, namely, to rid himself of neurotic symptoms. Goethe's discussion of drama as therapy was seen by Diener and Moreno as anticipating later developments in psychodrama (more playwrights have seen this use, too, for example, Shakespeare in *Hamlet's* play within a play). Goethe's other contribution to psychology, color theory, was reviewed by Brown. Harmes has discussed the challenge to this theory by the physiologist Helmholtz.

Skard reviewed the many ways in which color has been used for psychological effect in different periods of literature prior to its study by psychology, for example, the extensive and subtle color vocabulary of Milton. Abraham's study of Balzac's *Human Comedy* series is particularly interesting. His descriptions of the eye and hair color of 2,000 men in crowd passages differed from their estimated distribution in a real population of Frenchmen. Abraham interpreted this disparity as having a symbolic purpose. Others have looked to the color vocabulary in the literature of ancient, primitive, and cross-cultural sources, as well as the works of the last 200 years, as an indication of the effects of the environment on perception and thinking.[30] Trevor-Roper has written on the influence of defective vision on the work of artists. He also examined a wide variety of different works in relation to their authors' nearsightedness, color blindness, or other possible visual defects based on their autobiographies and their references to color visual imagery. He speculated, among other things, that Homer may not have been blind.

Creativity is a topic the analysis of which would be valuable to both psychology and literature. Ghiselin's collection is representative of the approach which uses interviews and self-reports on creativity by writers, as well as by artists and scientists, as a means of understanding underlying processes. However, Rosner and Abt note in their own collection the limits of relying on autobiographical information: "This is only a beginning to the exploration and appreciation of the various factors, both subjective and objective, that compose the creative experiences of persons in the arts and sciences."[31] Nevertheless, in relating artists' self-disclosures to gestalt psychology—that is, the demand requirements and field forces present in the creative situation—Rosner and Abt found that subjective reports were congruent with empirical analyses of creativity. Both intuitive and empirical approaches to creativity indicate that it is a unitary process; its operation is similar in both artists and scientists; it reflects an independence rather than conventionality of thought and emotions; and it involves being open and flexible to experience. Perhaps most surprisingly, creative individuals apparently need to collaborate with others; and they evidently express many of the frustrated ambitions of their fathers. Others, like Martindale, Reeves, and Dreistadt, have obtained statements by artists about their imagery, thinking, and imagination, either directly from tests and interviews, or indirectly from dreams, fiction, or autobiographical material.[32] They have related this information not only to creativity but to the nature of genius and intelligence. Similarly, Durr has taken literary examples reflecting the revelatory (in contrast to the hallucinatory) aspects of the psychedelic experience from the unusual themes and patterns of poets such as Coleridge and Blake.

LITERATURE AND THE STUDY OF CONSCIOUS EXPERIENCE

Of the various psychological topics to which literature might contribute, whether as fact, analysis, or illustration, the most obvious and relevant are the topics of consciousness and experience. Literature's presentation of the content and meaning of conscious experience is especially useful to psychology, which normally relies more extensively on data from animals and physiology than on that from humans, and on human behavior rather than on consciousness. Psychologists like Kelly have acknowledged the need for an openness to new methodological models which can take into account the importance of experience. MacLeod has noted that the experiential characteristics of man, a "distinctive phenomenon of the human mind," is often absent among the topics and interests of psychology. This, he adds, makes psychology incomplete: "A proper science of man must draw upon man's unique ability to observe and report on his own experiences."[33]

Duncan suggests that one good source of information about experience could well be great literature. Its expression and communication of the experiences of a people at a particular time might enable us to understand them and ourselves better. Dewey has expressed the thesis that art can represent and clarify man's experience, arguing that there is a critical and intimate relationship between art and psychology: art has its source in human experience and finds its fulfillment in the experience of an observer. Both of these experiential functions of art, in its origins and reactions, are patently psychological. Hence, art and psychology are not as different or separate as they might appear: "A world of art tells something to those who enjoy it about the nature of their own experiences of the world."[34]

Critique and evaluation

Most discussions of the psychological uses of literature blur the lines between its factual, interpretive, and illustrative functions, implying that literary content may contribute to psychology in one or more ways simultaneously. The idea that literature is generally useful to psychological concerns—without indicating whether as fact or analysis—characterizes this statement by Mace on the value of aesthetics:

> [Aesthetics] contributes to general psychology by reason of its special concern with some of the "higher" and most distinctive functions and activities of the human mind. It serves to correct the over-preoccupation of "general" psychologists with the simpler and more primitive functions and activities, and with the more primitive "physiological" and "biological" needs. . . . It opens the way to a distinctively human psychology in which psychological needs are clearly distinguished.[35]

The initial task of an objective study of literature may not therefore be to decide whether or how to use it. Instead, the primary task may be to separate literature's various functions—as illustration, fact, and analysis—from one another and to clarify each of its multiple roles.

Whatever literature's exact role may be, many psychologists recognize that literary content is too good a source of important information about man to ignore. This recognition is shown by Wilson's statement on the usefulness of the arts to the study of social relations:

> Patently, the richest mine of material in existence here is that amassed by generations of artists, for nowhere else has self-analysis with its resulting insight into behavior been so extensively practiced.

Because of its rich potential, argues Wilson, aesthetic material cannot be neglected without serious consequences:

> Failure to recognize that man and his activities have

been most faithfully delineated over the centuries by painters, sculptors, and writers is equivalent to renunciation of any real effort to understand the human species.[36]

The subject matter of literary works is too vital to be neglected for its scientific shortcomings. To the degree psychology is committed to the importance of the personal and subjective world of experience, literature cannot be ignored. Whatever literature's specific functions in psychological study may be, the eventual outcome could be the liberalization of psychology's subject matter and, ultimately, its methods and theories:

> The richness and variety of human experience, to be taken into account in any system . . . may help keep the breadth of life in psychology itself, pointing to new dimensions of experience which the psychologist may have neglected.[37]

Yet in considering literary content as useful to psychological purposes, whatever its specific status, even a sympathetic observer would say that the information is in raw and biased form. Whether literary content is fact, hypothesis, analysis, or example, it was not reached by the careful, objective, and systematic procedures of science. Its origins, comprehensiveness, and intent are unclear. The deficiencies of literature's applicability to scientific psychology have long been recognized, beginning with its earliest attempts in literary characterology:

> The literary approach to the study of character [personality] can help us only with clues. It lacks most when it lacks the conscious effort to analyse the subject, instead of being guided by random inspiration.[38]

Other long-standing faults have been acknowledged: selectivity of its coverage rather than comprehensiveness; uniqueness of its descriptions, and at the same time, its overgeneralizations and contradictions; and the moralizing, sermonizing, and philosophizing contained within psychological narrative.

Despite the many similarities between literature and scientific psychology, the two disciplines differ in the way they obtain, use, and verify their observations. Like any historical record, but even more so because of its personal implications, literature as a source of information needs to be carefully mined, refined, and classified. An author's statements and insights have to be translated into a language which allows them to be investigated and confirmed by objective techniques.

Because this translation has hardly begun, psychology has generally failed to entertain seriously the possibility that literary creations can make a significant contribution to the understanding of human behavior. Swartz has called this oversight "a one-sided and narrow orientation [which is] alien in the House of Science." His plea for a greater appreciation of literature and tolerance of its methods, and his condemnation of psychology's indifference are expressed in this passage:

> As long as psychologists continue to deny their birthright and leave to others—novelists, poets, playwrights, social critics—the responsibility of analyzing, describing, or explaining the natural-behavior world, we had best make whatever effective use we can of their insights and observations. . . . If psychologists believe that the methods of science are superior ways of understanding the natural behavior-world, let them turn to this world and demonstrate the superiority of their methods. . . . The psychologist's obsessive concern with scientific respectability may blind him to the avenues of understanding opened up by a non-experimental observational type of analysis.

Swartz caps his criticism with this biting quote from Krutch on the narrowness of psychology in contrast to the broad significance of literature: "Perhaps Hamlet was nearer right than Pavlov. Perhaps the exclamation 'How like a God' is more appropriate than 'How like a dog! How like a rat! How like a machine!' "[39]

After decrying "the opposition between poetry and science," McCurdy nevertheless asserts that there can be a reconciliation between objective science and the subjective topics of psychology, arguing that intuitive materials which lack a scientific basis can nevertheless be made useful through their careful integration with supplementary objective knowledge:[40]

A kind of truth is conveyed by the writer, a kind unattainable by science alone, and this truth is an indispensable element in [a] full understanding of personality. Literary technique is a tool of scientific study [for it would not be] fair to strip man of the only vehicle he possesses for conveying to others the shadings of his thoughts and feelings . . . to whom such language is an integral part of thought processes and social life.[41]

Stegner sees literature as imaginative, intuitive, and nonlogical, yet complementing scientific sources of knowledge by revealing, asserting, and expressing human truths.

Truth in science and philosophy is a cold, logical, and rational truth, reached through nonhuman and emotionless methods. Truth in art is alive, vital, and rich in human significance. Art reaches wisdom through the imagination, science through logical rigor and understanding.[42]

In order to properly evaluate literature's relevance to psychological interests (and psychology's relevance to literature: chapter 2), an important distinction must be made between literature as art and literature as knowledge—a necessary oversimplification which ignores their overlap. Literature as art is read for personal enjoyment; literature as knowledge is studied as a source of data. Whether read for enjoyment or for information, however, the writer discovers and communicates facts and their meanings about human experience and behavior relevant to all men.

Further, one should realize that many of the conceptual and methodological ambiguities of literature can also be found in more typical kinds of psychological input—in written but nonliterary records, clinical and case studies, and introspective and verbal self-reports, as well as in the interpretation of the behavior of animals, children, and adults—no matter how rigorous one's methods for obtaining such information may be. The facts and hypotheses of psychology, whatever their origins, are not self-evident; they are discovered in a difficult search. The analysis of data, whatever its basis, is not obvious. Further, facts must be related to one another and to different conceptions and interpretations (that is, to hypothesis and theory). Facts by themselves are insufficient to disclose their meaning and significance.

Literature can be thought of as one of many sources of psychological information which vary in their degree of rigor and comprehensiveness. Literature's problems as a source of data, arising because it is an historical record of fiction by dead authors who were more concerned with literary than scientific criteria, are balanced by its major advantage: it gives the insights of talented people about important problems. Bindman's claim that authors are the acknowledged masters in the communication of their life experiences may be an exaggeration, but it does suggest that what they say may tell us something important about psychology. "The careful study of the forms of literary expression cannot fail to bring us into contact with processes which are fundamental in the activity of the mind."[43] Their contributions may only be indirectly checked, by means of what Swartz has called clinical validation: literature's insights are valid to the extent they lead to an improvement in our understanding, prediction, and control over variables which can be studied in more conventional settings. In this sense, the hints and suggestions of literature serve as a spur to further clarification.

Even if the usefulness of literature as data is seriously questioned and its distinctiveness from psychology strongly emphasized, literary insights nevertheless present a challenge. The intensely creative efforts of an author may contain distortions in the service of art and unresolved perplexities that prevent its full objective utilization. But they will also contain some essential validity, if the work is to be accepted by its creator, and understood and appreciated by its readers.

Subsequent chapters will go beyond speculative and conceptual treatments of literature, and will instead focus on the objective and statistical study of literary materials. The success of an empirical approach to literature will depend more on the accomplishments of actual investigations than on the attractive but still programatic exhortations found in this and earlier chapters. Barron's methodological critique of expository materials used for exemplary purposes, although directed specifically at a collection of artists' autobiographical statements on creativity, can also be applied to speculative nonempirical writings that attempt to relate psychology and literature in discursive terms only:

Such work ... in the end ... leaves one with many dissatisfactions because of the resistance of such complex data to classification. Yet the effort must be made [although] we must do better.[44]

Notes

1. H. G. McCurdy, *Personality and science* (Princeton, N. J.: Van Nostrand, 1965).

2. The didactic use of literature can be found in G. W. Allport, "The study of personality by the intuitive method: An experiment in teaching from *The locomotive god, Journal of Abnormal and Social Psychology* 24 (1929): 14–27; C. H. Fellner, "Paperback psychiatry," *Journal of Medical Education* 44 (1969): 585–588; R. Fernandez, ed., *Social psychology through literature* (New York: Wiley, 1972); E. P. Hollander, "Popular literature in the undergraduate psychology course," *American Psychologist* 22 (1956): 95–96; I. N. McCollom, "Psychological thrillers: Psychology books students read when given freedom of choice," *American Psychologist* 26 (1971): 921–937; R. J. Sardello, "Toward a reorganization of the psychology curriculum," *American Psychologist* 26 (1971): 1037–1038; J. S. Sherwin, *Social and psychological assumptions about human behavior in selected literary works,* Ph.D. dissertation, New York University, 1954. *Dissertation Abstracts* 15 (1955): 245–246; M. Librachowa, "The fiction from between the two world wars as a source of scientific material for the psychologist," *Psychological Abstracts* 22 (1948) #2808; A. B. Wood, "Psychodynamics through literature," *American Psychologist* 10 (1955): 32–33; R. J. Zbaracki, *A curriculum design based on cognitive psychology for teaching narrative and dramatic literature in the secondary school,* Ph.D. dissertation, University of Nebraska, 1970. [*Dissertation abstract* 31 (1970) #1700-A].

3. Fernandez, 1972, p. xvi.

4. H. Cantril & C. H. Bumstead, *Reflections on the human venture* (New York: New York University, 1960), p. 1.

5. Ibid., p. 77.

6. F. M. Teagarten, "Some psychological trends in modern literature," *Kadelpian Review* 9 (1930): 309–310.

7. E. T. Hall, *The hidden dimension* (Garden City, N. Y.: Anchor, 1969), p. 75.

8. Ibid., p. 100

9. D. E. Berlyne, *Conflict, arousal, and curiosity* (New York: McGraw-Hill, 1960), chap. 9.

10. F. C. Bartlett, "Types of imagination," *Philosophical Studies* 3 (1928): 78–85; M. S. Lindauer, "The sensory attributes and functions of imagery and imagery evoking stimuli," in *The function and nature of imagery,* edited by P. W. Sheehan (New York: Academic Press, 1972).

11. R. N. Wilson, "Literary experience and personality," *Journal of Aesthetics and Art Criticism* 14 (1956): 47–57.

12. In Elizabeth Hall, "Hebb on hocus-pocus: A conversation," *Psychology Today* 3 (1960): 21–28: M. H. Hall, "A conversation with Henry A. Murray," *Psychology Today* 2 (1968): 56–63; B. B. Wolman, "Poetry and psychotherapy," *Voices* 6 (1970): 56–59.

13. In P. Swartz, "Perspectives in psychology, VII. The criteria of validity in observational analysis," *Psychological Record* 8 (1958): 82.

14. Berlyne, 1968, p. 21.

15. J. S. Bruner & R. Taguiri, "The perception of people," in *Handbook of social psychology,* edited by G. Lindzey (Reading, Mass.: Addison-Wesley, 1954), vol. 2, p. 639.

16. Mannheim in Swartz, 1958, p. 83.

17. D. M. Johnson, "Psychology vs. literature," *Harper Books and Authors* 12 (1961): 1–4; R. L. Van de Castle, *The psychology of dreaming* (New York: General Learning Press, 1971): 2–6.

18. C. Clark, *Shakespeare and psychology* (London: Williams & Norgate, 1936). [*Psychological Abstracts* 12 (1938) #379]; D. E. Alcorn, "New Testament psychology," *British Journal of Medical Psychology* 16 (1937): 270–280.

19. J. Ruesch & W. Kees, "Function and meaning in the physical environment," in *Environmental psychology,* edited by H. M. Proshansky, W. H. Ittelson, & L. G. Rivlin (New York: Holt, Rinehart & Winston, 1969), p. 144.

20. R. Dreistadt, "The prophetic achievements of geni-

uses and types of extrasensory perception," *Psychology* 8 (1971): 27–40.

21. D. G. Singer, "Piglet, Pooh, & Piaget," *Psychology Today* 6 (1972): 71–74, 96.

22. D. W. MacKinnon, "The structure of personality," in *Personality and the behavior disorders,* edited by J. Hunt (New York: Ronald, 1944), vol. 1.

23. A. A. Roback, *A bibliography of character and personality* (Cambridge, Mass.: Sci-Art, 1927).

24. Roback, *The psychology of character,* 3rd ed. (London: Routledge & Kegan Paul, 1952), p. 556.

25. Ibid., p. 24.

26. Ibid., p. 556.

27. Ibid., pp. 556–557.

28. Swartz, "A rose for behaviorism," *Psychological Reports* 27 (1970): 364.

29. D. C. McClelland, *The roots of consciousness* (Princeton, N. J.: Van Nostrand, 1964), pp. 93–116.

30. M. H. Segall, D. T. Campbell, & M. J. Herskovits, *The influence of culture on visual perception* (Indianapolis: Bobbs-Merrill, 1966). See especially the review of Allen and Gladstone's works, pp. 37–41.

31. S. Rosner & L. E. Abt, *The creative experience* (New York: Grossman, 1970), p. ix.

32. Dreistadt, "An analysis of how dreams are used in creative behavior," *Psychology* 8 (1971): 24–50; C. Martindale, "Degeneration, disinhibition, and genius," *Journal of the History of Behavioral Sciences* 7 (1971): 177–182.

33. R. MacLeod, Review of *Experience and behavior,* by P. McKeller, *Contemporary Psychology* 15 (1970): 332–333. Quotes are from p. 333 and p. 332, respectively.

34. J. Dewey, 1934, p. 83.

35. C. A. Mace, "Psychology and aesthetics," *British Journal of Aesthetics* 2 (1962): 15–16.

36. R. N. Wilson, "Literature, society and personality," *Journal of Aesthetics and Art Criticism* 10 (1952): 297–305. The quotes are from p. 229 and p. 298, respectively.

37. Cantril & Bumstead, 1960, p. xiii.

38. Roback, 1952, p. 39.

39. Swartz, 1958. Quotes are from p. 54, p. 82, and p. 84, respectively.

40. McCurdy, 1965, p. 1.

41. R. N. Wilson, 1952, p. 299.

42. W. Stegner, "One way to spell man," *Saturday Review* 41 (1958): 30.

43. J. T. Metcalf, "Psychological studies of literary form," *Psychological Bulletin* 35 (1938): 337.

44. F. X. Barron, Review of *The creative experience,* by S. Rosner & L. Abt, *Contemporary Psychology* 17 (1972): 4–5.

6

Literature and the Social Sciences

Thou shalt not answer questionnaires
Or quizzes upon World Affairs,
Nor with compliance
Take any test. Thou shalt not sit
With statisticians nor commit
A social science.[1]

General

Literary materials are used extensively in empirical studies by the social sciences. This fact, along with the conceptual advantages raised in previous chapters, is a major argument in favor of the use of literary data by psychology. Literature and social concerns naturally share the same interests:

A large majority of the questions raised by literary study are ... social questions: questions of tradition and convention, norms and genres, symbols, and myths ... the relations of literature to a given social situation, to an economic, social, and political system ... to describe and define the influence of society on literature, and to prescribe and judge the position of literature in society.[2]

Many of these social issues are illustrated in Coser's collection of almost a hundred literary selections, *Sociology through Literature*. Coser sees the writer's comments on man's social life as an important source of data:

> Literature, though it may also be many things, is social evidence and testimony . . . on manners and morals . . . tensions between men and their society [and] modes of response to peculiar social and cultural conditions.[3]

The novelist, continues Coser, has the advantage of "trained sensibilities [and an] intensity of perception [with the] capacity to articulate."[4] While Coser recognizes that fiction is not scientific knowledge ("systematically accumulated and certified"), he accepts it as material which can be profitably used for theory and research. The reflection of society in literature, argues Coser, can be used to learn more about those aspects of society that may be overlooked by traditional studies, resulting in a broadening of sociological perspectives. The perspectives of literary criticism are also enriched by an understanding of the social sciences. For example, a knowledge of the social sciences can lead to a greater appreciation of cultural influences on the responsiveness of an audience.

Sociology has made the greatest use of literary material; early reviews are found in Kern, Sewter, and Witte and, more recently, in Barnett. Berger's analysis is an example of the sociological description of an audience, whether defined as the classroom or the more typical group seeking entertainment. Other disciplines have also included literary materials. Literature's relevance to anthropology, which includes folktales, myths, and oral literature, is reviewed by several writers: Maranda, Marett, Shapiro, Thompson, and de Voss and Hippler. Charvat has reviewed the area of economics and literature. The relevance between linguistics and literature is discussed in Adams and Powers, Duncan,

McGranahan, and Paul. Journalism's use of literature is found in Clay. The general contribution of the social sciences to the arts is amplified in Hoggart's "Humanistic Studies and Mass Culture."

The social sciences, sometimes relying on units as small as the phoneme, and taking into consideration a reading audience as large as a national group, society, or culture, have investigated the classics of literature as well as best sellers. The distinction between these two types of fiction and their relevance to sociology are aptly presented by Lowenthal.[5] Also included among the types of literature studied is drama presented on stage, film, TV, and radio. In addition, there are also biographies and autobiographies of nonliterary persons. Greenstein and Little have examined this sort of material in an historical-political context, while the psychoanalytic approach to biography is represented in the work of Barnes, Fearing, and Merriam. Social psychological treatments of biography are reviewed in chapter 8, in the section on the reader. Among all the various types of literature, short stories in mass media magazines are the most frequently studied.

The issues are often controversial problems of immediate public interest: poverty, race, the city, alienation, and anomie in a changing modern civilization; or focused on special groups: bureaucracy, the intellectual, and youth. These and other contemporary social issues in a literary context are discussed by Lowenthal.[6]

A variety of quasi-literary materials have been used, indicating the amenability of prose to quantitative treatment. These include propaganda, oratory, marketing, advertising, public relations copy, and even greeting card verse. The use of nonliterary prose material in a political science context, for measuring public opinion and the content and function of communication, is discussed by many writers in the Berelson and Janowitz reader, especially by Berelson in his own article, and in the collections by Gerbner et al. and Lasswell et al. (The study of communication in a psychological rather than sociological context, which may more directly bear on the literary message received by the reader, is treated by Hovland and Weiss.)

A wide range of other subtle, unusual, and apparently difficult types of prose materials have proved amenable to the testing of hypotheses, the use of quantitative analysis, and the gathering of objective data. Musical lyrics and songs have attracted much attention. Their thematic content was examined by Brook; the relation between words and music was discussed by Schwadron; attitudes toward courtship expressed in lyrics were analyzed by Horton; and lyrics in non-Western societies as a form of communication were reviewed by Lomax. Other apparently intractable materials have been objectively studied. Fischer contrasted cross-cultural art styles; Sebald compared German and American song books; Kris and Leites examined the propaganda content of various media; Shils and Janowitz investigated the recall of propaganda leaflets; Hatch and Hatch surveyed marriage announcements; Lewin reviewed the yearbooks of Nazi and American youth; Schneider and Dornbusch relied on religious best sellers; Stoetzer analyzed postage stamp pictures; and Auster used cartoon characters like Little Orphan Annie. While they are not literary, the empirical study of such materials illustrates the resourcefulness and versatility of the empirical approach and the susceptibility of apparently intractable prose materials to objective study.

Literature provides highly communicable and realistic social information, in an expressive and articulate way, about institutions (for example, politics, economics, education, community structure, class, urbanization, and religion); and a wide variety of social facts about groups, classes, and societies, including their values, norms, mores, roles, beliefs, aspirations, and attitudes. Thus, Martel and McCall used magazine fiction for the information it provided on the changing interests of a society with respect to the family, work, leisure, and, in particular, the effects of industrialization: "Stories often contain many valid ethnographic components and, further ... these are sensitive to broad social changes."[7]

In addition to providing descriptive information about society, literature may also foresee social change or even bring it about. Literature acts as a kind of pressure, which like any other type of communication is "verbally transmitted information [used] to modify the behavior of another individual or group."[8] That literature has the power to disrupt society and threaten the social order is attested to by the censorship imposed by authoritarian governments.

Changes in society can come about as different types of experiences and events are articulated by literature, leading to their recognition, which then produces public action. An interesting survey of literature as productive of change is Davies' analysis of over fifty books of political fiction (for example, Harriet Beecher Stowe's *Uncle Tom's Cabin*). These books dealt with the issues of their times: power relationships, protest, class struggle, social conflict, the goals of equality and dignity, and the opposition or support of anarchy, tyranny, and oppression. Analyzing literary statements, including their references to the state, government, and citizenry, Davies demonstrated that there was a close tie between political theory and literary fact and that fiction did anticipate the occurrence of real events.

Literature may also integrate, stabilize, and strengthen social events. Hoggart in *The Uses of Literacy* has argued, for example, that the values of contemporary working class culture are supported by the mass circulation magazines read by this group.

Literature may also function to dissipate emotions that might otherwise lead to harmful actions, through role playing and identification with confessional literature, detective and horror stories, and pornography. Literary types (for example, the fool), according to Klapp, may also play a special cathartic function for the reader, as they provide an object with which to safely identify without self-conscious embarrassment.

Along with the content and the reader, the writer of literature has attracted sociological interest (although to a lesser degree). Albrecht and Wilson, among others, have discussed the writer within a social framework in which he can be classified as a particular occupational type, with a unique lifestyle (that is, in dress, leisure, residence, self-image), holding a specific place in a particular system, and identified with values that correspond to this system.[9] Further, members of the various arts may be recruited differently into the social order, have different relations to their publics, and differ from one another in other ways: economically, socially, ethnically, and in origins, status, and educational background. Not only is the writer's choice of career influenced by the social system, but so too is his subject matter, style, creativity, and extent of recognition. The acceptance of a writer, a literary form, and a style is dependent upon broad sociological forces. Fashions in literature and writers may fluctuate in relation to changing social phenomena and other collective events. More narrowly, the artist's work, status, and role, and his acceptance by an audience are related to the economics of an industry, including that of the bookseller and publisher.

However, studies of the industry which supports a particular art form are rare; even rarer are empirical studies of the contemporary book publishing industry. However, Hirsch's study of the economics of the popular music industry serves as a model for empirical research. In general social-economic terms, the aesthetic product can be seen as a result of the producers' and artists' attempts to fit their work to an audience by remaining within the context of the prevailing values of the society.

THE SOCIAL SCIENCES IN CONTRAST TO PSYCHOLOGY

Although their involvement with other written materials (for example, official documents) is much greater, it is clear from this survey of the social sciences' varied and extensive interests in literature that the importance of literary content is recognized and accepted by most sociological scholars. Their interdisciplinary involvement with literature has developed its specific subject matter, methodology, and point of view. A count of content analysis studies in Holsti's review (the method most frequently used for literary materials) indicates that only about 10 percent of the studies done in the social sciences have been carried out in the field of psychology. The disparity of interest in literature may be explained by the traditional difference in the groups' attitudes on the acceptability of subjective data, historical methodology, and descriptive analysis. Psychology has generally favored objective data, experimental methodology, and predictive analysis because they imply greater rigor. The contrasting orientations of each group have also been influenced by the extent to which their major figures have used literature. Those of the social sciences—Marx, Weber, Spencer, Sorokin—have made serious and important references to literature in their works.

In contrast, the major figures of psychology (excluding the nonacademic clinician Freud) have rarely if at all done this. (The difficulties in separating psychology from the social sciences should be recognized since the traditional gross distinction given—an interest in the individual versus an interest in the group or institution—is often inappropriate and oversimplified. Complicating any distinction is the subdiscipline of social psychology, which includes psychologists if their concern with the social context is directed toward an interest in the individual and individual processes.) Reflecting on the disparity between psychology and social sciences, Leenhardt has pointed out the extensive, pervasive, and continuing contribution of foreign sources in the social sciences. This historical and philosophical influence, which is more likely to include the humanities in its thinking, is less frequently found in the more insular field of psychology; hence the neglect of aesthetics and literature. However, as discussed below, relatively little of the social sciences' admittedly greater interest in literature has been converted into empirical investigation.

Investigations of literary materials

Although relatively few problems have been empirically investigated in the social sciences, those few concretely attest to the applicability of a scientific approach to literature. Most are by sociologists, and they are usually of popular works, such as short stories in mass circulation magazines. The intent of this review, which is organized by type of literary form studied, is not to examine details about the procedures, results, and conclusions of these studies as much as it is to survey the kinds of literary and quasi-literary materials that have been used for different types of sociologically oriented problems.

THE NOVEL

Although there have been fewer empirical studies of the novel than of other literary forms, such studies have usually been quite ambitious, with results more qualitative than quantitative. For example, Gossman examined and compared fifty works of popular fiction in two early periods of English literature, largely on the basis of impressionistic analysis buttressed by counts of several variables (for example, the setting, the leading characters, and their problems). His subjective and objective analyses dealt with the motives of the readers of that time and their feelings about the religion and political system of their society. Lowenthal reviewed the characteristics of novels of eighteenth century England, along with information on libraries and booksellers, in order to reveal such facets of life in society at that time as the readers' attitudes of optimism and despair.[10]

Watt also relied heavily on qualitative terms in interpreting his statistical analysis of the public and critical reaction to *Robinson Crusoe*. He discussed these as a projection of the readers' and critics' needs; that is, they saw Crusoe as a rugged individualist and entrepreneur although this was not the author's intent. Lowenthal also examined the reception of Dostoevski's work in Germany in the context of the political ideology of the audience, which he felt disposed them to react to literature in particular ways.[11] While these studies were largely impressionistic, Rosengren's study of reviews of fiction in two time periods was almost entirely based on quantitative analysis. He did not arrive at any substantive conclusions about sociological issues, but he showed that the reviews were statistically analyzable, proving that they were a reliable and valid tool for sociological analysis.

SHORT STORIES

Social science investigations have concentrated on short story fiction in popular mass magazines perhaps because their brevity makes for more efficient (or faster) statistical analysis. Berelson and Salter studied about two hundred short stories written over two different periods of time for their references to minority groups' economic status, occupations, and roles. They compared the portrayal of minorities with that of the majority culture and with available demographic data. Inglis conducted a survey on women as a specific disadvantaged group, dealing with the portrayal of heroines in one magazine over the first third of this century (for example, occupation). It was found that women's status in these stories reflected, and to some degree also preceded, actual trends in their roles as determined by census data.

Other characteristics of heroines in fiction have been studied in different types of magazines. For example, Flora found feminine stereotypes in several hundred U.S. and Latin American short stories (for example, dependence, passivity, ineffectuality, pride) to be consistent across cultures, classes, and occupations of readers.

Johns-Heine and Gerth examined male fictional heroes, their ages, occupations, and other characteristics in one large circulation magazine over a forty year span. They found that the heroes reflected readers' values (based on known circulation data) on several dimensions (for example, love and success). W. Hirsch determined that the portrayal of scientists in 300 science fiction stories changed between 1926–50 as a result of historical and social trends: the scientific solution has become only one of several types of answers to social problems, rather than the major one (that is, technology, courage, and intelligence also count); and the scientist as a major character has declined.

Other studies have been more concerned with basic values than with descriptions of groups. Albrecht examined the dominant motives in several hundred short stories (for example, marriage as an exclusive life goal), finding that different types of magazines were similar in their portrayal of these values, despite their popularity with different socioeconomic readerships.[12] A study by Taviss indicated that the existential themes of alienation and isolation and their resolution could be scored in stories of different time periods. Whipple traced various expressions of success in the early issues of the *Saturday Evening Post* (to 1928).

Manfredi concluded that stories in two different magazines could be scored as providing escape and release for their readers' dissatisfactions by comparing the characteristics of the stories with various known parameters of the readership. Martel and McCall paid especially close attention to the methodology of sample selection and content analysis technique in analyzing mass circulation fiction over the first half of this century. They quantified many dimensions: the locales used at different periods; the social status of males and females arranged by age, class, occupation, schooling, and marital status; and even as subtle an index as the placement of the story's theme on a liberalism-conservatism continuum. They concluded, as have most other investigations, that the source of fiction's pleasure was its resemblance to the readerships' interests, values, ideals, and aspirations.

Cross-cultural variations in magazine fiction have also been investigated. Ginglinger used the fifty dimensions of White's value-analysis to inspect American and French magazines and their representation of different cultural values. Wayne contrasted American and Soviet values on the basis of graphic material in the stories of two popular magazines in each country. The story illustrations of the Soviets were more economic and aesthetic than those of the Americans; the latter were more religious and social.

Cross-cultural interests are also reflected in anthropological studies of other types of brief literary materials. The folktales of various primitive groups have been regarded by de Voss and Hippler as institutionalized expressive behavior that parallels the more spontaneous materials of projective tests, as well as the content of dreams, music, art, and humor. Less clinically oriented, Colby and his co-workers quantitatively analyzed myths of the Navajo and the Eskimo with respect to such dimensions as the characteristics and values of the home and play, the expressions of anger, and attitudes toward space, good, and evil. Ethiopian folktales have been similarly treated by Korten.

Unfortunately, researchers have not directly tested readers' reactions, but they have instead relied on story content. This omission of individual reactions reflects a bias in the methodology and conceptualizations of the social sciences. This bias is consistent for all examinations of literature by socially oriented researchers.

DRAMA

Drama has also attracted investigators in the social sciences. McGranahan and Wayne studied the most popular American and German plays of two time periods in terms of the frequency of different themes, plots, endings, and types of conflict. They found several differences between the two countries, for example, American plays placed a greater emphasis on love and morals, while the German plays focused on idealism and power. They corroborated these findings using nonliterary sources of information (for example, questionnaires). Head compared American and German TV dramas and plays. While the frequency of different themes in American TV and plays was similar (for example, love), the themes in the two types of German productions were not correlated. L. W. Gardner has compared types of TV programs in America and Japan. While both groups showed the same degree of interest in drama, there were more educational programs on Japanese TV and more children's and variety shows on American TV.

Examples of various types of investigations of radio content and its listeners, of different degrees of rigor, can be found in Lazarsfeld and Stanton's collection. The articles by Arnheim on soap operas and by Peatman on taste in popular music are especially significant because of their extensive reliance upon quantitative data taken from survey research methods and questionnaires. Lazarsfeld has also discussed audience research along several dimensions.[13] Empirical studies by Erdelyi, Jakobovits, and Wiebe have correlated several factors with audience behavior: the number of repetitions of popular songs with listeners' preferences, and in more economic terms, with sales; and preference for popular music on the radio was correlated to an audience's movie-going behavior, across different time periods and for different age groups. However, there are many more discussions than studies of radio and TV drama available in a wide range of sources, including those found in Herzog, Warner and Henry, and E. C. Wilson. While they deal with drama and the reactions and characteristics of the audience, most are not concerned with quantitative studies. These discussions do, however, suggest possibilities for quantifying the reactions of any audience, including the readers of literature.

FILM

Film has attracted the interest of several empirical investigators because, as R. A. Smith and Hovland et al. have noted, of its broad relevance to aesthetics, education, and propaganda. D. B. Jones tallied one year of Hollywood's productions in straightforward quantitative terms on a wide

variety of dimensions: the values reflected by the characters (for example, security); demographic features (for example, marital status); the predominance of certain themes (for example, love); and the degree to which values and themes were fulfilled. Thurstone developed an attitude scale and questionnaire about the movies. Building on this instrument, Panda and his co-workers, and Patal have measured various groups of viewers and their demographic characteristics (for example, age, sex, educational background), including personality and cross-cultural differences. Williams surveyed student feelings about and interests in different types and themes of films, and Anast examined frequency of attendance.

More theoretically, Wolfenstein and Leites surveyed films from several countries over two time periods from a psychoanalytic point of view. On a quantitative level of analysis, they first counted the most typical manifest themes, which then became the basis for the authors' speculations on the emotional significance of the films to their audience, and to their respective cultures. Schiff took viewers' judgments of apparent time durations for two types of films, one documentary and the other art education, and used these estimates as an index of the audience's interest in the films. Viewers overestimated time equally for both types of films, both immediately and after an interval.

Asheim investigated the interesting question of whether a book gains or loses when made into a film by examining the changes made in the filming of twenty-four classic literary works (for example, *Pride and Prejudice, Anna Karenina*). As a means of measuring the deviation of the film from the original, he compared a content analysis of various themes of the book and film, for example, whether the ending affirmed or denied the original story's thesis. Among the various findings, Asheim ascertained that the chronological sequences in the story were more likely to be followed than not; that most of the films had the same kind of ending as the books, especially if the books ended happily; and that

unhappy themes were retained only if they were not negative, that is, they did not question the convictions of the
audience, nor deal with indecision, frustration, helplessness,
and despair.

Critique

The social sciences other than psychology have not
been reluctant to examine literature and related prose forms.
Although popular and quasi-literary examples from the
mass media are studied more often, social science theorists
and investigators have not hesitated to deal with relatively
unusual and atypical sources of information. They have
found literary sources useful and have analyzed them in
methodological and quantitative terms.

However, many of these efforts have serious flaws, as
the investigators themselves have pointed out. Further, despite the prominent role of literature in the social sciences,
there remain complaints that the treatment is inadequate: it
is "sporadic and unsystematic even though considerable in
volume,"[14] and "sociologists have but rarely utilized works
of literature in their investigations."[15] One still finds both
humanists and social scientists resistant to the idea of research with literary materials. There has been confusion,
affirms Block, as to literature's particular relationship to
society, that is, as reflector, interpreter, anticipator, or initia-
tor of social events. Another general criticism is that sociology has paid more attention to literature than to art. This
is because sociologists, according to Kavolis, feel that literature is easier to study. It should be noted that this priority
of attention, and its justification, are just the reverse of
psychology's (chapter 1).

There are a variety of more specific weaknesses in social
science studies. One frequently finds a statistical naivety in
empirical studies of literary content, in which analysis is
limited to tallies and percentages without probability tests
of significance. Data are simply described without indicating their statistical reliability, validity, and meaning. There

are other notable deficiencies in methodological and technical rigor and sophistication. For example, some sort of base line (or control group) is often absent, thereby making it difficult to talk meaningfully about differences and other comparisons between data and trends. There is frequently a failure to use corroborative information from nonliterary sources (for example, demographic, historical) in order to supplement literary data. These methodological omissions make it difficult to interpret the significance of the obtained results. Are the results, effects, or relationships due to those factors postulated, or to other and irrelevant factors, or to chance? Further, because few details on procedures are usually given, it is often hard to tell how problems of reliability and sample selection, and the choice of measurable categories were handled by the investigator. The difficulties of content analysis, the major tool of the social sciences in literature, have already been indicated. Compounding these problems, subjective impressions are often interwoven with quantitative analyses in unknown ways and to an uncertain degree. Also of serious import, different investigations are not interrelated with one another or followed through with related studies. There is instead an isolation between studies, perhaps because a good deal of the research is merely busy work—work in which specific hypotheses are infrequently tested, done with the general notion of describing whatever can be found, or the procedural goal of proving that a technique is useful. This means that a high priority of effort is placed on showing that investigations of literature are possible.

There are other problems which have been noted in the context of historical psychobiography, in Greenstein and Lerner's *Sourcebook,* but which are also generally applicable to most literary analysis. These problems include the exaggeration of psychosocial determinants, the emphasis on the negative influences on man, and the arbitrary assignment of terms borrowed from the social sciences. Consequently, much of the work seems to be relatively unimpressive because of its poor methodology and its unrelatedness to broader issues and theory. Although there are a large number of speculative discussions on literature in a social science context, empirical investigation lags far behind. The number of empirical studies is small relative to the number of discursive, speculative, critical, and descriptive essays. As an additional handicap, the empirical study of literature is fragmented from the mainstream of the social sciences, in which nonliterary but prose materials (for example, documents) have been successfully used in broader theoretical frameworks. Despite the greater empiricism and quantification, literature in the social sciences has not fared much better than it has in psychology.

However, as serious as the shortcomings are, many of them can be avoided, compensated for, or ameliorated, especially if more theoretically oriented scholars and methodologically sophisticated investigators were to become interested in literary material and recognize its worth. Even when the problems of literary analysis cannot be completely overcome (for example, because of its impressionistic basis), other kinds of data, including those from more objective sources (for example, interviews) and other traditional materials (for example, written records), can be used to corroborate and extend what might otherwise be circumscribed information.

Despite the difficulties of literary study, it is clear that the social scientist, unlike the psychologist, accepts the writer as especially sensitive to problems relevant to his interests. Many of these interests may not be the same as those of the psychologist (for example, the group rather than the individual), or they may have a different focus (for example, the role of social institutions rather than of personal processes). A particular interest literature shares with psychology, on the other hand, is the individual's experiences. Literature selects, focuses, organizes, and heightens the experiences of a people. As two social scientists have asserted, "The basic material of literature is thus experience."[17] The language and words of a culture, whether literary or not, but especially if they are, reflect the feelings and attitudes of the members of society.

The social sciences' attention to literature as a germane source of information, their willingness to study it, and their ability to do so with at least a fair amount of success, should encourage and support psychology's own involvement with literature. The social sciences have at least begun to develop a methodology and appropriate techniques with which to empirically investigate literature. They have generated research hypotheses about literary materials which have yielded quantitative data. Further, they have recognized, to some extent, the dangers of over-relying on literature as a completely representative, adequate, and undistorted reflection of society. Thus they have included the more mundane social facts, taken from records and documents, in order to avoid what Albrecht finds to be the major abuse of literary analysis by social scientists, namely, overemphasis on sociology and oversimplification of literature.[18]

The possible biases of the writer, the artistic distortions of his material, and the fact that he writes for a small elitist audience have not been considered insurmountable handicaps in using literary information for empirical purposes. The special considerations that reduce the objectivity of a literary work differ only in degree from those of other types of data, and are common to any historical record. Further, there are compensations: "A writer is a specialized thinker about the individual," argues Lowenthal.[19]. He is therefore a kind of reporter whose breadth and depth of insight are valuable despite the possible ambiguities in his work.

The positive attitudes of social science investigators toward literature cannot help but reinforce psychology's interest. To the degree literature is relevant to the social sciences, it should also be relevant to psychology. In the next two chapters, psychological studies of literary materials are reviewed. They more directly support the argument that literature is a valuable source of information to psychology.

Notes

1. W. H. Auden, "Under which lyre," in *Nones* (New York: Random House, 1951), p. 69.
2. R. Wellek & A. Warren, *Theory of literature* (New York: Harcourt, Brace, 1952), p. 89.
3. L. A. Coser, ed., *Sociology through literature* (Englewood Cliffs, N. J.: Prentice-Hall, 1963), p. 2.
4. Ibid., p. 3.
5. L. Lowenthal, "The sociology of literature," in *Communication in modern society,* edited by W. L. Schramm (Urbana, Ill.: University of Illinois, 1948) and L. Lowenthal, *Literature, popular culture, and society* (Englewood Cliffs, N. J.: Spectrum, 1961).
6. Lowenthal, "Literature and sociology," in *Relations of literary study,* edited by J. Thorpe (New York: Modern Language Association, 1967).
7. M. U. Martel & G. J. McCall, "Reality-orientation and the pleasure principle: A study of American mass-periodical fiction (1890–1955)," in *People, society and mass communication,* edited by L. S. Dexter & D. M. White (Glencoe, Ill.: Free Press, 1964), p. 298.
8. C. I. Hovland, "Psychology and the communication process," in Schramm, 1948, p. 59.
9. M. C. Albrecht, "The relationship of literature and society," *American Journal of Sociology* 59 (1954): 425–436; I. Watt, "Literature and society," in *The arts in society,* edited by R. N. Wilson (Englewood Cliffs, N. J.: Prentice-Hall, 1964), pp. 299–311; R. N. Wilson, "The poet in American society," in R. N. Wilson, 1964, pp. 1–34, and "F. Scott Fitzgerald: Personality and culture," in R. N. Wilson, 1964, pp. 271–298. Similar arguments are found in J. H. Barnett, "Research in the sociology of art," *Sociology and Social Research* 42 (1958):

401–405; L. H. Buckingham, "The development of social attitudes through literature," *School and Society* 52 (1940): 446 –454. [*Psychological Abstracts* 15 (1941) #1489]; A. Carter, "Sociology in the new literature," *Sociological Review* 20 (1928): 250–255; Charvat, 1949; S. M. Dornbusch, "Content and method in the study of the higher arts," in Wilson, 1964, pp. 363–372; R. Escarpit, "The sociology of literature," in *International encyclopedia of the social sciences*, edited by D. L. Sills, vol. 9 (New York: Macmillan & Free Press, 1968); R. Fernandez, "Dostoyevsky, traditional domination, and cognitive dissonance," *Social Forces* 49 (1970): 299–303; M. Lerner & E. Mims, Jr., "Literature," in *Encyclopedia of the social sciences*, edited by E. R. A. Seligman (New York: Macmillan, 1935), vol. 9, pp. 523–543.

10. Lowenthal, 1961.

11. Lowenthal, "The reception of Dostoevski's work in Germany: 1880–1920," in Wilson, 1964, pp. 122–147.

12. M. C. Albrecht, "Does literature reflect common values?" *American Sociological Review* 21 (1956): 722–729.

13. P. F. Lazarsfeld, "Audience research," in *Reader in public opinion and communication*, edited by B. M. Janowitz (Glencoe, Ill.: Free Press, 1953), pp. 337–346.

14. J. H. Barnett, "Research in the sociology of art," *Sociology and Social Research* 42 (1958): 403.

15. Coser, 1963. p. 2.

16. F. I. Greenstein & M. Lerner, eds. *A source book for the study of personality and politics* (Chicago: Markham, 1971), pp. 78–98.

17. Lerner & Mims, 1935, p. 525.

18. M. C. Albrecht, Review of *The novel and society*, by D. Spearman, and *The rise of the novel*, by I. Watt, *Transaction* 6 (1969): 54–55; see also, Wilson, 1952.

19. Lowenthal, 1961, p. xiii.

PART TWO

IN SUPPORT OF AN

OBJECTIVE STUDY OF LITERATURE

The previous chapters have indicated that serious reservations exist about objective psychology's involvement with literature; there are real problems and warranted skepticism regarding a closer relationship between the two. Nevertheless, there are several reasons for viewing a tie between literature and psychology as meaningful and useful and the obstacles to such a tie as not insurmountable. At this time, an open-minded attitude toward literature's relevance to psychology is appropriate.

There are many ways in which psychology's serious involvement with literature can be supported. The potential for the objective study of literature is greater than so far indicated. Literature shows its relevance and usefulness to psychology in several ways: (1) literature provides data for further psychological investigation; (2) literature offers analyses and explanations of psychological themes which can subsequently be objectively amplified and corroborated; (3) literature anticipates answers to psychological questions, thereby suggesting hypotheses for further study; and (4) literature illustrates and thereby clarifies known psychological themes. Literature therefore has both a direct and an indirect bearing on psychological investigations: it acts as a source of content, explanation, and ideas for further study, as well as dramatizing what is already known.

Most of the arguments presented against psychology's empirical use of literature have either been countered or put in perspective in part I. The differences between the two disciplines are neither as great nor as insurmountable as they may have originally appeared. Psychology can justifiably look to literature: objective methods are available and statistical abstractions are possible; the social sciences have demonstrated that literary materials can be studied with some success; and literary information can be useful to psychology as illustration, data, hypotheses, and analyses. There are therefore a number of reasons for including literature as one of several sources of psychological information about man's experiences and behavior.

However, regardless of the number and worth of these arguments, discussions, logical presentations, and examples, they remain insufficient. Literature will continue to be outside of the boundaries of scientific psychology or, at best, remain peripheral to it, if only exhortation and speculation are the bases for evaluating its relevance to psychology. It must also be demonstrated that concrete empirical studies of literature can in fact be carried out; and that these quantitative investigations do indeed contribute to psychological, aesthetic, and literary issues. If there is to be any worth to the proposed tie between literature and psychology, its fruitfulness must be demonstrated, and its future possibilities outlined. Otherwise, those in literature and psychology will remain skeptical of there being more than a superficial link between psychology and literature, regardless of the number and kind of rationale one might offer.

Concrete examples of research demonstrating the meaningfulness of an empirical psychological study of literature are summarized in chapters 7 and 8. Not only do these scientific investigations directly contribute to an understanding of literature (its creative origins, structure, function, and response) but they also, less directly, clarify various areas of psychology which have used literary materials for their own nonaesthetic purposes. At the risk of artificially categorizing these studies and of ignoring their similarities and interrelationships, they have been grouped under three major headings: studies of the author (his personality and creativity) in chapter 7; and investigations of the reader and the work itself in chapter 8. The final chapter evaluates empirical psychological efforts in literature in light of the criticisms made by both literary critics and psychologists, and concludes with several directions for future research.

7

Studies of the Author:

Creativity and Personality

The personality and creativity of the writer are of interest to the psychologist, who has historically dealt with these topics. Psychological research in these areas is also of value to the literary critic if an understanding of the personal dynamics of the writer contributes to an understanding of a work, the literary process, and an audience's reactions. The topics of personality and creativity are related to one another and overlap—creativity is usually considered an aspect of personality—but psychologists who work in each area differ in their approach to and treatment of literary material. While the study of personality usually examines the works of one author, the study of creativity typically focuses on the lives of a group of contemporary creative people, most of whom are neither literary nor aesthetic types.

Most of this chapter will center on the topic of creativity, even though little creativity research has been specifically directed toward authors. Creativity research has been carried on much more vigorously than literary personality studies, especially since the event of Sputnick in the 1950s, when the discovery and support of talented people assumed high priority. Recent collections of articles and studies of creativity are found in Anderson, *Creativity and Its Cultivation;* Gruber et al., *Contemporary Approaches to Creative Thinking;* C.

W. Taylor, *Widening Horizons in Creativity;* and Vernon, *Creativity.* A general review is found in Golann; and a survey of creativity research in the visual arts was carried out by Beittel. Despite these signs of interest, research in creativity compared to other psychological topics is still quite limited; Guilford points out that it accounts for less than 1 percent of current entries in *Psychological Abstracts.*[1] Perhaps because of the practical and pedagogical origins of the study of creativity, one finds less attention directed to men of literature and the other arts than to nonaesthetic persons, that is, scientists and other professionals, businessmen ("brainstorming"), college students, and school-children. Investigations of creativity do not usually distinguish literary creativity from other creative endeavors. Instead, all types of creativity are typically grouped together. The review of research in creativity will therefore concentrate largely on investigations of nonliterary creative artists and creative types outside of the arts.

Creativity and the intellect

The empirical study of creativity began with Galton, who examined the family lines of several hundred geniuses and eminent men in different fields, including novelists, playwrights, and poets. In showing that the ancestors and offspring of successful men also had high intelligence, Galton hoped to prove the hereditary character of genius. However, similarities in intelligence among relatives could also have been due to common enriched environments. Nevertheless, Galton's work was the first systematic study of genius, and he initiated and encouraged sound methodology and the use of statistics.

The inheritability of genius or of creativity and the relationship between intelligence and creativity remain controversial questions today, although not in an aesthetic context. The issues are focused on the study of gifted children and in finding the means to encourage creativity in the educational process. The view that creativity and intelligence are independent is represented by Getzels and Jackson's *Creativity and Intelligence: Explorations with Gifted Children;* a critique and an alternative approach to the problem is Wallach and Kogan's *Modes of Thinking in Young Children: A Study of the Creativity-Intelligence Distinction,* especially chapter 8. A good review of the controversy regarding intelligence and creativity is Hudson's article, "The Question of Creativity." He has also contributed a major study on the educational aspects of creativity, *Contrary Imaginations.* A good survey of the definitions, theories, and problems of creativity within the educational context is Kneller's *The Art and Science of Creativity.*

Historical biographies, relied upon by Galton as a source of data about men of genius, have also been used by other investigators. Cox had judges estimate the IQs of several hundred men of eminence on the basis of their biographies. Poets, novelists, and dramatists (together with statesmen and scientists) fell at the mean IQ for this group (160); philosophers were estimated to have the highest IQ at 170 (soldiers had the lowest IQs, 125, but still greater than the population average of 100); and the IQs of musicians (145) and artists (140) were somewhat lower than those of writers. White also relied on a biographical analysis of genius in examining the versatility of 300 eminent men who lived between 1450–1850. The groups which were rated as having the greatest range of competence among the twenty-three professions surveyed were the philosophers, statesmen, and scholars (competent in 7.5 areas), closely followed by poets and novelists (at 6.7). Among the other arts, represented by eleven to twenty-six persons in each field, musicians ranked lowest in versatility, while artists were at an intermediary level (4.0). Among the creative fields in which competence was shown, poetry was the area most frequently mentioned (ranked 3rd out of twenty-three), followed by drama (13th), art (14th), music (15th), and fiction (18th). Goethe and Benjamin Franklin were two of the most versatile men in this sample, and Rembrandt was one of the least, although the group as a whole was overwhelmingly versatile compared to ordinary people.

Biographies have been used to study various other traits of talented people. Raskin compared the biographies of over a thousand eminent men of science and letters, including artists and authors, whose eminence was determined by the number of lines written about each person, on many dimensions: length of life, creative period, family influence and other early environmental factors, the presence of various social and temperamental traits (for example, cheerfulness, persistence), evidence of neurosis, and cause of death. Her survey indicated that mental instability appeared to be greater for literary men than for scientists (an issue that will reappear in this review); that all types of genius displayed an unusual diversity of abilities (as White above reported); and that men of literature were characterized as more dependent, emotional, and sickly than scientists. Rubinow's study of biographies examined the development of personality in 250 men, including poets and writers among other artists and nonartistic professionals. Different and progressive stages of growth were consistently expressed in the work, events, and experiences of their lives.

Although the biography is directly relevant to both the study of personality and creativity—after all, it is intentionally oriented toward these topics—this literary form has received relatively little empirical attention from psychologists. While the studies reviewed above used biographical material, they did not relate it to other personality analysis of authors, especially if living; neither were other resources of creativity examined (for example, productivity), nor were their products directly analyzed for corroborative evidence (for example, a content analysis of themes). Squire's study of the musician Franck is exemplary in this regard. Some of the reasons for these omissions on the part of investigators of creativity may be the inadequate development of critical biographical techniques, a shortcoming Edel has emphasized in accounting for the neglect of this form when literature per se is studied. In addition, the prominence of nonempirical and psychoanalytic approaches to biography, as noted in Garratz's review, has discouraged objective approaches. In general, however, the main problem is psychology's difficulties in objectively classifying and analyzing subjective protocols.

Galton's approach has been continued in several directions other than in the use of biographies. In general, his approach defines success by the number of specific accomplishments, maintains a strong interest in the role of intelligence, and vigorously champions the value of measurement. Terman, who uses a longitudinal method of research based upon on-going rather than historical lives, views intelligence as the dominant factor in success. He and his coworkers have for several decades studied the achievements of several hundred people whose IQs were obtained when they were children. However, they have not particularly focused on creativity.

Guilford's work with its emphasis on intellect and its measurement, is more directly related to creativity.[2] He specializes in the factor analytic method, a kind of multiple correlational technique which seeks a few communalities within a vast array of data. The method can be used to extrapolate those intellectual traits that distinguish the different abilities of the various arts, or to contrast the arts with other creative endeavors. Although the wide array of factors discovered are still largely provisional, in general they define the creative person as a thinker and a problem solver. This cognitive orientation to creativity contrasts with the more personal dimensions stressed by most other investigators. Cognitive factors in creativity include fluency (of ideas and expressions, and of words and associations), flexibility, and originality.

Guilford has also made much of the distinction between divergent and convergent thinking: the former type moves away from expected and previously known responses, while the latter type moves toward responses that are already known and more specifiable. Whether divergent thinking is more typical of creative thinking or whether both types are used equally is a question which has not yet been satisfactorily resolved. The notion that creativity simultaneously involves contradictory modes of thought has historically been and remains a provocative idea. Within the psychoanalytic tradition, Rothenberg has termed the creative use of opposite images as "Janusian thinking." Although similar to Guilford's notion of divergent thinking, it is used more as a metaphor than as a measurable concept.

The approach to creativity which concentrates on intellect has developed sophisticated psychometric techniques. However, sophisticated technique may not always be an advantage, in that one may become overdependent on tests and overvalue their intercorrelations. Too great a faith can be placed on measurement indices as automatically revealing the creative process. For example, there is an over-riding preoccupation with measurement in intelligence testing, a field closely linked to the study of genius and creativity, and one in which there is a great technical virtuosity and a seemingly substantial classification scheme. Nevertheless, the topic of intelligence is characterized by a paucity of explanation, a lack of theory, and an absence of experimental research on the nature of the underlying processes and their functioning. These general difficulties of psychometrics may have led to Dellas and Gaier's pessimistic summary of Guilford's factor analytic approach to creativity:

[There is a] lack of success of these instruments in predictive efficiency and in correlating with demonstrated creativity and other indices of creative performance.[3]

They blame the "inconclusiveness of the data"[4] on a variety of specific causes, including the questionable adequacy of the particular factor analytic techniques used, of which there are several in contention, and the methods of obtaining the data that will be used in the factor analysis, for example, how the subjects are selected, and which of several criteria of creativity are chosen. Additional difficulties in an intellectual treatment of creativity include not only the slighting of personal determinants, especially motivation (a provincialism matched by those studies of creativity emphasizing personality while ignoring intellect), but the neglect of cognitive functions other than intellect, for example, perceptual openness, awareness, and attention.

Other offshoots of the Galton tradition, in its concentration on the number of concrete achievements as an index of success, are those studies which are based on the products of creativity. The productivity of geniuses has the advantage of being more directly observable than their intelligence, and is therefore more susceptible to quantification and criteria of reliability. The best example of a researcher using the productivity approach to creativity is Lehman, who has simply counted the number of superior works produced by eminent men in different professions at various ages. The result is a graphic plot of the relation between creativity (that is, productions), age, and profession. Among different forms of literature, the general trends are as follows: lyrics and ballads have been written at the earliest ages (25–30), followed by short stories (30–35), and then tragedies (35–40); novels were written latest in life (40–45).

Critical to Lehman's method is the use of sophisticated procedures to insure that the works of creative men and not just prolific hacks are being counted. To this end, the status of creative persons and works is based on judgments by experts and the analysis of biographical data. The sensitivity with which an apparently gross counting technique can be used is illustrated in Lehman's study of writers' creative years, as reflected by their best works. Using several hundred works of fiction by over a hundred deceased authors who were judged by experts as significant, Lehman found that the greatest number of these significant books were produced when the authors were in their early forties, an age at which their books were also most likely to become best sellers. However, the age at which the *first* significant book was published was somewhat earlier, in the late thirties. Further, men and women authors differed, in that women produced the greatest number of significant books in their late thirties, somewhat earlier than men did. (However, the sample of women authors, presumably considerably fewer in number than males, limits the validity of this generalization.) These age distinctions (at least among men) appear to be quite general: they held for other compilations of great books, for living authors, and for authors from four different European nations.

A limitation of Lehman's analysis is that his data over-represent the productivity of younger people, and therefore the earlier years of creativity, since his procedure does not take into account the loss of older subjects through death. Thus there are more younger than older people in his sample. To overcome this bias, Dennis examined the productivity of a sample of dramatists, novelists, and poets, along with creative people in other fields, all of whom lived to be at least eighty. He found that the peak years of productivity for all professions were the forties (a period which is a little later than Lehman's sample), followed by the thirties. Further, the artists (unfortunately, the data are not differentiated by specific types) declined more in productivity during their later years than the scholars did, and, to a lesser degree, than scientists.

Among several reasons offered for the more rapid decline of the artistic group, the most reasonable seems to be that artists are less likely to work with collaborators, a form of assistance available to scholars and scientists that might compensate for the lower energy level of old age. However, the decline of artists may be only relative. Artists are more productive than other types in their early years since they require less time for training, the gathering of data, and research activities than either scholars or scientists do. The productivity of the latter groups only appears greater in later years, in that the relative number of nonartistic contributions is disproportionately more than the quantity of work accomplished during their earlier years.

Related to age and creativity, but at the other end of the life span, Bliss found that the birth order of writers and poets was later than that of scientists; scientists were more likely to be first born, and they were more frequently only children. Further, among the authors, novelists and short story writers tended to be born later in the sequence of children than poets. This type of research contributes to Adlerian notions of birth order and feelings of powerlessness.

While the counting techniques of Lehman and Dennis pinpoint the ages at which creative products are most likely to initially occur and be sustained, they do not directly investigate the reasons for these events (or why they differ between professions). An examination of personality variables in creativity attempts to get at some of the causative factors.

Creativity and personality

Classical psychoanalysis holds the general view that creativity is rooted in personality. In particular, it interprets creativity as a disguised form of unconscious urges and as a sublimated defense against neurosis. Whatever the merits and usefulness of this position, it remains largely immune to empirical attack in psychology. Psychoanalytic arguments are based on generalizations from a few reported case studies, the details of which are sketchy at best. However, several recent works by psychoanalysts suggest a trend toward more objective efforts, although still only minimally comprehensive in research design and quantification. For example, Milner has argued that the creative efforts (drawings) of patients undergoing therapy confirm clinician's diagnosis of the problem and dramatically reveal the current status of its treatment. Closer to literary interests, Rothenberg analyzed the symbols in O'Neill's play, *The Iceman Cometh,* using data from manuscript versions and revisions, biographies, and interviews. Another aspect of the study of creativity which fits into the clinical context is the use of personality tests for creative people, especially projective instruments like the Rorschach (inkblot).

In contrast to the psychoanalytic and clinical approach, which concentrates on the unconsciously morbid and pathological aspects of creativity, psychologists such as Vinacke have interpreted creativity as a normal capacity found to varying degrees in everyone. Accordingly, talented people are seen as subject less to the ravaging influences of childhood than to the benefits of special experience and training. Indicating how far the pendulum has swung away from a view of creativity as madness (despite its continuance in popular thought) is Martindale's hypothesis of disinhibition.[5] It holds that lack of control is not a neurotic characteristic but rather, a cognitive process which facilitates enthusiasm, expansiveness, and resoluteness; in short, disinhibition is originality. If correct, this view may reflect the limited truth of the popular stereotype of the artist as impulsive (a theme to be discussed subsequently). Another reversal of the Freudian influence is a current interpretation of creativity, represented by the clinician Rogers, as synonymous with good mental health and satisfactory adjustment.

The Freudian influence is still dominant in the work of MacKinnon, one of the major researchers in creativity. However, although psychodiagnostic and clinical themes are prominent in his work, his studies are nevertheless empirical. Further, they are holistically oriented, interpreting creativity as reflecting the total personality rather than an isolated trait or habit. MacKinnon's general procedure (widely followed by others) is to select a sample of creative people in different professions on the basis of judgments by their peers (for example, editors of journals, deans of schools). Those named then volunteer to undergo a wide battery of intensive personality, aptitude, and intelligence tests. The results are compared with a noncreative normal group (the controls), matched to the creative group on most relevant dimensions (for example, age, sex, occupation, and importantly, success), in order to find differences that may highlight the nature of creativity. The methodology could be characterized as a shot-gun approach to creativity, a technique useful in the early descriptive stages of research. Data are collected not because of a specific hypothesis or theory but rather in the expectation that something useful will show up.

Characteristic of most workers in creativity, MacKinnon has not usually investigated aesthetic creativity, nor has he often compared different aesthetically creative types; his subjects are mostly scientists, engineers, and mathematicians. An exception is his extensive study of architects, chosen perhaps because of their special position as simultaneously artists, engineers, designers, and businessmen. Illustrative of his procedures and findings, he had a group of psychologists familiar with the creative architects (after testing them for several days) check off the following adjectives as particularly descriptive of this group: alert, artistic, intelligent, responsible, ambitious, capable, cooperative, civilized, dependable, friendly, pleasant, resourceful, active, confident, industrious, reliable, conscientious, imaginative, reasonable, enterprising, independent, widely interested, adaptable, assertive, determined, energetic, persevering, sincere, and individualistic.[6] A wide variety of additional paper-and-pencil tests, together with projective tests, have also led to the characterization of architects and other groups by similarly large lists of traits.

In general, this sort of cataloging of personality traits does appear to distinguish creative from noncreative people, whose scores on the above traits are not particularly outstanding. Creatives also show more self-confidence and self-acceptance; resoluteness; independence of judgment, attitudes, and behavior (that is, nonconformity); an openness to their own feelings and to new experiences; and a preference for the complex. Further, differences in IQ do not seem relevant after a particular minimum is reached, a point which varies for different professions. The correlation between IQ and creativity is, at most, found to be around .40, which is a moderate (but still statistically significant) relationship (the maximum is 1.00; and values as high as .65–.80 are unusual). However, the magnitude of this figure is still low enough to allow for many exceptions to any relationship that may exist between intelligence and creativity.

With respect to the mad genius stereotype, MacKinnon finds that although creative people may outwardly display more personal problems than controls, they nevertheless handle them more satisfactorily. As a consequence of this adjustment, creatives have better mental health than controls. This apparently paradoxical finding both confirms and contradicts the popular caricature of the artist. While he may look and act disturbed, these signs are but outward and superficial. In comparison to ordinary people, he has better control over unrecognized, unconscious, and sublimated urges. Also contradicting prevailing myths, MacKinnon finds that creative people do not differ from normals in the incidence of happy life histories and other favorable circumstances of development.

These conclusions, which increase rather than mitigate the mystery of the normality of creativity, are also reflected in the imaginative responses of artists and writers to the Rorschach test, which Dudek compared to those of other creative professionals (for example, businessmen) and noncreatives. No quantitative differences were found between the artistically creative and nonartistically creative groups (both equally showed more complex responses than an average group), but they did differ from one another in their qualitative reactions. The comments of the artistically creative group were said to fit the stereotype of the mad genius.

Other clinical comparisons between successful people, based on projective tests like the Rorschach, selected as either aesthetically or nonaesthetically creative, have suggested to Myden additional qualities of creativity along traditional Freudian lines (for example, the role of regression, anxiety, and ego-id integration).

> The creative artist [is] a person of superior intelligence who functions close to his potential. He is intellectually oriented toward the outer world, with a rich inner life and a strong sense of his role-in-life. He is healthily non-conformist, interested in achievement, and more sexually ambivalent [compared to controls], probably due to lack of repression of id feelings.[7]

Munsterberg and Mussen compared the responses of art and nonart students to the Thematic Apperception Test or TAT (among other tests) to one another with respect to twenty-one psychoanalytic hypotheses (for example, artists would show more conflicts with their parents). All but four of the hypotheses were confirmed, although they do not necessarily fit only Freudian theory.

The only study contradicting the thesis that creatives and noncreatives differ on important dimensions (whether psychoanalytic or other) is the work of Roe. She studied the paintings, biographies, and published criticisms of twenty living and recognized American painters, along with interview data and the results of the Rorschach and TAT. Using established norms, she found little difference between artists and others:

> There are no personality or intellectual traits and no constants in their life history which characterize them all and set them off from all other persons.[8]

Even more unexpected, half of the artists were "startlingly

lacking" in perceptual facility or in creative imagination (on the Rorschach);[9] nor were any common environmental factors found in their background, art experiences, or famly influences. Because of Roe's foremost status as an investigator of the traits that characterize people in different occupations, her negative conclusion regarding the special qualities of the creative artist is particularly noteworthy.

[Nothing] can be considered a unique determinant of their choice of painting as a vocation or of their success in it.[10]

However, Roe's study is the exception in failing to find important distinguishing features of creativity, and therefore it bears replication before its results can be fully accepted.

Differences between types of creative people have received less attention in research than differences between the creative and noncreative. MacKinnon has maintained, on the basis of his considerable research experience, that there are more similarities than differences between various types of creative people, and that the distinctions between creatives and noncreatives are greater than those between creatives. One noteworthy difference said to distinguish the artistic from the scientific type, suggested by MacKinnon and others in the field, is that the former externalizes, identifies, empathizes, and projects himself onto the environment, while the scientist more actively manipulates the external world.

A group which receives less attention than other creative types is the creative author. In one of the few studies of the personality of authors, R. N. Wilson studied established poets using projective tests and interview data.[11] He felt that their subjective self-evaluations were special and unique since their isolated and anomolous status in American society conflicts with their need to communicate.

The limitations on the types of creative persons studied

have led to the neglect of the traditional modes of aesthetic expression. An unavoidable problem is the difficulty of getting writers and other artists to cooperate in empirical ventures, since members of these professions often judge statistical and laboratory studies, if not any systematic effort to explore creativity, as crass and philistine activities. Even if sophisticated, experienced, and trained authors were to cooperate more fully, their professional literateness and highly developed subjectivity might be too difficult to reliably study, categorize, and quantify.

The problem of using and evaluating comments about creativity by artistic people is illustrated in Henderson and Lindauer's examination of the autobiographic works of approximately a hundred writers, musicians, and artists. Although over five hundred statements related to creativity could be culled from their writings, the two investigators could reliably classify only half of them into psychological dimensions (for example, source and speed of their ideas: quickly, from inspiration, versus slowly, from hard work). While the investigators independently agreed that the statements did refer to creativity, they could not agree on how to categorize them in order to discover any consistent patterns in the creative process that would differentiate the three creative types. In an attempt to sort the material into some order, they could agree upon only general and vague categories of limited usefulness (for example, conscious versus unconscious factors, emotional versus rational sources of inspiration, insight versus hard work). Rather than abandon this potentially useful data completely, they plotted the number of statements (regardless of content) for each of the three professions, over three centuries. This analysis made possible the examination of gross differences in the quantity of self-analytic statements made by three creative types over time.

Surprisingly, artists and musicians have made a greater number of autobiographical comments on creativity than writers (a trend consistently found over time). Perhaps this is because painting and music express an artist's conceptions of creativity only indirectly, if at all, so these aesthetic types need to communicate their feelings in sources outside of their work. In contrast, authors have a more direct means of self-expression in their fiction. Other attempts to obtain first-hand self-analysis, mainly from scientists and mathematicians, have been reviewed by Patrick (in her introduction to the study of poets), who also includes a poem by Amy Lowell voicing objections to this request. A brief comment on the value of introspective reports by creative people is also found in Sinnott.

Psychologists' notable lack of interest in either retrospective or introspective reports by creative people on their creativity, whether expressed in interviews or in autobiographical material, is attributable to psychology's pervading and historical reluctance to deal with the subjective (chapter 1). The ambiguity of any sort of personal data is compounded further when the subject is artistic and the object of self-analysis is the subtle and intimate phenomenon of creativity. Vernon puts the problem this way:

> Artists and scientists are seldom likely to be careful and reliable observers of their own mental processes and methods of work; and in music and painting it must be doubly difficult to describe the nature of inspiration verbally.[12]

MacKinnon is aware of the possible consequences of the apparently unavoidable problem of studying restricted samples of creative types. However, he has stressed that the creative accomplishments of those who refused to participate in his studies did not differ from the accomplishments of those who did. Nevertheless, he also admits that there may be other differences between participants and nonparticipants (for example, in personality) which may not be as readily apparent. The essential similarity between all creative types is asserted by Barron, an active researcher who has continued in the MacKinnon tradition of using tests to describe the personalities of creative people. Although his samples are largely limited to the nonaesthetic professions, Barron feels that the available evidence would be applicable to all creative types:

> It would be a mistake . . . to oppose the artistic imagination or the poetic imagination to the scientific imagination.[13]

Wilson, who worked with poets, takes an opposite view:

> One must distinguish creative artistic effort from other forms of creativity. Although many similarities seem to exist between artistic creativity and other kinds of creativity, especially the scientific, it would be dangerous to generalize too far.[14]

The difference or similarity of aesthetic types in diverse fields remains an unresolved question, awaiting further research with more specialized groups of subjects.

Dimensions of personality among creative people, especially those traits with a strong cognitive component (originality, independence of thought, and aesthetic judgment), remain a dominant interest among researchers of creativity. In particular, a preference for complexity and novelty among creatives, as measured by the Barron-Welsh art scale, has received much attention.[15] The preference for complexity reflects an attitude that stems from a person's attentional and perceptual orientation, and it is more general and pervasive than a specific personality trait or set of traits and abilities. Rosen showed that the Barron-Welsh scores of art students do not differ from art professionals, not do they change with the amount of art training, indicating that the test measures something other than a specific artistic ability. Comparisons between different professions also show that preference for the complex is highest among artists (scores

of 39) and architects (37), followed by writers (31.5), research scientists (24), and nonartists (13.9).[16] These scores
indicate a sharp difference between creative and noncreative
types; they also suggest differences (but of a lesser degree)
between the creative groups.

CRITIQUE OF CREATIVITY AND PERSONALITY RESEARCH

Despite the care and extensiveness of the research on
the personality of creative people, the field lacks theoretical
cohesiveness and, as a consequence, an adequate explanation of the development and processes of creativity. Mackler and Shontz's extensive review of the field reached this
critical conclusion:

> No theory, narrow or broad, adequately describes the
> process of creativity. No small wonder creativity is a
> confusing theoretical and research area. . . . The worth
> of theory and research . . . has not been thoroughly
> evaluated.[17]

Dellas and Gaier's review of creativity research, while it
finds much to commend in the field, nevertheless notes a
wide variety of faults: undefined or vague criteria of
creativity; small sample size; the neglect of many variables,
including intelligence, socioeconomic level, social setting,
past experience, and sex; the difficulty in comparing studies
which use different response measures, as well as non-
validated measurement instruments; the presence of un-
wanted response biases; the absence of longitudinal studies,
follow-up, and replication; and confusions between statistical analyses and their interpretation. Because of these
theoretical and methodological inadequacies, Rothenberg
has concluded that there is little one can reliably accept
about creativity:

> The problem of creativity is beset with mysticism, con-
> fused definitions, value judgments, psychoanalytic ad-

monition, and the crushing weight of philosophical speculation dating from ancient times.... As a result, an adequate empirical methodology for the study of creativity has not been developed.[18]

The definitional confusions of creativity have been especially condemned by Hudson.[19] Creativity has been equated with all sorts of good and admirable traits (for example, newness, originality, productivity, mental health); old topics have been redefined with a new terminology, thereby giving the false impression that solutions have been found; and many concepts are maintained simply because they are faddish. Another definitional problem noted by Shapiro has been the inattention to the criteria of creativity. Because there are different ways of identifying the creative person (for example, by his products, his reputation, his life history, expert judgment, or general consensus), each may require different techniques of study.

Another general set of criticisms has come from social scientists, who have noted the omission of sociological analysis in the study of creativity. Lasswell has commented on the slighting of several sociological issues: the influence of the social context on the work, and on the use of a particular form; the relationship between different aesthetic products; the role of the audience; and most broadly, the author's, reader's, and work's relationship to the history, values, and motives of the group, society, and culture.[20] Similarly, Mead has criticized psychological research for ignoring the function of creativity in a society, whose groups and institutions provide norms and a context which may facilitate or interfere with its expression and content. She has pointed out the role of collective rather than individual influences on creativity, offering examples of cultures which differ in their susceptibility to and definition of newness and originality.

Another major criticism is the unexpected failure of creativity research to study the creative products of those whose personalities they test. The factor analytic study by Skager et al. of the evaluation of art by experts and laymen suggests how one might approach creativity through an examination of the creative product. Not surprisingly, it was indicated that the two types of subjects used different criteria of evaluation. Perhaps more unexpected, laymen showed more agreement than experts. Importantly, it was also revealed that different qualities of art appealed to different types of personalities. This factor analytic approach could also be extended from an analysis of the nature of the stimulus object and observer to that of the personality of the artists who produced the judged works. Although the Skager et al. study dealt with both the product of creativity and its observer, it did not, unfortunately, include the artist's place in this triad. Csikszentmihalyi and Getzels' study did focus on the artist and his work, by directly probing his attitudes as he worked. Artists were asked such questions as: "Why did you arrange the materials as you did? What were you thinking about? Could you change your drawing?" Nevertheless, the study is again incomplete, in that it neither obtained the responses of others (whether laymen or experts) to the work nor explored the personalities of either artists or observers.

It is surprising to find researchers in personality, given their holistic orientation, failing to examine the creative object or the observer's reactions. The study of the artist is important in arriving at a full picture of creativity, but there are also the products of his self-expression and the reactions of others to his work. In the study of literature, the combining of personality study with an examination of that person's writing, along with the study of the reactions of the reader (and a consideration of the social context), would surely increase our knowledge of creativity. A comprehensively interrelated approach to aesthetics would be invaluable in answering the classic psychological questions about literature: how, if at all, does the personality of the writer influence his writing; to what degree, if any, does a literary work reflect the writer; and to what is the reader responding?

The more traditional type of research on the personality of authors, in contrast to creativity research, examines the creative product only (occasionally supplemented by biographical material), perhaps because the person is not available for study. Unlike creativity research, the psychological study of literature is historical and rarely examines living figures. While personality research is often limited, by necessity, to reconstructing the lives of dead authors through guesswork based on their writings, creativity research does not have this excuse for excluding an examination of an artist's product. (The omission is partially due to the unavailability of artists as subjects.) The field begs for a joint meeting between those interested in personality, as reflected in literary works, and those doing creativity research, carried out with living personalities.

Personality as reflected in authors' work

The attempt to abstract an author's personality from his work and then use it as an adjunct to literary analysis is best represented by the extensive research of McCurdy. He analyzed the works of Sophocles, the Brontë sisters, D. H. Lawrence, and Shakespeare with a variety of quantitative techniques: page counts for the appearance of different characters, the number of lines spoken by different persons, and a tally of the nouns and personality traits mentioned. These statistics, together with subjective interpretations, enabled McCurdy to extract themes, patterns, and relationships between characters. The analysis aided the literary comprehension of the work and also provided information about the authors' personalities.

Another major effort is that of C. S. Hall and Lind, who performed a content analysis of the three novels of Kafka. They placed the fictional characters along a friendliness-aggression continuum and interpreted the characters' views of the goodness of people. They compared this analysis with biographical information, particularly Kafka's recorded dreams. They found, in general, that the novels revealed a much more complex individual than one might have expected on the basis of biographical information alone.

White also used content analysis, applying it to Wright's autobiographical novel, *Black Boy,* using categories taken from Murray's clinical dimensions of motivation (which form the basis for the TAT). His results did not contradict generally accepted subjective impressions of the work but supported them; and in some cases, the objective data modified and extended previously established findings based on traditional analysis.

Rosenberg and Jones analyzed Dreiser's perception of women, basing their study on several quantitative techniques of trait analysis, applied to one of his novels. Their intention was to illustrate the usefulness of a particular methodology rather than to directly apply the results to literary analysis. Their results were corroborated by Dreiser's biography and were congruent with judges' ratings of the literary characters' traits.

Only the Buirski and Kramer study has countered the prevailing view that an author's personality and his work are related. They found no relationship between ten published authors' personal need for achievement and affiliation, as measured by the TAT, and the presence of these themes in their short stories. However, as the experimenters concede, this apparent failure may only indicate that unconscious determinants of personality play a subtler role in story content than anticipated. In addition, the social context in which a writer works may substantially influence the content of his unconscious needs. Their analysis highlights the intricate and indirect tie that must characterize the relationship between an author's personality and his work, and the need for accounting for the expected complexities with sophisticated techniques that do justice to the underlying intricacies.

The experimental study of creativity

Creativity research and studies of the personality of authors as reflected in their works almost exclusively concentrate on individual differences (for example, in intelligence and personality) and necessarily depend heavily on descriptive techniques of investigation (for example, content analysis, tests, correlations). Although these interests and the methodological approach required to study them are popular and useful, by their nature they tend to overlook the more general psychological processes found in everyone. Nor do they lend themselves to experimental research, in which relevant variables can be manipulated and better controlled. More universal dimensions, which most people commonly share, are traditionally part of general experimental psychology. They include the topics of perception (concerned with the nature of the situation and task), learning (the role of training, insight, and remembering), attention (set), and thinking (problem solving, imagery, and imagination). These topics and their experimental study are infrequently found in studies of creativity. Instead, as has already been indicated, there is less concern with the creative object and situation, and the various reactions of an observer to that object, than with the personality of the creative person. Hilgard, speaking as an empirical psychologist, has pointed out the omission of these experimental topics in creativity research, a lack which has probably led to his unhappy conclusion:

> The field is in a rather unsatisfactory state, and ... psychologists have thus far raised more questions than they have answered.[21]

There have been only a few attempts to study creativity from an experimental orientation, perhaps because the method is more limited in scope and less dramatic than personality investigations. Creativity has been generally interpreted within the framework of thinking, that is, as non-verbalized problem solving. Thus Wescott refers to creativity as incidental concept formation, and Mednick and Mednick speak of it as the result of combining associative habits. However, studies that stem from this cognitive point of view only indirectly touch on creativity. They typically use normal rather than creative subjects and ordinary rather than creative tasks (for example, a random sample of college students is asked to solve a learning problem). Several controlled studies more directly relevant to literary aesthetics are unfortunately quite old. Murphy found that scientists and literary subjects were similar to one another in the speed with which free associations were evoked, but differed in the number of items repeated; and Washburn et al. found that poets gave more responses than scientists did to nonsense syllables and colors.

In contrast to these limited efforts, a good amount of experimental research has been inspired by Wallas' classical formulation of the stages of creative thought. He described creativity as a progression, beginning with preparation (gathering of information), followed by incubation (a period without overt or covert activity), insight, and verification. Different aspects of this descriptive analysis of creativity, supported by many anecdotal observations, have been studied. In a nonexperimental study based on the sequential conception of creativity, Dreistadt examined the symbolic content of the reported dreams of artists, scientists, and inventors in order to understand their role in preparation and incubation. He found that the dreams of scientists and inventors were more likely to directly express solutions to problems, while the dreams of artists, musicians, and novelists were only indirectly related to ultimate solutions.

The complexity of the stages of creativity was indicated by R. N. Wilson's study using retrospective analysis: poets chronologically described the sequence of events when they wrote.[22] Although the data were not systematically presented (instead, examples of the poets' comments were given), the intimate role of personal feelings and attitudes in the stages of creativity was apparent. Hyman presented different types of information immediately before problem solving, finding that this input established sets which had both positive and negative effects on the preparation stage. The artist's concern with discovery during on-going creative efforts, and his problem-solving strategies, have also been investigated by Csikszentmihalyi and Getzels.

The most direct and comprehensive experimental investigation of the role of all four stages of creativity was carried out by Patrick. In a laboratory situation, she presented poets and nonpoet controls with the same stimulus (a landscape scene) and asked them to write a poem. This controlled setting permitted the careful observation of the two groups' behavior and the recording of their comments, spontaneous and otherwise, both during and after the task. Among the major findings of this important research (unfortunately, data are presented in descriptive tables without statistical analysis), Patrick found that the stages of creativity were fluid and interchangeable events rather than separate and successive. Further, although the creative subjects' poems were judged by four poets as more meaningful and significant than the productions of the control group (their absolute value is not given), the two groups were more similar than dissimilar on many other dimensions: both groups manifested the four stages of creativity, took the same time to write, wrote similar types of poems, and used similar words. Among the differences, the poets' work contained more and different topics, was less tied to the initial visual stimulus around which they wrote their poems, and was more personal.

Artists (and scientists) in a controlled situation have performed essentially like the poets, thereby supporting the view that there are few (albeit critical) differences between artistic and literary types, between aesthetic and scientific types, and between all creative types and normals. Artists, like poets, showed more similarities to than differences from their control subjects; for example, both reflected the four stages of creativity, although artists differed from controls more than poets did (perhaps because the skills of drawing and painting, unlike those of writing, require special training). Although the research is obviously limited by its artificiality (as is all experimentation), when asked to compare their products with those done under more spontaneous conditions of creativity, about 80 percent of the poets said that their poems were fairly representative of their usual work. Also attesting to the realism of the laboratory work, judges were able to identify the poets' work on the basis of their knowledge of previously published poetry; one poem was published; and many poets intended to publish the results of their laboratory work.

When work is done with creative subjects in a laboratory setting, the problems include overcoming the artificiality of the situation, deciding whether to observe directly or secretly, judging the reliability of their comments, and offsetting the subjects' difficulties in introspecting. Tsanoff some time ago suggested that many of these dilemmas might be obviated through studying the first drafts of a poet's writing, which might indirectly yet realistically reveal his thinking. (Patrick also refers to an examination of Coleridge's notebooks in an effort to reconstruct his creative processes.[23]) However, this approach contains its own set of difficulties, which have probably led to its disuse. These include the general unavailability of first drafts, the need for literary knowledge in order to understand a manuscript and its various revisions, and, most seriously, doubts about whether an author's first ideas are necessarily represented in his first draft. Despite these problems, Rothenberg has recently used manuscript drafts, together with interviews, in his analysis of poetic inspiration.[24] Although not carried out as a formal study, his impressionistic analysis suggests that inspiration is not always a starting point of creativity, and may be less critical than the poet's mood or state of tension.

A study of H. Gardner and J. Gardner, although it dealt with children's story writing and storytelling skills, especially as these abilities relate to such variables as personality, is nevertheless noteworthy for its methodological possibilities for the study of professional writing.[25] On the basis of how stories were completed and their recall, objective data were obtained on plot understanding, originality of endings, sensitivity to style, and the retention of major facts and details. This type of data (which could also be obtained from student and professional writers) was seen as reflecting the development of comprehension, creativity, and communication, and the retention of complex material.

The experimental approach may appear to be unnatural and to deal with what seem to be relatively minor questions of aesthetics, especially when compared to the richness and relevance of personality and creativity research. However, less of this type of research has been done than of any other kind (for example, content analysis), so that it may be premature to judge its adequacy for literary issues. Moreover, experimentation has certain strengths (for example, control over the situation and its dimensions) that may compensate for its necessarily limited scope. Topics concerned with the work and the reader, which are reviewed in the next chapter, may lend themselves more easily to experimentation than to attempts to understand the more individualistic characteristics of personality and creativity.

Although creativity is an intrinsically interesting, important and attractive topic, and has consequently led to many discussions and research efforts, there has nevertheless not been an appreciable gain in empirical knowledge about the processes and traits involved. Conceptual and methodological problems abound, probably because the focus of inquiry is the person rather than the creative object or its response—dimensions which may be more amenable to objective attack because of their external status. It may therefore be good strategy to turn to other psychological functions which bear on creativity and personality. These include the nature of cognitive and motivational processes in the observer, and the content and structure of the literary work which evoke particular responses. They are treated in the next chapter. The study of these topics has another advantage over that of creativity: they have been more directly tied to literary materials. Further, the research reviewed next has relevance to a wide range of psychological topics, many of which, while not directly tied to aesthetic interests, may yet indirectly relate to the basic processes involved.

Notes

1. J. P. Guilford, "Creativity: Retrospect and prospect," *Journal of Creative Behavior* 4 (1970): 149–168.

2. Guilford, "Creative abilities in the arts," *Psychological Review* 44 (1957): 110–18; "Traits of creativity," in *Creativity and its cultivation,* edited by H. H. Anderson (New York: Harper, 1959), pp. 142–161; a recent updating of his work is found in "Creativity," *Journal of Creative Behavior,* 1970, note 1. A good general review of the factor analytic approach represented by Guilford can also be found in T. A. Razik, Psychometric measurement of creativity," in *Explorations in creativity,* edited by R. L. Mooney & T. A. Razik (New York: Harper & Row, 1967), pp. 301–309.

3. Dellas & E. L. Gaier, "Identification of creativity," *Psychological Bulletin* 73 (1970): 59.

4. Ibid.

5. C. Martindale, "Degeneration, disinhibition, and genius," *Journal of the History of the Behavioral Sciences* 7 (1971): 177–182.

6. D. W. MacKinnon, "The personality correlates of creativity: A study of American architects," in *Creativity,* edited by P. E. Vernon (Baltimore: Penguin, 1970), p. 293.

7. W. Myden, "Interpretation and evaluation of certain personality characteristics involved in creative production," *Perceptual and Motor Skill, Monograph Supplement* no. 3, 9 (1959): 158.

8. A. Roe, "Artists and their work," *Journal of Personality* 15 (1946): 2–3.

9. Ibid., p. 3.

10. Ibid., p. 7.

11. R. N. Wilson, "The poet in American society," *The arts in society,* edited by R. N. Wilson (Englewood Cliffs, N. J.: Prentice-Hall, 1964), pp. 1–34.

12. P. E. Vernon, ed., *Creativity* (Baltimore: Penguin, 1970), p. 53.

13. F. X. Barron, "The psychology of creativity," in *New directions in psychology II,* edited by T. M. Newcomb (New York: Holt, Rinehart & Winston, 1965), p. 88

14. R. N. Wilson, "Poetic creativity: Process and personality," *Psychiatry* 17 (1954): 163.

15. Barron, "The disposition toward originality," *Journal of Abnormal and Social Psychology* 15 (1955): 478–485.

16. MacKinnon in Vernon, 1970, pp. 289–311.

17. B. Mackler & F. G. Shontz, "Creativity: Theoretical and methodological considerations," *Psychological Record* 15 (1965): 237–238.

18. A. Rothenberg, "The Iceman Cometh," 1969, p. 549.

19. L. Hudson, "The question of creativity," in Vernon, 1970, pp. 217–234.

20. H. D. Lasswell, "The social setting of creativity," in Anderson, 1959, pp. 203–221.

21. E. R. Hilgard, "Creativity and problem solving," in Anderson, 1959, p. 163.

23. C. Patrick, "Creative thought in poets," *Archives of Psychology* 26 (1935), #178.

24. Rothenberg, "Inspiration, insight, and the creative process in poetry," *College English* 31 (1970): 172–183.

25. H. Gardner & J. Gardner, "Children's literary skill," *Journal of Experimental Education* 39 (1971): 42–46.

8

Studies of the Literary Work

and Its Reader

Studies of the content of literature and studies of the reader's reaction to it are difficult to distinguish from each other. It is obvious that the psychological meaning of a work cannot be separated from a reader's response to that work—nor can it be isolated from the author's personality and creative processes, all of which are tempered by the social context. While recognizing the close ties between all these phenomena and processes, one can nevertheless attempt to concentrate on one aspect at a time. This chapter reviews studies of the content and structure of literature, the use of literature in psychological investigations, and research on the reader of literature.

The psychological content of literature

Literature refers to a variety of topics of psychological interest, particularly those of attitudes, motives, and emotion. In addition, literature has a cognitive referent, as its content and structure evoke imagery, meaning, and a sense of style in a reader. Many different literary forms have been investigated for their psychological content, including the traditional forms (especially poetry), quotations, metaphoric expressions, and children's readers. These different materials have been used to answer many kinds of questions, some of aesthetic interest, others psychological.

LITERATURE'S EXPRESSION OF ATTITUDES, MOTIVES, AND EMOTIONS

The most general quality of literary content is its reflection of personal and cultural attitudes. McClelland examined the Harlequin complex (which symbolizes death as a female lover) in myth and other forms of literature.[1] Although the literature survey was largely impressionistic, some evidence for the presence of this complex was found in interviews and case studies of dying women. Ogilvie traced another myth, that of Icarus (the flight fantasy), across fifty primitive groups, and related it to each society's child-rearing practices. He found, among other things, that the fantasy was negatively correlated with parental dominance. (In the same article, he discussed Marc Chagall's autobiography in terms of this flight motif.) McClelland and Friedman related the coyote folktale, a religious allegory found among several Indian tribes, to child-rearing practices as an expression of the need for achievement. A study of McClelland et al. correlated such themes as anxiety and dependency in the folklore of various groups with the incidence of drunkenness in their cultures. Drunking was not correlated with anxiety about sustenance, but was less likely in a culture with such values as respect and support for males reflected in its tales. Klineberg used Chinese literature to examine the question of facial expressions of emotion. He found both similarities to and differences from Western mannerisms, supporting both relativistic (learned) and universalistic (innate) theories of human nature.

McClelland's extensive studies of need achievement (summarized in *The Achieving Society*), a motive to strive for success according to internal standards of excellence, have made liberal use of literary sources as indirect indicators of this need. He has used a variety of literary forms: folktales, ballads, legends, English literature of the sixteenth to nineteenth centuries, the fiction of medieval Spain, and ancient Greek poetry, speeches, and epigrams. Seeing literature as a reflection of society's values, he employed it as an indirect source of information about achievement motivation in earlier societies for which other data are sparse or unavailable. McClelland showed that high need achievement in the literature of earlier societies preceded the economic rise of a society, using the amount of trading or number of buildings constructed as economic indicators. At a society's economic zenith, personal habits of independence and striving are no longer relevant since the wealthy can purchase services from others; in particular, children receive less independence training. Achievement motivation consequently subsides, thereby anticipating the eventual economic and general decline of the society.

More recent studies of the achievement need (as well as power and affiliation) have also used literature. Children's readers, in particular, have been viewed as good indices of a society's motives, as the modern equivalent of the myths and legends of primitive societies. These stories are considered as reflecting the values of a group in an imaginative and interesting way, while not limited in content to any one social class or set of historical events. Supporting these assumptions, DeCharms and Moeller revealed that the needs expressed in children's readers of the United States during the period 1800–1950 did antedate objective economic indices. Further, Rudin was able to use the readers of fifteen countries and their motivational content to predict successfully the extent to which deaths in these societies could be attributable to different psychogenic causes. Where the power motive was found in readers, deaths were more likely to be aggressive (for example, murder, suicide, alcoholism). In contrast, inhibitory deaths (ulcers, hypertension) correlated with expressions of the achievement motive. Analysis of other data in relation to the primers indicated that citizens in high achieving societies, in comparison to low achieving societies, attended more films (presumably as a release for inner tension) and showed a lower per capita book productivity (presumably because reading requires a more contemplative temperament).

Need achievement may be more directly studied in light of individuals' literary preferences and productions. Knapp and Garbutt correlated need achievement with subjects' preferences for different types of metaphorical references to time. McClelland and Friedman found that short stories written by subjects who differed in their achievement motivation (as well as in hunger), appropriately reflected these needs. Henley surveyed short stories written by professionals in a popular magazine over a sixty year span, discovering a decline in the need for achievement; the need for affiliation remained constant, rather than increasing as expected.

Studies of attitudes besides those that refer to achievement, as they are reflected in literary materials, have centered on attitudes toward numbers, emotions, and life and death. In a study by Lindauer, judges evaluated the positive or negative themes of over a hundred quotations dealing with numbers and other quantitative concepts. Regardless of when or where they originated, quotes indicated a negative attitude toward statistics, an attitude that matches the resistance most people show to the use of numerical concepts, and the wariness of humanists toward numerical analysis of aesthetic topics.

Lindauer also contrasted psychology's concentration on negative emotions, like anxiety, fear, and psychopathology, in its research and theories, with the frequency of positive and negative emotions in the titles and content of five different literary forms. All types of literature—poems, epigrams, novels, plays, and short stories—consistently and over a wide time range referred more often to positive than to negative emotions. This pervasively positive literary index, which may reflect societal and cultural values, suggests that psychology's negative view of man, as shown by its preoccupation with negative emotions, is not necessarily the only view. Psychology's attention to the morbid and pessimistic may be the result of several factors: the unique importance of these topics to psychology; their convenience for study; or historical accident.

Hall's quantitative treatment of the content of literary materials is a psychoanalytically oriented investigation of positive and negative attitudes toward life and death in quotations. He summarizes the literary views on death:

> Leading the list is the belief that death is good, but it is closely followed by the opposite conception, that death is bad. Then in order of frequency are the [themes of] inevitability of death, death as sleep, the might of death and its impotence, the mystery of death and the shadow of death, and the ennobling mantle of death.... Man's fear of death turns out to be much weaker than his attractions to it [for] there is much more yearning than fearing.[2]

Life, as expressed in quotations, is seen as follows:

> Negative feelings lead the list with 75 quotations. [It is a] bitter cup, a fitful fever, a calamity, a long disease, a galling load, protracted woe, a cheat, a weary pilgrimage, a dull round, gray and weary, harsh, a grind, and a vale of tears. [In more positive terms, life is] good, sweet ... precious, glorious, amusing, gay, pleasant, dear ... a game.[3]

Life and death themes, which had about the same number of positive and negative entries, were then compared:

> Only one poet likens life to sleep but 29 liken death to sleep. On the other hand, life is regarded as being active and developing 49 times and death is regarded only once this way. The inevitability and certainty of death are frequent (33 instances); the inevitability and certainty of life are rare (one instance). Life is mighty only once but death is mighty seventeen times. Life is ennobling only once, but death is ennobling seven times.

Life and death are conceived of as being omnipotent
and trivial a similar number of times (twenty for life
and seventeen for death). Life is rarely a shadow as
death is. Death is never considered to be short, as life
is. Life is more often a journey than death.[4]

In comparing these poetic conceptions of life and death
with Freud's, C. S. Hall concludes that "probably no poet
anticipated Freud's formulation of the dialectical nature of
the life and death instincts."[5]

Helson has run a quantitative study of attitudes within
the Jungian framework of depth analysis. She examined
over seventy works of fantasy written for children since
1930, representing a wide spectrum of content, and interpreted them as reflecting authors' (rather than children's)
projections. She also had judges, familiar with children's
literature, rate the works' originality and various other dimensions (for example, setting, mood, style, needs). Helson
found that works judged as creative could be reliably differentiated from those not so judged on several dimensions
(for example, in expressing more feelings). Mullen compared Freudian and Jungian orientations for sexual symbols
by examining the gender of French, German, and Spanish
definite articles for masculine and feminine sex objects.
There was no correspondence between the gender of nouns
and their articles for both schools of psychoanalysis and for
all three languages, a finding that argues against the universality of some types of sexual symbolism.

Many researchers have surveyed the attitudes and
emotions reflected in musical lyrics, a form of prose tangen-
tially related to literature. Hannett organized the content of
thousands of old and contemporary hit songs into several
classifications (for example, romantic, sentimental, war-
like) and compared the historical trends. Narcissistic and
love themes and fantasies had increased over time, and
songs mourning the death of a loved one had decreased.
These findings, together with others (the favorite songs of

patients in therapy) and historical analysis, led to the conclusion that popular lyrics express unconscious infantile attitudes, especially about the mother-child relationship, and perhaps surprisingly, express predominantly depressive rather than happy themes. Less psychoanalytic in orientation, Carey demonstrated that almost two hundred lyrics of different types of contemporary songs (for example, blues, rock and roll) should be classified in terms of beliefs about self and society, dissatisfactions, the need for autonomy, and one's relationship to nature. The philosophical and historical relationship between music and its lyrics—their role, use, and the achievement of a successful fusion—and the distinction between music with words and music without words are discussed by Schwadron.

LITERATURE'S EXPRESSION OF COGNITIVE PROCESSES

Psychological investigations of thinking processes reflected by literary content are more likely than studies of attitudes to use experimental rather than descriptive and correlational procedures. Investigations of imagery in response to poetry exemplify this analytical approach to aesthetic problems. Early studies, however, were limited by unsophisticated methodology and statistics.[6] In general, subjects read (aloud or silently) poems or fragments of poems by different established poets. On the basis of verbal introspections, data on the types, frequency, and vividness of the evoked images were obtained. These data usually revealed consistencies between and within subjects' images, differences in the imagery-arousing capacity of different and same poets and poems, and the relation of images to a poem's meaning, symbols, and difficulty. One conclusion, by Valentine, was that poetry's pleasureableness and aesthetic enjoyment depended on whether the aroused imagery was spontaneous or not.[7]

Most of the early research in imagery is characterized by several flaws that limit its usefulness: the absence of systematic statistical tabulations, or their minimal use in analysis; the small number of subjects used; the unreliability of the introspective method; the reliance on poetry to the neglect of other types of prose; the unknown background, training, and imaginative capacities of the subjects; and the lack of a measure of the complexity and other qualities of the materials. Many of these difficulties are particularly evident in an ambitious study carried out by Lay in the 1890s. Artists (including sculptors and painters but not writers) read and recalled several fictional and nonfictional passages. Their retention, measured by both questionnaire and interview data, was compared with that of nonartists and related to the materials' imagery type (either visual or auditory) and vividness. Unfortunately, only the detailed protocols were presented for each subject, without numerical analysis, synthesis, or organization of all the variables studied. Despite all these shortcomings, the early studies illustrate at least the beginnings of an empirical approach to imagery in literature, a topic which has received an overabundance of speculative discussion. They merit replication with greater methodological sophistication.

A more objective procedure than introspection is counting the images in literary works. For example, Spurgeon tallied the number and types of images in Shakespeare's plays in order to compare his works and test their authorship. Dudley used the types of imagery found in different forms of literature as a basis for classifying literary content and themes.[8] However, critics like Friedman have complained that literary analysis based on this sort of counting method is too simple because it overlooks other and more important qualities of prose (for example, author's intent).

Cognitive qualities of literary content other than imagery have received attention, especially metaphors, clichés, and slang. The metaphor is much discussed because of its obvious importance to literature, as well as to science (in its models) and psychology. In one empirical study, Knapp examined several classes of metaphor (for example, about death and conscience) as indicative of deep-seated and symbolic motives and attitudes. He first had metaphors judged for their appropriateness to several themes; he then correlated them with the imagery evoked. Asch surveyed the common physical and psychological properties (that is, physiognomy) to which metaphors jointly refer (for example, warm person and warm colors) across six unrelated language groups, finding more frequently than expected that there were common metaphorical references to the perception of objects, events, and persons across cultures. Siegel tallied figures of speech and similes in Schopenhauer as a means of facilitating the understanding of his work. Honkavaara used visual stimuli and to a lesser degree, words, to study children's physiognomic mode of perception (a process that may underlie metaphoric meaning; a general discussion of this phenomenon is found in Werner).

Lindauer investigated the response to clichés, with or without direct psychological content (for example, "human nature," "believe it or not"). Judges rated clichés as meaningful even though they recognized them as clichés, a finding that contradicts the claims of rhetoricians that clichés are by definition meaningless. However, affirming expectations, the judges did not think clichés were particularly interesting. Whether or not subjects used clichés depended on their training: English majors were less likely than those with other backgrounds to use clichés, although psychology majors, who had some basis for evaluating clichés with psychological referents, found psychological clichés acceptable. Cliché use also varied with intelligence (as reflected in grades): students with the lowest grade averages tended to use clichés more frequently than those with better averages. The acceptability of clichés may therefore be related to the quality of thinking, as rhetoricians contend.

The meaning of slang has also been investigated, particularly its parallels with the symbolic function of dreams, that is, both slang and dreams indirectly express unconscious processes. C. S. Hall categorized over seven hundred slang expressions and about three thousand dream symbols that referred to the genitals and sexual intercourse into thirteen different groups. His analysis indicated that both dreams and slang similarly refer to suppressed and disguised mental processes:

> Long before Freud and his associates were discovering the extent to which man sexualizes the world, there existed the evidence from slang. Surely no other function of the body as sex suggested so many figures of speech. . . . The world of dreams is replete with sexual symbols and they . . . run pretty much the same gamut of fantasy representations as is found in waking speech.[9]

Lindauer studied durational connotations of several hundred expressions of time, including metaphors and clichés ("as quick as a flash"), as well as single words ("soon"). Subjects placed the expressions into ten categories of time, ranging from seconds to millenia. Expressions which referred to the past suggested greater periods of time to the participants than did those of the present or future. Contrary to popular stereotype, there were no sex differences in the assignment of duration to the various expressions of time.

The most general yet subtle feature of literature is its style. H. Gardner has shown that children of varying ages are sensitive to the nuances of artistic styles. The children were able to complete stories written in different styles with the right ending, indicating their ability to identify the subtleties of style without necessarily being able to verbalize what they were responding to.[10] Martindale has boldly experimented with various stylistic features of poetry, both real and simulated, using criteria of incongruity, novelty, expectation, and imagery. He used the data, taken from both historical analysis and laboratory simulation, to account for differences and changes between poetic traditions and to develop a theory of creativity.

The structure of literary prose

Not only does style evoke a cognitive response in the reader, but it is also a basis for describing the structural characteristics of prose materials and the differences between them. (This inter-relationship between topics highlights the arbitrariness of subdividing the psychological approach to literature.) Lee demonstrated an extremely narrow orientation to style, relying on rather isolated linguistic elements, for example, the verbs in De Quincey's writings, and Carlyle's use of the present tense. More broadly, Gilman and Brown compared essays by Emerson and Thoreau, equivalent in content, and showed them to be similar on such counts as references to the single person, number of negatives, ratio of abstract to concrete nouns, and various types of sentence constructions. The stylistic similarity reflected the personal similarity of the two essayists on several dimensions, for example, self-image and aggressiveness.

A severely quantitative approach to style can be achieved through factor analysis. J. B. Carroll extracted a wide variety of numerical values from various forms of prose, including novels, essays, and magazines, on the basis of such measures as word counts, ratios of classes of words and sentences, and the semantic differential. Several factors emerged as quantitatively indicative of style: a general evaluation dimension (good-bad); personal affect (emotional-rational); ornamentation (flowery and wordy as opposed to plain): and abstractness. Brinton and Danielson's factor analytic study of fictional literary content included as its basic input for analysis not only isolated language elements, such as sentence length, but larger units, such as figures of speech, in an attempt to incorporate more contextual factors. The twenty factors that emerged from this analysis referred less to the characteristics of literary form than to the nature of the reader (for example, his age and personality). These results again indicate the difficulty of separating the reader's response from the psychological content and structure of literature.

Structural characteristics of poetry have been similarly studied from a rigorously reductionistic point of view. For example, Roblee and Washburn had judges rate the agreeableness of different sounds (that is, vowels, consonants, gutterals) and E. S. Jones obtained preferences for nonsense words. Such materials are considered comparable to the real words and sounds of poetry. The use of simple forms permits greater control over the materials than can be achieved with the complexities of meaning found in actual poetry. Hopefully, one can then arrive at the pure qualities of letters, phonemes, and syllables, from which broader analyses presumably can be built. In Hevner's work, one of the more comprehensive of a fairly large number of similarly atomistic studies (summarized in Chandler's *Beauty and Human Nature*), the various attributes of meter, vowels, and consonants were manipulated through the use of nonsense materials, and their meanings were then reported by subjects on an adjectival checklist.

Hevner found that meter was the most effective structural determinant of the passage's meaning: the "two-syllable foot is solemn, dignified, and sad, in contrast to the three-syllable foot, which is joyous, light, sparkling, spirited, and gay."[11] The study also used a few real poems (by Keats and Browning), which were studied in the same way as meaningless material: subjects selected descriptive terms that matched the emotions evoked by the material. A more contemporary example of the reductionist approach to poetry is found in Lynch, who published his work in 1953 (Hevner's study was published in 1937). He tabulated the phonetic structure of the sounds of well-known poems and then related the distribution of these sounds to the poem's images and meaning. He found that sound patterns changed systematically with the images portrayed by different passages.

In another attempt to discover the building blocks of language and writing, Alluisi and Adams' research on preference and pleasingness used judges' ratings of the appearance (and sounds) of letters (including capitals and pairs) found at either the initial or terminal positions of a word. Studies of psycholinguistics, although not usually dependent on literary materials, also use a reductionistic approach to the problem of communication. Wickens' review treats meaning, for example, by studying the structure of isolated units of prose, for example, words, sentences, or paragraphs. A general review of psycholinguistics and the structure of language, which makes some mention of literature, is Miller's *Language and Communication.*

The most ambitious attempt to study the structure of literature, which is also unusual in that it did not rely on a reductionistic approach, is that of Vygotsky. He surveyed various literary forms (for example, the fable, epic poem, short story, and drama) in order to discover the underlying structure of the aesthetic response. In his terms, the essential literary response is the reader's resolution of contradictions in the form of the work. His analysis is broad, and his assertions are provocative. For example, pleasure and satisfaction in the reader and the beauty of the material are irrelevant for the aesthetic response, which is mainly an intellectual grasp of a work's structure. However, his theory is expository and intuitive rather than empirical. These limitations (shared with most literary analyses) have probably prevented further research on his thesis in the fifty or so years since it was promulgated. In contrast, more limited and reductionistic orientations, like Hevner's and Lynch's, continue.

Contemporary research has continued to look for the units of prose most susceptible to measurement. Of the different literary forms, the elements of poetry again have received the most attention. Skinner analyzed alliteration (sound patterns) in Shakespeare's sonnets on the basis of certain rules which treated verse as a form of verbal behavior. He demonstrated that some patterns were more effective than others in contributing to an effect on the reader. He also included the alliteration measure, together with that of assonance (resemblance of sounds in words), in another study of the phonetic elements of the poet Swinburne. Recent work on the nature of sound patterns in poetry and their possible contribution to a poem's meaning, as well as how these patterns differ from those in prose, has been reviewed by Child.[12]

Birkhoff's classical contribution to the quantification of aesthetic materials also used a reductionistic approach to structure. While his search for the "good figure" and a formula for pleasingness was directed toward art, he also gave some consideration to poetry. He derived a formula based on the ratio of complexity to order, defining these variables in terms of rhyme, assonance, and alliteration. Metcalf has more extensively applied an aesthetic formula to literature. In brief, the aesthetic value of literature is represented by the ratio between orderliness (O), defined by alliteration, assonance, rhyme, and musical vowels (to name just a few of the variables) and complexity (C); the latter measure is mainly represented by the total number of speech sounds and word junctions. The structural qualities of the words in music have also been quantitatively described by Seashore and related to musical notations.

SPOKEN LITERATURE

An interest in the sounds of literature can also be found, although to a minor degree, in those who study speech. Scripture quantitatively described poetry read aloud by living poets on the basis of sounds, melody, rhythm, syllables, accents, stress, and feet. Schramm used the distribution of these objective characteristics to compare different poems. Investigations of the relationship between speech and personality, reviewed by Sanford, have occasionally used literary materials. More commonly, however, studies of spoken literary prose (mostly poetry), most of which are old, have concentrated on measuring formal elements of prose (for example, rhythm, rhyme, alliteration), on the theory that isolating the units of prose would help in determining the aesthetic value of different works, and accounting for the emotions they arouse. For example, Lipsky showed that the distinctive rhythms of the spoken words of over twenty authors, together with materials taken from the Bible and newspapers, could be reliably differentiated from one another. He felt the rhythm would be a key to understanding the meanings and emotions these materials aroused (but he did not pursue his theory further).

Although the various sounds of prose have been successfully recorded and reliably differentiated by sophisticated techniques, such as those developed by Gottschalk and Gleser, materials of literary merit have not been fully explored, even though they are as susceptible to quantitative description as ordinary prose is (and more interesting). An exception, Glasgow's study of speech mannerisms using prose and poetry of merit, shows how fruitful such research can be. She manipulated changes in the quality of the materials' spoken presentation, changes that clearly affected different groups of listeners in their appreciation of the passage. Thus, the use of good speech mannerisms led, according to judges' ratings, to a more positive response to the materials read.

READABILITY OF LITERATURE

Studies of readability quantitatively examine the physical features of written rather than spoken language, in an attempt to establish a quantitative formula to describe the ease with which reading materials can be understood. However, most investigators, like Dale and Chall, or Flesch, have relied on ordinary rather than literary prose. An exception is W. L. Taylor's "Cloze procedure," which essentially relies on the ease with which deleted words from sentences are filled in. In order to more clearly demonstrate the usefulness and validity of his technique, which scores the frequency of correct guesses, he applied his method to the works of Boswell, Huxley, James, Caldwell, Stein, and Joyce.

The limitations of readability formulas, whether based on literary or other materials, have been summarized by Kearl. Their major difficulty is their crudeness: they measure only what is measurable—comprehension. Other aspects of prose, including its format, lucidity, appeal, context, and author's purpose as well as the contribution of the reader's expectations, are by necessity omitted.

AUTHORSHIP

Of all statistical analyses of literary structure, attempts to decide disputed authorship have the longest tradition. A basic issue is the proper unit to be tallied in order to best represent an author's work. Different investigations have favored a variety of measures: the noun was used by Yule, the total number of words was relied on by C. B. Williams, and Brinegar preferred word length.

These rather simple and straightforward approaches to authorship have been criticized by Leytham for neglecting content, style, and other subtle features of prose. Another limitation to their relevance to literary study is that many studies, according to C. B. Williams, merely exercise and illustrate the usefulness of statistical techniques, and are only incidentally interested in materials as complex and interesting as literature.[13] For example, Ellegard used Chaucer, Shakespeare, the Bible, and Joyce's *Ulysses* to illustrate the reliability of a technique for estimating vocabulary norms for different types of writing. He discussed this technique as a device that would enable speakers and writers to quickly determine whether their level of prose was compatible with their audience's; he did not explore its relevance to the differences between works, authors, or styles.

Instead of relying on such obvious and direct units of languages as words, nouns, and sentence length, Paisley has proposed that certain minor cues can be used.[14] These cues could reliably and efficiently describe authorship in several aesthetic areas: literature (the number of definite articles used); art (the way fingertips are drawn); and music (the first five notes of a piece). Paisley has extended his approach to the examination of the basic structure of language in terms of information theory.[15] For example, the simple measure of letter redundancy or repetition, an indirect index of how well the information in prose is communicated, could be used to test authorship, and in addition, could reliably differentiate the themes, structure, and conceptions of time in nine Greek plays, the *Iliad,* and the New Testament.

Paisley argues that redundancy, a high amount of which is reflective of uncertainty, is a more accurate measure of language structure than the more traditional measures of content such as sentence length and vocabulary. Others in the information theory framework have also indicated that the frequency with which letters occur can be useful in understanding the communicative content of prose.[16] This argument was illustrated by the frequency distribution of letters in the works of William James, a magazine article, and the Old Testament writings of the prophet Isaiah. Alluisi and Adams' study of letter preferences, referred to earlier, is also within the tradition of information theory.

The use of literary materials in psychological studies

Most of the topics and studies reported in these chapters, including that of the personality and creativity of the author, the content and structure of literature, and the reader of literature, are less directly related to general psychological problems than to aesthetic issues. However, psychological studies have also used literary materials in a manner which gives secondary consideration to their literary and other aesthetic qualities. For example, a few studies of learning and remembering have used literary prose instead of ordinary material or disconnected words.

An area of psychological investigation close to literary concerns is the study of the effects of prestige and suggestion on prose evaluation. The effect of manipulating attributed authorship on the evaluation of prose material has been investigated by Asch and Osgood and Tannenbaum in the theoretical terms of perception, attitude change, and meaning. The material used has been largely nonfictional or nonliterary prose, with only occasional use of literary materials. Whatever material is used, the procedure is similar: the same passage is presented to different groups of subjects; in each group, the passage is attributed to authors of contrasting merit (for example, a passage about liberty is assigned to either Hitler or Roosevelt). Since the authors' status usually has an effect on the subjects' judgment of the passage, the main issues have been the explanation of this effect and the prediction of the amount of change.

However, in the Michael et al. study, the judgments of paragraphs from good and bad novels and poetry were not affected by attribution to well-known authors. These results were unexpected, and the researchers were forced to blame them on the independent personalities of the particular subjects used in their study. More typically, prestige works, even in different cultures. Thus Das et al. found that the merit of Indian literary passages (as judged by Indians) changed according to their attributed authorship. Philip found that the assignment of an author's name had a powerful effect on the ratings of single lines of poetry when compared to passages for which no author was named.

Learning is a major research area of psychology that sometimes uses prose materials, though usually not literary, since the more commonly relied upon nonsense words and disconnected serial and paired lists of words allow the experimenter more control. An early exception to this reductionistic strategy is a study by Woodrow. He compared poetry, prose, facts, and vocabulary in terms of their rates of learning and transfer characteristics, and how these were affected by different types of instructions. However, the use of such complex and meaningful materials in learning and remembering studies is atypical.

Yet as early as the 1930s Bartlett, in his now classic *Remembering*, objected to the widespread dependence on meaningless and limited materials (which still characterize the procedures and models of verbal and rote learning). He argued that results based on such studies were restricted, narrow, and irrelevant to real learning situations. As an alternate strategy of research, Bartlett examined qualitative changes in the recall of complex materials, such as folktales. He was thereby able to show the active nature of remembering and its modification according to the learner's past experience and attitudes. One of the folktales studied, "The War of the Ghosts," has been used by many other researchers. Recently, King subjected the passage to two different methods of measuring learning and recall, counting either the number of words or sequence of words remembered, in order to demonstrate that the technical difficulties usually found in measuring connected discourse in laboratory studies of learning and remembering can be overcome. Dooling and Lachman have used Bartlett's general approach to the study of qualitative changes in memory, but they have written their own stories. They investigated such variables as the influence of titles on comprehension.

Meaningful connected prose, to which literature bears many similarities, is being used increasingly in the learning laboratory. Ordinary prose (sentences and paragraphs) is found in studies of many facets of learning, such as the effects of retroactive and proactive inhibition in forgetting; the Zeigarnick effect in the memory of incomplete (interrupted) and completed tasks; and the acquisition and recall of controversial material congruent or discongruent with one's attitude.[17] Runquist's recent review of various aspects of verbal behavior is indicative of an increasing trend toward the use of prose. He included, along with the traditional serial and paired associates types of materials, a section on the growing use of multiple language units (that is, prose).

Prose, whether or not it is literary, has the advantage of being more interesting and meaningful than ordinary materials; however, it also has the technical difficulties of control and measurement that have hampered its greater use. In order to obtain acceptable data on the acquisition and recall of prose, one first needs a reliable and quantifiable measure of the materials' structure, content, and meaning, as well as an efficient way of classifying the response. Runquist has suggested that a procedure similar to Taylor's "Cloze analysis"—a type of sentence completion technique —might solve some of the scaling and scoring problems of prose. In this procedure, subjects fill in the blanks of test sentences based on the original material presented during learning; successful completion is determined by the number of correctly recalled items. The technique has been successfully used by G. R. Miller and Coleman to measure nonliterary passages' stimulus complexity, which was then compared to difficulties in comprehension.

The definition of the stimulus and response of prose learning is a serious problem in carrying out research in the learning and remembering of complex materials. Without a quantifiably meaningful and manageable unit of analysis (that is, is it the word, clause, phrase, or idea?), reliable measurement and analysis are not possible. It is difficult, consequently, to insure that the content of different materials is matched in meaningfulness and emotionality. Further, once the stimulus unit has been established, it is also necessary that the responses be reliably measured.

While the use of literary prose in the area of verbal behavior is on the verge of acceptance, complex prose materials, literary or not, have hardly made any appearance in the area of perception. An interesting exception, which suggests the potential of relying on intrinsically interesting material, is the Wilding and Farrell study. Two different passages by the novelist Hardy were presented to each ear through separate earphones. This interference procedure demonstrated the competing roles of visual and auditory masking effects in attending.

The reader

Investigations of the reader of literature are intimately related to those studies reviewed earlier, whether of the creative process, person, work, or social milieu. The study of the reader necessarily includes a broad range of topics, such as his personal and intellectual characteristics, what he reads, his specific reactions to different forms and styles of literature, the effects these have on him, and ultimately why he reads. Despite the scope of these questions—or perhaps because of it—research on the reader is the least extensive of the three major areas that describe the empirical study of literature. While research on literary topics inevitably and naturally depends on the reader—he is after all the source of data upon which analysis of the work is built—his characteristics, experiences, and reactions are nevertheless frequently taken for granted. It seems to be implicitly assumed that there is a sort of neutral and generalized reader who uniformly reads, responds to, and appreciates a literary work.

While it may seem that the concerns of sociologists, reviewed in chapter 6, would be appropriate in this area, sociological interests lie in the audience, a more global and less individualistic definition of the reader. However, these distinctions blur in discussions of the social-psychological approach to the reader.

THE VARIETY OF VARIABLES STUDIED

Although there are many important questions raised and statements made about the reader, there have been few empirical studies of the differences between readers in their reactions to either the same or different works. Thus, Child makes only brief reference to different readers' response to the same set of poetry in a recent review.[18] One of the most ambitious investigations of the reader is by Richards. His *Practical Criticism* reports an informal study that deals with responses to poetry. These written reactions to various poems were collected and examined in terms of preferences and imagery. This information was then related to the frequency of word forms in the different poems and, more ambitiously, to the motives expressed in these poems. In a less complex but more circumscribed study, Jakobovits found that readers were able to accurately label literature characterized by the author as either erotic or obscene, a finding the author thought might help in evaluating legalistic criteria of pornography. (Surprisingly, the reaction to pornographic literature, especially in relation to different personality types, has received less attention than the reaction to pornographic art.[19])

The study by Wells, although done in 1907, is outstanding in its attempt to study the reader empirically. He quantitatively examined readers' reactions to different authors by having them rank their preferences for ten American writers (for example, Poe, Hawthorne) on several dimensions previously established as relevant by expert judges, for example, general merit, clarity, force. Wells used the same procedure to compare ten works by a single author (Poe). His approach deserves more attention than it has received, especially because of its usefulness to teachers of literary appreciation courses. More recently, McGranahan has studied readers' emotional reactions to different forms of literary language; he compared these with the response to scientific language.

An important question is whether literature influences the personality of the reader. Some indirect support for this presumed effect was found in Barron and Rosenberg's study of an actor. Measuring his personality before, during, and after a series of performances of *King Lear*, they found that in the course of playing the major role in the play, the actor's personality did change (at least temporarily) in a direction congruent with the character he played.

Drake demonstrated changes in readers' interpretations of a concept (as measured by the connotative scales of the semantic differential), resulting from the reading of a poem. He compared the attitudes of subjects who read poetry on a particular subject with those of control subjects who read either a bad poem similar in content or prose information on the same subject. Berlyne has initiated further efforts along these interesting lines, including measures of recall.[20] The study by Arcamore and Lindauer also proved a previously presumed but not empirically demonstrated effect of literary training, namely, that people can be taught to recognize styles and their authorship merely by exposure to these authors' works. Subjects were first shown six unidentified modern poems which they were asked to identify; this task, on which they did poorly, was a base line for later comparison. They then briefly read and studied several identified examples of the poets' other work. Finally, subjects were tested on a new set of six unidentified poems by the same authors. They identified more of this last set than they did originally and more than a control group which had not received any training. Presumably, the subtle cues of style, although not verbalized, had somehow been identified by exposure, learned, transferred, and recalled.

Studies on the structure of written material have related its placement and other characteristics, such as length of text on a page, to the reader's attention. In these studies, reviewed by Nafziger, nonliterary and nonaesthetic materials, such as newspapers, have been the major source of information. Closer to literary interests, J. B. Haskins found that the degree of abstraction in short stories was positively correlated with reader satisfaction but, paradoxically, not with their attention.

There are several studies of the stimulus qualities of prose and their effect on reading which stem from general interests in experimental psychology. Particularly noteworthy is Kammann's finding that readers preferred poetry of intermediate complexity over poetry of either high or low complexity. Although he worked with only one type of literary material and defined complexity only on the basis of word predictability, his results are important because they parallel those of other investigations with art and nonaesthetic materials, such as Berlyne's, in perceptual, attentional, and motivational areas of experimental psychology.

A current thesis of experimental psychology, which also touches on literary aesthetics, holds that preference is a function of familiarity, that is, that mere exposure to stimuli will lead to increased liking. Among the many illustrations of the familiarity thesis (in addition to the correlational and experimental evidence offered), Zajonc makes reference to the positive role of frequency in prose generally (including letters) and in literature specifically (although musical examples are more often used). Thus Zajonc showed that the content words in a happy poem of Blake were more common or familiar than those in one of his comparable sad poems. A similar pattern was found for the emotionally contrasting poems of Browning and Shelley. It is currently controversial whether the relationship between preference and exposure remains linear or becomes curvilinear, as is often the case for the relationship between preference and complexity. Bearing on this question, Jakobovits found that the popularity of hit parade songs was curvilinearly related to the number of times they were played per week: with increasing repetition, preferences rose and then declined.

There are approaches to the reactions of the reader relevant to both sociology and psychology. These have examined his attitudes and other individualistic and personal traits, as indirectly reflected in the market behavior of best sellers. For example, Austin divided nonfiction best sellers for the period of 1912–50 into fourteen types. Almost half of the books fit into the following categories (which varied somewhat at different time periods): biography, autobiography, social problems, self-help, and war. The list suggested to him that readers were more interested in people than in events and in the analysis of other people rather than in themselves. Sewter's tally of fiction and nonfiction best sellers over time was less clear in its implications. There were dramatic (but unexplained) shifts in the popularity of different styles of writing and subjects. Harvey's more selective and intensive study of popular books of 1930–46 compared twenty-two best sellers with poor sellers, matching the subject matter of the two groups. The books were evaluated on several hundred variables, for example, action, emotion, personality of major characters, plot themes, romance, and simplicity of characterization. Sixteen of the dimensions distinguished best sellers from poor ones. Especially critical to sales were the emotional characteristics of the male central character (for example, in popular books he was sentimental and affectionate). Such variables as wordage, the recency of events reported, and the amount of publicity received also affected sales. Kappel used best sellers in order to probe the relationship between book club selection and literary standards; that is, did the books chosen receive positive or negative critical evaluation? While the merit of book club choices varied with different clubs, their selections on the whole were of high literary quality, suggesting (at least for the period studied, 1927–46) that book club choices were not detrimental to the maintenance of high literary standards.

In a more direct evaluation of reading habits, Starch asked qualified judges (literary critics and professors of literature) to select the 100 greatest books. Except for the Bible, ranked first by most judges, nine of the top ten books were fiction, as were about half of the first 100 on the list. The fiction was equally divided between drama and poetry, the works of Shakespeare receiving the most substantial vote. College seniors, at least in the 1940s, were familiar with fewer than half of the works on the list and had read less than 25 percent of them.

Another broad and indirect source of information

about a reading audience is found in biography. Lowenthal recorded the type and number of biographies of the past and present celebrities in popular magazines to measure readers' changing attitudes toward society's heroes and the status of different occupations. The data indicated that an interest in serious authors (and artists) has declined over time (from 77 percent to 9 percent of the total number of biographies examined) and been replaced by an interest in popular entertainers, businessmen, and politicians. Similarly, Winick compared the occupational types found in the biographies of one popular magazine with the types represented in a TV interview series. Writers ranked second in frequency of appearance on TV; and among related aesthetic occupations, actors, singers, musicians, artists, and dancers ranked first, third, seventh, ninth, and fifteenth, respectively. Although the rankings of these artistic occupations on TV were higher than in the magazine, the overall differences were not statistically significant; and the period of time covered was too brief to indicate trends.

However, generalizations from marketing and mass media data to the characteristics of the specific reader may be misleading. The dangers are illustrated by Waples, who found no relationship (that is, a nearly zero correlation) between what people say they read and what they say they like to read. His findings indicate the difficulties of relying on what people say about their reading, or on less direct indices, for example, lists of best sellers. His results also suggest that readers' responses and reading habits are as likely to conform to social expectations as to more psychological dynamics. A general discussion of the reader, including some questionnaire data, is found in Waples et al.

TESTING OF THE READER

More direct information on the reader is acquired by using tests. H. A. Carroll's prose appreciation test measures the ability to distinguish literary qualities, using examples of good and bad prose taken from various literary sources;

their qualities were established by expert judges. Weisgerber showed that an understanding of literature (as measured by a comprehension test) parallels accuracy in identification of emotions as portrayed in photographs. Gordon's dissected story test, based on the ability to rearrange the scrambled parts of prose passages (that is, nonliterary anecdotes), measures the person's facility with language and use of ideas. Imagination and intelligence have been measured by Hargreaves in a test which requires either the completion of a story when given only its opening sentence or the building of a story around a few given words. Tests of intellect by Lindquist and Peterson have also used the response to literary materials. Duffy has developed a reliable scoring system to evaluate children's poetry, based on seven rating scales (for example, types of themes, quality of organization, emotional depth, and word choice), whose validity was corroborated by experts' judgments.

Several tests of personality also contain literary materials. H. A. Murray reports Diven's use of literary passages, poems, and paintings as part of a battery of personality tests. He felt that the pattern of responses to these materials, including comparisons with expert evaluations of the words, revealed important motivational themes and symbolic aspects of a subject's personality. Gorham has used the selection of a proverb's meaning from a set of alternate choices as the basis for a test of mental illness (as well as a measure of vocational aptitude and intelligence). Bass has relied on the choices subjects make from alternate interpretations of famous sayings as a diagnostic test of personality.

DIAGNOSIS OF THE READER

Literary materials can be used in a clinical manner, diagnosing the reader. Lindauer examined the biases of psychoanalysts, considering them a specialized type of reader of literature, in light of their treatment of Shakespeare and his works in almost two hundred psychoanalytic studies. The particular preoccupations of psychoanalytically oriented interpretations revealed themselves in several ways. For example, psychoanalysts have given the personality of Shakespeare disproportionately more attention than the psychological themes contained in his various types of plays (that is, histories, comedies, or tragedies). Further, they have extensively examined less than half of Shakespeare's plays, with the tragic category predominating; about 75 percent of all studies were directed toward *Hamlet, Macbeth, Othello,* and *King Lear.* There are other indications of limited interests: only about 6 percent of over three hundred Shakespearean characters have received any extended attention; and about half of the personality traits receiving extensive treatment are of the serious pathological type. The omission of many plays and characters, and the neglect of normal personality dimensions (research trends which have not changed over time) reflected the relatively narrow and specialized reading habits of psychoanalysts.

Leedy has collected writings by psychoanalysts on the benefit of poetry reading in the treatment of neurosis, presumably paralleling the therapeutic roles of art, music, and drama in a clinical setting. In a characteristic treatment, patients read poems by recognized authors, sometimes in a group setting. Harrower reports the less frequent use of the poems of the patients themselves. In a similar vein, Rockland reports tracing a patient's preferences for popular songs during the course of his treatment. Whatever the technique used, it is claimed that poetry provides an acceptable release for feelings, leads to increased self-understanding, and results in useful diagnostic insights for the therapist. However, systematic studies are rare, samples are small, control groups are infrequently used, and there is little statistical treatment of the data. (Curiously the benefit of other literary forms [for example, plays] is not discussed.) Without an empirical framework, it is difficult to determine whether or not poetry (or other prose) is effective, the degree to which it is, and the factors responsible for its presumed effects. (These methodological shortcomings generally describe research efforts in clinical settings which have used aesthetic materials.)

Related to the use of literature for diagnosis is the study of the reader's identification with what he reads. Anast has argued that the reader identifies with fictional heroes and heroines. He analyzed the popular characters in stories in the mass media, concluding that their traits were complementary to the reader's personality. In contrast, most other sociological researchers, also using short stories, have argued that readers identify with similar characters. Barron's study could support either the complementary or similarity hypothesis.[21] Students took a battery of tests as they ordinarily would and as they thought the protagonists in ten works they had read would. Their ability to do this without evident strain indicates that an identification process occurred, but the results do not specify whether identification was easier with characters similar to or different from the readers.

The diversity of studies reviewed in this chapter precludes any attempt to make a reasonable synthesis or overall evaluation. However, comments regarding research in general are made in the concluding chapter. The heterogeneity of the studies reviewed does indicate the resourcefulness of the empirical researchers and the variety of psychological problems they have related to literature.

Notes

1. D. C. McClelland, *The roots of consciousness* (Princeton, N. J.: Van Nostrand, 1964), pp. 182–216.

2. C. S. Hall, "Attitudes toward life and death in poetry," *Psychoanalytic Review* 52 (1965): 73.

3. Ibid., p. 74

4. Ibid., pp. 75–76.

5. Ibid., p. 79.

6. Early experimental studies of imagery to poetry, reviewed in the text, were carried out by J. E. Downey, "Literary self-projections," *Psychological Review* 19 (1912): 299–311; Downey, "Literary synesthesia," *Journal of Philosophy* 9 (1912): 490–498; Downey, "Emotional poetry and the preference judgment," *Psychological Review* 22 (1915): 259–278; E. A. Peers, "Imagery in imaginative literature," *Journal of Experimental Pedagogy and Training College Record* 11 (1914): 174–187; J. C. Hill, "Poetry and the unconscious," *British Journal of Medical Psychology* 4 (1924): 125–133.

7. C. W. Valentine, "The function of imagery in the appreciation of poetry," *British Journal of Psychology* 14 (1923): 164–191.

8. L. Dudley, *The study of literature* (Boston: Houghton-Mifflin, 1928).

9. C. S. Hall, "Slang and dream symbols," *Psychoanalytic Review* 51 (1964): 42–43.

10. H. Gardner, "The development of sensitivity to artistic styles," *Journal of Aesthetics and Art Criticism* 29 (1971): 515–527.

11. K. Hevner, "An experimental study of the affective value of sounds in poetry," *American Journal of Psychology* 49 (1937): 434.

12. I. L. Child, "Esthetics," in *The Handbook of social psychology,* edited by G. Lindzey & E. Aronson (Reading, Mass.: Addison-Wesley, 1969), pp. 853–916.

13. C. B. Williams, "Statistics as an aid to literary studies," *Science News* 24 (1952): 99–106.

14. W. J. Paisley, "Identifying the unknown communicator in painting, literature and music: The significance of minor encoding habits," *Journal of Communication* 14 (1964): 219–237.

15. Paisley, "The effect of authorship, topic, structure, and time of composition on letter redundancy in English texts," *Journal of Verbal Learning and Verbal Behavior* 5 (1966): 28–34.

16. F. Mosteller & D. L. Wallace, "Inference in an author-

ship problem," *Journal of the American Statistics Association* 58 (1963): 275–309; E. B. Newman & L. J. Gerstman, "A new method for analyzing printed English," *Journal of Experimental Psychology* 44 (1952): 114–125; Newman & N. Waugh, "The redundancy of texts in three languages," *Information and Control* (1960): 141–153.

17. A review of the early use of nonliterary but meaningful prose is in M. S. Lindauer, "The role of attitude and needs in the learning and retention of relevant meaningful prose." Unpublished paper, State College at Brockport, 1960. A classic example of the use of controversial prose material and how its learning and recall are affected by one's favorable or unfavorable attitudes is found in J. M. Levine & G. Murphy, "Learning and forgetting of controversial material," *Journal of Abnormal and Social Psychology* 38 (1943): 507–515.

18. Child, in Lindzey & Aronson, 1969.

19. I. R. Stuart, "Personality dynamics and objectionable art: Attitudes, and opinions, and experimental evidence," *Journal of Art Education* 4 (1970): 101–116.

20. D. E. Berlyne, "Affective aspects of aesthetic communication," paper read at symposium, "Affect and Communication," Ervindale College, University of Toronto, 1971, pp. 19–22.

21. F. X. Barron, *Artists in the making* (New York: Seminar Press, 1972), chap. 7.

9

Summary and Conclusions

The survey of conceptual and methodological ties between science, psychology, and literature in chapters 4 and 5, and the review of empirical, sociological, and psychological studies of literature in chapters 6, 7, and 8, answer many of the objections to an empirical orientation to literature raised earlier. This chapter summarizes these arguments, adds further reasons why resistance to an objective treatment of literary material is unjustified, and offers suggestions for developing the empirical relationship between psychology and literature.

In answer to literary objections

Literary critics' antipathy to an empirical treatment of literary materials stems largely from a misinterpretation of psychology's purposes. Psychological investigation distinguishes between literature's function as a source of knowledge and its more personal and idiosyncratic function of giving insights and revelations to specific readers. It is literature's impersonal status which is of empirical interest; literature's intuitive, private, and less communicable role is not of primary concern to psychology. Consequently psychology's intention is not to challenge literature as art nor to reduce literature's personal value to the anonymity of science. Psychology tries to translate art (not transform it) for its own particular purposes. These are largely irrelevant to the aesthetic goals of art, the motives of the author, and the interests of the reader. The fears of the literati are misplaced: literature's roles as art and as an aesthetic experience are not the primary issues for psychologists; literature's role as data is. Quantitative research on literary materials is not meant to have the broad relevance of literary analysis.

Empirical analysis not only uses more restricted methods but asks more limited questions. As a result, objective findings in psychology cannot be as dramatic or appealing as the literary sources from which such data were derived. In short, the psychological study of aesthetics cannot itself fulfill an aesthetic criterion: it does not give the same sort of pleasure to the reader or inspiration to the critic as literature does. Further, not all literature is applicable to psychological investigation: only that segment dealing with material which lends itself to empirical attack. It is therefore unfair to judge the value of psychological investigations of literature on the irrelevant grounds of literary standards, aesthetics, and personal tastes. Psychology's aims are more modest than those of the writer, reader, and critic.

Psychology's modest claims should not, however, put literature's special status as art into false perspective. The personal, intuitive, and revelatory effects of literature occur rarely, for just a small number of readers and in response to only a few great books in each generation. Not all literature is art, and even great art is often flawed. Further, science at its best, like literature at its best, can also transform facts so as to arouse in man a new perspective of and sensitivity to himself and nature. Therefore Stegner's argument in chapter 3, which cogently contrasts the high ideals of literature to the philistine goals of science, is overdrawn. Literature is rarely so unique, special, provocative, and full of insights as to preclude scientific analysis. The recognition of the special province of literature and the acknowledgment of its distinctiveness from science do not mean an unquestioning acceptance of its total inviolability to objective analysis.

Emphasizing literature's specialness and hailing its empirical untouchability as an advantage are not only antiscientific, but also anti-intellectual and essentially pessimistic, because doing so sets limits to man's pursuit of knowledge.

The assertion that literature is not open to quantification is inappropriate and extreme. Much of literary analysis indirectly depends on what are essentially mathematical concepts: ordering, categorizing, and classifying. Poetic forms are explicitly numerical. Ranta has noted that several authors (for example, Poe, Thoreau, Pound) have discussed in detail the mathematical qualities of literature or have informally and implicitly relied on statistical concepts. On this basis, Ranta has defended the usefulness of statistics to literary critics. They offer a means of grasping complex relationships and patterns in the structure and forms of literature:

> The method is simply a way ... of coping with the intricacies of the physical properties, whether textual or structural, of a work, and of gathering data for making descriptive statements about those properties that perhaps could not be made in any other way.[1]

Ranta sees measurement as a descriptive and reportorial procedure from which literary interpretation and opinion can more easily follow. As a means of amplifying traditional types of literary interpretation and analysis, Ranta has obtained counts of different elements of prose (for example, images, motifs, key words) and used a wide range of units (for example, sections, paragraphs, capital letters, and punctuation). He feels that the quantitative approach may be particularly useful in understanding the nontraditional and unique forms of modern poetry, the meaning of which is particularly unclear. (A limitation to his argument is that he recommends using the statistical approach with little or no specific conception of what one hopes to find; hence, much analysis seems unnecessarily wasteful.)

There are parallels other than quantitative ones between science and art (chapter 4). These include their common reference to experience and observation and their joint reliance on metaphors, subjectivity, and creativity.

Literary critics are on more justifiable grounds when they complain that an overconcern with psychological issues and objective methods leads empirical investigations to ignore literary facts and analysis. Most psychological studies of literature are in fact directed less toward the issues and content of literature than to traditional psychological topics of personality, creativity, social psychology, and thinking. There is relatively little direct interest in the psychology of creative writing, literary content, and the readers' reactions. Consequently, hardly a beginning has been made in the study of such critical aesthetic questions as why one reads, what is good literature, how did the creative literary process originate, and are the truths contained in literature valid? The dominance of psychological rather than aesthetic interests is evident in the diverse range of studies reviewed in chapters 7 and 8. However, the relevance of literature to psychology should eventually increase as psychology's involvement with literature matures. A balanced and reciprocal exchange of ideas, data, and conclusions between literature and psychology will eventually occur, to the advantage of both fields.

Another justifiable complaint of literary critics is that psychological research in literature is not marked by sustained and systematic empirical efforts on any one problem; nor are there more than the rudimentary beginnings of theory. Instead, there are tentative research efforts, characterized by a groping for a suitable methodology, and a cautiousness of hypothesis (if any).

In order for technical, theoretical, and factual advances to occur, psychologists have to become more involved with literature. But this cannot happen unless psychologists exhibit an acceptance of less rigorously empirical topics which deal with conscious events. The dilemma is illustrated by the vigorous state of theory and research in the closely related psychological areas of humor, play, and laughter (little of which has, surprisingly, been related to literature, despite many parallels).[2] One finds there an abundance of testable theories, hypotheses, and studies—but the topics nevertheless remain largely neglected in experimental psychology because of their subjectivity.

Another reason why psychology's approach to literary material is often only indirectly related to literature is because it begins with and focuses on psychology rather than literature. This priority of interests stems from the belief that questions of literature (or any other applied topic) are best answered from a basis in general psychology. It is presumed that specific applications of psychology will more successfully occur if they are first grounded in the fundamentals. This strategic assumption and the advantages attendant upon dealing with "purer" issues account for an orientation which attempts to make literature relevant to psychology rather than the reverse; that is, one begins with psychological rather than literary questions. Psychological investigations of literature are therefore initiated less by literary analyses than by psychological theory, a goal which appears scientifically justifiable as well as more realizable.

Thus it is true that psychology needs to learn more about literary analysis and to at least appreciate more of literature's possibilities for research. Yet it is also true that those in literature need to know more about psychology. Literature's conceptions of psychology are generally outmoded; they are largely limited to classical psychoanalysis, introspective psychology, and early behaviorism. Nixon and Richards wrote the two major works that seriously attempted to make general psychology relevant to literature in the late 1920s; no recent work comparable to theirs in scope has emerged. The psychological content of much literary criticism therefore has a flavor of the past and refers to historical rather than contemporary research efforts. Literary critics seem largely unaware of the value of statistical and computer analysis of the structure and content of language. They have not seriously studied literary expression with sophisticated methodologies based on empirical and quantitative techniques.

Literature's rejection of quantitative techniques and empirical research reflects an attitude that has led to several negative pedagogical consequences. A superficial comparison of art education with English education indicates a predominance of research efforts intent on fostering art education and appreciation. Thus Matchotka can talk about applying the principle of learning to the field of art education only. There is little in the educational field of English literature which is comparable to the applied and technological orientation, emphasis, and accomplishments of art. Perhaps because of these diverse and concentrated efforts, one finds many courses in art education but few in literature education in the early grades. Pronouncing, spelling, vocabulary, and composition—the usual forms of literary education in the early years of school—are emphasized, to the neglect of the reading or writing of a story or poem. Similarly, the art amateur finds many more opportunities for the expression of his interests, whether for pleasure, health, or therapy, than the amateur writer. Comparable avocational opportunities in the reading and writing of literature are less available: appropriate courses are often restricted to advanced levels or available only to those students who have demonstrated a minimum level of talent or skill. Another possible consequence of literature's technical naivety is the rare use of reading and writing in a clinical setting, in comparison to a frequent dependence on art for diagnostic and therapeutic functions.

In answer to psychology's objections

Psychologists' resistance to the possibilities of literature is as inappropriate as the resistance of those in literature to psychology. Most psychologists appear to be unaware of the extensive ties that exist between psychology and literature, both conceptually and (to a lesser degree) empirically. Psychologists seem ignorant of the advantages of the study of literature to psychology's humanistic and experiential themes.

Psychologists, like literary critics, have failed to distinguish between literature as personal entertainment and as impersonal data. They have not recognized the possibilities inherent in literary content and its response, from which not only illustrative materials but also facts, analyses and hypotheses can be taken. They have not considered literature as data, which like any other kind of data, can be empirically investigated. Instead, they have emphasized the problems of literary analysis, without recognizing that they also exist among readily accepted paradigms of animal and laboratory research.

Psychologists have not been reluctant to use the pathological data of the clinic, which, although also a unique form of data, are considered (with reservations) a legitimate source of study. Writers and the special effects their work has on a reader could be considered as lying at the extreme end of the continuum of normality, but on the positive rather than pathological side. Extremes, whether positive or negative, serve to clearly and dramatically represent the events and processes which lie in the less clearly defined middle area of the normal curve that most of us occupy. Both polarities serve as unusual yet relevant sources of information about ordinary psychological processes. However, the pathological rather than the creative end of the continuum has received most attention.

Some of the limitations inherent in literature's less rigorous origins may be offset by the special status it has in relation to most other sources of data in psychology. Literature extensively refers to and relies upon the distinctively human traits of consciousness and experience. Contemporary psychology's neglect of these extremely interesting and important aspects of human behavior has been the basis for humanistically oriented psychologists' pessimistic and discouraging evaluation of the field. The study of literature could provide a welcome and refreshing addition to the traditional reliance on simpler problems, materials, and responses. A viable psychology of literature would help loosen the bonds of those historical forces which have restricted psychology's development, including the rigidity of stimulus-response and atomistic conceptions of man. Severe and narrow restrictions on subject matter were more relevant when psychology was struggling for recognition as a science. Hopefully, this search for status can now be replaced by a more liberal and relaxed methodology and spirit of inquiry. The empirical study of literature would add to, not detract from, psychology's status as a human science.

Many who acknowledge literature's potential contribution to psychology may still feel that methodological difficulties in its objective study outweigh any advantages. However, it is one thing to say that the attempt to relate literature to psychology has serious problems; it is quite another matter to argue that the attempt should therefore be abandoned. A psychology of literature can be evaluated only in terms of its fruitfulness to both psychology and literature, in light of the data, hypotheses, and theories which will eventually emerge. A priori prohibitions (or, for that matter, a priori advantages) should not be the basis for an evaluation. Despite difficulties, the study of literature along empirical-objective-quantitative lines has made a meaningful beginning filled with much promise. Sufficient time should now be given for the psychological study of literature to prove itself in concrete accomplishments. The number of discussions of literature's usefulness far outweighs the number of objective investigations that have actually taken place. The two fields would be better served if more concrete research efforts were initiated and completed, and were substituted for further arguments, justifications, and exhortations.

The major reason for the paucity of psychological research in literature is not so much the lack of will on the part of researchers but the absence of the means to carry out such investigations. There is a serious shortage of suitable and sophisticated methodologies with which to empirically investigate literary materials. The development and refinement of appropriate research techniques are absolutely necessary if the rich and subtle content of literature is to be adequately managed and translated into meaningful psychological analysis. The major method of literary study, content analysis, is insufficient as a complete research tool, although the technique has proven its usefulness in showing that literary material can be quantified. Osgood and Tannenbaum's semantic differential technique, although more subtle and statistically powerful than content analysis as a descriptive tool, also risks overuse and overdependence. Descriptions of literature, which these techniques emphasize, fail to come to grips with questions regarding the effects and consequences of literature; without further analysis, they also do not functionally reveal the causes and correlates of writing, reading, and the appreciation of literature. For these more analytic purposes, other methodologies and research designs are required.

Directions for research

If a psychology of literature mutually acceptable to both disciplines is to be developed, the contribution of literary experts to psychological inquiry must be encouraged. Students of literature provide a promising subject pool, one frequently relied on in art research. As Barron notes: "The place to begin [is] with beginners."[3] Knowledgeable participants can assist in the abstracting and classifying of literature, providing the necessary analysis of literary content and structure upon which psychological research can build. Literary experts can highlight literature's relevance to psychological themes and suggest those literary dimensions to which empirical attention could be relevantly drawn. Literary contributions to psychological inquiry include analyses of authors (for example, Shakespeare); comments on the role of cognitive processes (for example, imagery); and summaries of the views of motivation and types of personality found in literature (as done by Nixon and Ashmun). There are other dimensions of literary analysis yet to be developed, which, if they were undertaken by experts, could then be objectively confirmed or extended by psychological investigation. Possibilities include precise and informed statements about the effects of different periods and types of literature on the reader; comparisons between literary expression in different countries; and inferences regarding the motives and emotions most typically found in literature at different times.

There are other roles for literary experts in psychological inquiry. Because they have a basic, familiar, and workable knowledge of literary materials, they can be used either as judges of literary material or as participating research subjects. The use of a specialized subject pool of literary experts would provide measurable and reliable answers to substantive questions about preferences and other qualities of different works and authors, questions which have been either taken for granted or answered intuitively by a few authorities. Data from specialized subjects would provide normative descriptions, standardized information, and established categories of literary content, structure, and style. These data would also be useful in formulating problems and hypotheses for further investigation. For example, sets of data taken from restricted but known and controlled subject pools could be correlated, illustrating the relationship between literary preferences and age, sex, types of experience, background, and personality. Further, in experimental paradigms of research, consensual descriptive statements about literature would provide known, concrete, operational, and therefore manipulable stimulus variables for the study of presumed literary effects, for example, the types of literary material which lead to the greatest pleasure, result in the clearest understanding, or evoke the highest degree of tension. The power of the experimental procedure would be increased to the extent that subject characteristics were also known and included.

Many studies in aesthetics have used art experts or students. The substitution of a literary sample of subjects in these studies would make them applicable to literary issues. Relevant studies include Getzels and Csikszentmihalyi's poll of experts' opinion on a set of drawings compared with the opinion of nonexperts;[4] Klein and Skager tested whether experts could distinguish beteween spontaneous and deliberate art; Getzels and Csikszentmihalyi correlated the personality and values of art students with the creative quality of their work;[5] B. Wilson had Picasso's *Guernica* evaluated by students of art, art experts, and laymen as a means of illustrating the effects of training and experience; and Peel systematically surveyed individual differences in tastes for various types of art. Comparisons of these kinds between different types of subjects and for different sorts of artistic works could be carried out with literary materials as well. While the results might confirm common sense, some interesting and surprising findings might also be revealed, as has been the case for art.

Some basic decision is also necessary about which types of literature are most appropriate for study. Enduring works of literary merit, rather than the more popular and fleeting forms of literature mainly studied by social scientists (that is, mostly best sellers and stories in the mass media), appear more appropriate for psychological investigation. The classics, standard works, and other literary forms of acknowledged and sustained merit, as consistently judged by experts over time, are more likely to provide information on universal and pervasive psychological processes and traits; and their validity is confirmed by continued and sustained acceptance from an informed readership. Unlike sociologists, who look to best sellers for their reflection of group and institutional forces, psychologists are more interested in literature's reference to individual processes in the person (for example, motivation, emotion, personality, cognition, perception, and imagination), whether found in the creator, his imaginary characters, or in the reader. The classics, unlike popular works and stories in the mass media, are less likely to be limited by the changing patterns of societal events.

Once the type of literature is chosen, the literary stimulus must be specified in such terms as to make it procedurally manageable. A strategy generally used in psychology is to simplify the stimulus. In art, nonsense shapes are relied upon. For literature this means, at its most extreme, the generation (by formula or computer) of nonsense syllables of exactly known specifications and qualities which are then treated as analogous to ordinary language. The danger in this extremely reductionistic tactic is that findings based on such simplified and artificial stimuli may no longer be relevant to aesthetics. A compromise solution, falling between the broad requirements of literary relevance and the narrowing restrictions of controlled methodology, is to depend on short literary forms such as poetry and quotations. Because these meaningful literary units are brief, they can be managed procedurally and quantitatively. Similarly, extracts from novels that tersely describe personality types would also be suitable. The use of small yet still literary units would serve the essential intent of a reductionistic strategy, that is, control, without at the same time sacrificing basic aesthetic and literary qualities. This strategy of research, according to Lindauer, would be a means of liberalizing experimental aesthetics because there would be less need to depend on nonaesthetic materials.

The impetus for psychological research in literature can take two broad directions. The less common approach is to begin with a psychological theme already suggested by literature or literary analysis. The content, issues, and assertions already raised in aesthetics and literature are amplified, extended, or confirmed by psychological investigation. For example, Lindauer's study of the cliché was initiated by the claims of rhetoricians that this form of literary expression is perceived as meaningless and that its use indicates a person's poor thinking. The more typical approach, perhaps because of the dearth of psychologically meaningful analysis by literary experts, has been to begin with psychological concepts and extend these to literary materials; major examples are McClelland's research on achievement motivation, and the illustrative role literature plays in psychoanalysis. The priority of this research strategy gives only incidental interest to aesthetic and literary goals. Only rarely does one find that the impetus or outcome of an empirical investigation is jointly relevant to both literature and psychology, as perhaps prestige and imagery studies are. The increased reliance on literary experts, whose potential contribution to research was discussed earlier, may help redress the balance to the advantage of the goals of both groups.

Another major problem of psychological research in literature is to account for the role of unconscious processes in both author and reader. The psychology of art may again serve as a model in meeting this issue. The presence of unconscious factors in the creation of art and the response to it has usually been ignored. The research procedure is to focus on overt events (at least at first), rather than on the more difficult underlying unconscious processes. Manifest events can then be taken as indirectly reflecting latent and underlying processes and structure.

This procedure can be extended to handle other covert and subtle mediators in aesthetic processes. For example, underlying processes are obviously a major factor in creativity. Nevertheless, it may be more practical to shift interest away from creativity's unconscious origins, mechanisms, and expressions and to turn instead to the more tangible study of the observer's overt responses to a creative object. The resultant data could be related to the similarly tangible stimulus characteristics of the creative object. This phenomenological approach accepts biographical and self-reports on creativity for what they *say* about personality and creativity, rather than what they might *imply*. Self-perceptions, regardless of their truth and dynamic sources, provide testable hypotheses about such important questions as the perceived role of childhood and parents in creative achievement and whether writers feel that the stages of creativity are necessary. A phenomenological strategy, beginning with the more overt characteristics of the literary response, is less incisive and dramatic than an analysis in depth, but it offers a start toward inquiries along more psychodynamic lines.

There are other reasons for deemphasizing the unconscious in research. A preoccupation with the unconscious has led to an overconcern with the abnormal and bizarre in the psychology of literature, the dominance of a few select research areas, such as personality and its motivational and emotional characteristics, and the neglect of the more positive and optimistic aspects of personality. But literature also represents man's successful adapting to stress, his growth, sense of self-realization, and feelings of adequacy.

There are literary treatments of topics other than psychodynamics. The conscious and cognitive qualities of man, as expressed in literature, are as intimately and appropriately relevant to psychological study as are personality dimensions. In general, these qualities include man's seeking of stimulation and order; his organization, integration, and synthesis of experience; his capacity to acquire and store information; and his ability to use it in imagination and problem solving (that is, the topics of attention, perception, learning, remembering, and thinking). Although art has been interpreted by writers such as Arnheim and Gombrich in cognitive terms (that is, in ways indicating how art enables man to grasp and cope with reality), the comparable functions of literature have been largely ignored by empirical analysis.

A cognitive approach to aesthetic materials opens up several new research directions, many of which have already begun in the study of art. For example, Child has applied a theory of cognitive style in personality expression to judgments of art.[6] Cognitive style, especially as represented in the nonaesthetic studies of R. Gardner and his co-workers, refers to those traits which characterize the individual's typical perceptual and cognitive approach to his world: analytic or holistic, field dependent or independent, tolerant or intolerant of ambiguity, wide or narrow, realistic or ambivalent, and explorative or incurious. One particular feature of cognitive style which has attracted a good deal of research in aesthetics (and elsewhere) is the preference for complexity. Barron has shown that its expression correlates with independence of judgment, social attitudes, and, most importantly, with creativity.[7] The complexity dimension of a stimulus may also be tied to attention and motivation; Berlyne has extensively examined the arousal capacity of visual stimuli of different complexity. However, neither cognitive style nor complexity has seriously been investigated in a literary context, although analyses similar to those using art could easily be accomplished with literary materials, for example, the correlation between cognitive style, stimulus complexity, and reader preferences. D. R. Evans and Kammann have made a beginning by quantifying the complexity of ordinary prose and poetry, then relating it to attractiveness and preference.

Besides complexity, other stimulus dimensions of nonliterary materials have been investigated. Zajonc has dealt with the effects of repetition and exposure on preference and interest. The relation between the direction and duration of looking behavior (including eye movements and pupillary opening) to different qualities of a stimulus (for example, the important and unusual details and ideas on the page, paragraph, or line) has been studied by Exline et al., Leckart and Faw, and Mackworth and Morandi. These variables could easily be applied to literary materials and would provide basic information on the literary response.

There are other areas of cognitive experimental psychology studied with artistic materials that should prove equally applicable to literary prose. A major example is

Walk's study of the learning, recognition, and transfer of the concept of artistic style, and Gardner's work on how these processes change with age.[8] Other literary research possibilities are to be found in less directly aesthetic areas of research. The successful scaling of the connotative meanings and personal attributes of given names, accomplished by Albott and Bruning, could be applied to the names of literary characters, as well as the titles of books. This procedure might indicate the subtle literary implication of labels. Dooling and Lachman examined the effect of titles on the comprehension and retention of nonliterary passages. Literary prose could also be substituted for ordinary materials. Such studies of learning as those by Blount and Johnson, and Crouse, who used highly meaningful prose, or by Booth, who examined the retention of news items from different media, are suggestive of how material as complex as literature could be successfully managed in learning studies. The use of literature would extend Bartlett's approach to learning and remembering to areas which have exclusively relied on simpler, less meaningful, and duller material.

There is also a place for literary rather than ordinary materials in teaching reading skills and comprehension (as well as speech) because literature has the advantage of inherent interest. Among the various critical aspects of reading that have been studied, those that may prove most applicable to the substitution of literary prose include patterns of eye movements and changes in pupil dilation. These measures, among others (for example, speed of reading), studied by Carver and Dearborn with ordinary text, would also be useful in the context of several aesthetic questions. For example, eye responses could be related to the quality of literary prose, differences between literary forms, contrasts between literature and other types of prose (for example, scientific), and distinctions between preferred and nonpreferred passages. Subject variables (for example, personality, creativity) could also be part of the study of the response to these stimulus features of literary prose. Some references to the reading of Shakespeare's sonnets were made in Yarbus' *Eye Movements and Vision,* although to Yarbus the literary qualities of the reading materials were only incidental.

Although social psychological studies, especially of attitudes, have already made great use of literary materials (chapter 8), additional applications are possible. Little has been quantitatively accomplished in comparing differences in literary expression between countries. A start might be made through interviewing translators. They would provide preliminary data on the types of difficulties faced in translating materials from one language to another. Of some possible relevance to this topic is Barik's examination of the various problems of simultaneous oral translation and the strategies used to overcome them.

Literature could also be used within a therapeutic context, paralleling the extensive reliance on art. This dependence on art has been too extensive, according to Wyschogrod, resulting in the neglect of other aesthetic forms of therapy. While a beginning has been made in the greater clinical use of literary materials, the effort, at least according to Schloss and Grundy's review, is largely psychoanalytic and nonstatistical rather than empirical. The general (untested) hypothesis is that the reading and writing of poetry, by stimulating associations, are cathartic and break down resistances. In addition to objectively corroborating this claim, more systematic study should also analyze patients' works of fiction (or diaries, essays, or other imaginative writings) for their themes, which might reveal either diagnostic or prognostic aspects of treatment. Further, different types of literature or authors, as well as writing tasks, could be given to patients, and the effects on progress systematically noted.

While these proposed directions for research with literary materials remain largely speculative, they do suggest many topics and approaches that could prove useful for the empirical study of literature. Extensions and elaborations of concepts from general experimental psychology, together with the suggestions of literary experts, should establish a beginning for the posing of meaningful research questions, the carrying out of research, and the amassing of data that would answer the essential psychological problems of literature dealing with the author, his work, and the reader. We need more empirical information about literature rather than more speculation. Authors, critics, and others have made more use of psychology, especially its psychoanalytic variant, than psychologists have made of literature. Yet literature-as-art cannot be empirically managed in its totality. However, treated objectively and considered as an elegant and refined form of common sense, literature can be scientifically approached. It has the same legitimate status as any one of the multitudinous topics that characterize psychological research interests. Literature illustrates psychological themes, and supplements psychology as a source of data, hypotheses, or analyses. In addition, literature may suggest tentative answers to psychological questions which empirical research has not yet asked or satisfactorily answered or which may never be susceptible to quantitative attack.

Notes

1. J. Ranta, "Counting and formal analysis," *Journal of Aesthetics and Art Criticism* 29 (1971): 455.

2. D. E. Berlyne, "Laughter, human and play," in *The handbook of social psychology*, 2nd ed., edited by G. Lindzey & E. Aronson (Reading, Mass.: Addison-Wesley, 1969), vol. 3, pp. 795–852.

3. F. X. Barron, *Artists in the making* (New York: Seminar Press, 1972), p. xvii.

4. J. W. Getzels and M. Csikszentmihalyi, "Aesthetic opinion: An empirical study," *Public Opinion Quarterly* 33 (1969): 34–35.

5. Getzels & Csikszentmihalyi, "The value orientations of art students as determinants of artistic specialization and creative performance," *Studies in Art Education* 10 (1968): 5–16.

6. I. L. Child, "Personality correlates of esthetic judgment in college students," *Journal of Personality* 33 (1965): 476–511.

7. Barron, "Complexity-simplicity as a personality dimension," *Journal of Abnormal and Social Psychology* 48 (1953): 163–172.

8. H. Gardner, "From mode to symbol: Thoughts on the genesis of the arts," *British Journal of Aesthetics* 10 (1970): 359–375.

References

Abraham, P. "Creations of Balzac." *Psychological Abstracts* 6 (1932) #747.

Abrams, M. H. *The mirror and the lamp: Romantic theory and the critical tradition.* New York: Norton, 1958.

Adams, S. & Powers, F. F. "The psychology of language." *Psychological Bulletin* 26 (1929): 241–260.

Albott, W. L. & Bruning, J. L. "Given names: A neglected social variable." *Psychological Record* 20 (1970): 527–533.

Albrecht, M. C. "Psychological motives in the fiction of Julian Green." *Journal of Personality* 15 (1948): 278–303.

_____. "The relationship of literature and society." *American Journal of Sociology* 59 (1954): 425–436.

_____. "Does literature reflect common values?" *American Sociological Review* 21 (1956): 722–729.

_____. Review of *The novel and society,* by D. Spearman, and *The rise of the novel,* by I. Watt. *Transaction* 6 (1969): 54–55.

Alcorn, D. E. "New Testament psychology." *British Journal of Medical Psychology* 16 (1937): 270–280.

Allport, G. W. "The study of personality by the intuitive method: An experiment in teaching from *The locomotive god.*" *Journal of Abnormal and Social Psychology* 24 (1929): 14–27.

_____. *The use of personal documents in psychological science.* New York: Social Science Research Council, 1942.

Alluisi, E. A. & Adams, O. S. "Predicting letter preferences: Aesthetics and filtering in man." *Perceptual and Motor Skills* 14 (1962): 123–131.

Anast, P. "Similarity between self and fictional character choice." *Psychological Record* 16 (1966): 535–539.

_____. "Differential movie appeals as correlates of attendance." *Journalism Quarterly* 44 (1967): 86–90.

Anderson, H. H., ed. *Creativity and its cultivation.* New York: Harper, 1959.

Arcamore, A. & Lindauer, M. S. "Concept learning and poetry." Paper presented at the 81st Meeting of the American Psychological Association, Montreal, 1973.

Arnheim, R. "Psychological notes on the poetical process." In *Poets at work,* by Rudolf Arnheim, W. H. Auden, K. Shapiro, & D. A. Stauffer. New York: Harcourt, Brace, 1948. Pp. 125–162.

_____. *Art and visual perception: A psychology of the creative eye.* Berkeley, Calif.: University of California, 1966.

_____. *Visual thinking.* Berkeley, Calif.: University of California, 1969.

_____. *Entropy and art: An essay on disorder and order.* Berkeley, Calif.: University of California, 1971.

Asch, S. E. "The doctrine of suggestion, prestige, and imitation in social psychology." *Psychological Review* 55 (1948): 250–276.

_____. *Social psychology.* Englewood Cliffs, N. J.: Prentice-Hall, 1952. Pp. 418–442.

_____. "On the use of metaphor in the description of persons." In *On expressive language,* edited by H. Werner. Worcester, Mass.: Clark University, 1955. Pp. 29–38.

_____. "The metaphor: A psychological inquiry." In *Personal perception and interpersonal behavior,* by R. Taguiri & L. Petrulla. Stanford, Calif.: Stanford University, 1958. Pp. 86–94.

Asheim, L. "From book to film." *Reader in opinion and com-*

munication, edited by Bernard Berelson & M. Janowitz. Glencoe, Ill.: Free Press, 1953. Pp. 299–306.

Ashmun, M. "A study of temperaments as illustrated in literature." *American Journal of Psychology* 19 (1908): 519–535.

Auden, W. H. "Psychology and art." In *The arts today,* edited by G. Grigson. London: John Lane the Bodley Head, 1935. Pp. 1–21.

———. "Under which lyre." *Nones.* New York: Random House, 1951.

Auster, D. "A content analysis of Little Orphan Annie." In *Sociology: The progress of a decade,* edited by S. Lipset & N. Smelser, Englewood Cliffs, N. J.: Prentice-Hall, 1961.

Austin, G. R. "Non-fiction best sellers: Types and trends." *Journal of Social Psychology* 38 (1953): 141–143.

Bakan, D. *On method: Toward a reconstruction of psychological investigation.* San Francisco: Jossey-Bass, 1967.

———. "Psychology can now kick the science habit." *Psychology Today* 5 (1972): 26–28, 86–88.

Baldwin, A. L. "Personal structure analysis: A statistical method for investigating the single personality." *Journal of Abnormal and Social Psychology* 37 (1940): 518–519.

Barbu, Z. *Problems of historical psychology.* New York: Grove, 1960.

Barik, H. C. "Some findings on simultaneous interpretation." *Proceedings of the 78th Annual APA Convention* 5 (1970): 11–12.

Barnes, H. E. "Psychology and history." *American Journal of Psychology* 30 (1919): 337–376.

Barnett, J. H. "Research in the sociology of art." *Sociology and Social Research* 42 (1958): 401–405.

———. "The sociology of art." In *Sociology today,* edited by R. K. Merton, L. Broom, & L. S. Cottrell, Jr. New York: Basic Books, 1959. Pp. 197–214.

Barron, F. "Complexity-simplicity as a personality dimension." *Journal of Abnormal and Social Psychology* 48 (1953): 163–172.

_____. "The disposition toward originality." *Journal of Abnormal and Social Psychology* 15 (1955): 478–485.

_____. "The psychology of creativity." In *New directions in psychology II,* edited by T. M. Newcomb. New York: Holt, Rinehart & Winston, 1965. Pp. 1–134.

_____. *Artists in the making.* New York: Seminar Press, 1972.

_____. Review of *The creative experience,* edited by S. Rosner & L. E. Abt. *Contemporary Psychology* 17 (1972): 4–5.

Barron, F. & Rosenberg, M. "King Lear and his fool. A study in the conception and enactment of a dramatic role in relation to self-conception." *Proceedings of the 76th Annual Convention APA* 3 (1968): 369–370.

Bartlett, F. C. "Types of imagination." *Philosophical Studies* 3 (1928): 78–85.

_____. *Remembering: A study in experimental and social psychology.* Cambridge: Cambridge University Press, 1932.

Bass, B. M. "Famous sayings test: General manual." *Psychological Reports, Monograph Supplement 6,* 4 (1958): 479–497.

Beardsley, M. C. "Aesthetic welfare." *Journal of Art Education* 4 (1970): 9–20.

Beittel, K. R. "Creativity in the visual arts in higher education: Criteria, predictors, experimentation, and their interactions." In *Widening horizons in creativity,* edited by Calvin W. Taylor. New York: Wiley, 1964. Pp. 379–395.

Berelson, B. "Communication and public opinion." In *Reader in public opinion and communication,* edited by B. Berelson & M. Janowitz. Glencoe, Ill.: Free Press, 1953. Pp. 448–462.

Berelson, B. & Janowitz, M., eds. *Reader in public opinion and communication.* Glencoe, Ill.: Free Press, 1953.

Berelson, B. & Salter, P. J. "Majority and minority Americans: An analysis of magazine fiction." *Public Opinion Quarterly* 10 (1946): 168–190.

Berger, B. M. "Audiences, art, and power." *Transaction 8* (1971): 26–30.

Berlyne, D. E. *Conflict, arousal, and curiosity.* New York: McGraw-Hill, 1960. Chap. 9.

_____. "The psychology of aesthetic behavior." Talk given to the Department of Art Education, Pennsylvania State University, 1968. Penn State Papers in Art Education, #5.

_____. "Laughter, humor, and play." In *The handbook of social psychology,* edited by G. Lindzey & E. Aronson. 2nd ed. Reading, Mass.: Addison-Wesley, 1969. Vol. 3, pp. 795–852.

_____. "Affective aspects of aesthetic communication." Paper read at symposium "Affect and Communication," Erindale College, University of Toronto, 1971.

_____. *Psychobiology and aesthetics.* New York: Appleton-Century-Crofts, 1971.

Bertalanffy, L. *Robots, men, and minds: Psychology in the modern world.* New York: Braziller, 1967.

Bindman, S. S. Review of *Challenges of humanistic psychology,* edited by J. F. T. Bugental. *Contemporary Psychology* 16 (1971): 158–159.

Birkhoff, G. D. *Aesthetic measure.* Cambridge, Mass.: Harvard University, 1933.

Bleich, D. "Emotional origins of literary meaning." *College English* 31 (1969): 30–40.

Bliss, W. D. "Birth order of creative writers." *Journal of Individual Psychology* 26 (1970): 200–202.

Block, H. A. "Toward the development of a sociology of literary and art-forms." *American Sociological Review* 8 (1943): 313–320.

Blondel, C. "The psychology of Marcel Proust." *Psychological Abstracts* 6 (1932) #1871.

Bloom, L. "Psychology and aesthetics: A methodological Monroe Doctrine." *Journal of General Psychology* 65 (1961): 305–317.

Blount, H. P. & Johnson, J. E. "Syntactic influences in the recall of sentences in prose." *Proceedings of the 79th Annual Convention APA* 6 (1971): 40–41.

Boder, D. P. "The adjective-verb quotient: A contribution to the psychology of language." *Psychological Record* 3 (1940): 310–343.

Booth, A. "The recall of news items." *Public Opinion Quarterly* 34 (1970–71): 604–610.

Boring, E. G. *A history of experimental psychology.* 2nd ed. New York: Appleton-Century-Crofts, 1950.

Bowles, E., ed. *Computers in humanistic research: Readings and perspectives.* Englewood Cliffs, N. J.: Prentice-Hall, 1967.

Brinegar, C. S. "Mark Twain and the Quintas Curtius Snodgrass letters: A statistical test of authorship." *Journal of the American Statistical Association* 58 (1963): 85–96.

Bringmann, W. G., Krichev, A., & Balence, W. "Goethe as behavior therapist." *Journal of the History of the Behavioral Sciences* 6 (1970): 151–159.

Brinton, J. E. & Danielson, W. A. "A factor analysis of language elements affecting readability." *Journalism Quarterly* 35 (1958): 420–426.

Brook, B. S. "Style and content analysis in music: The simplified 'Plaine and easie code.'" In *The analysis of communication content,* edited by G. Gerber et al. New York: Wiley, 1969.

Brown, J. L. Review of *Theory of colours,* by J. W. V. Goethe. *Contemporary Psychology* 16 (1971): 696–697.

Bruner, J. S. & Taguiri, R. "The perception of people." *Handbook of social psychology,* edited by G. Lindzey. Reading, Mass.: Addison-Wesley, 1954. Vol. 2, pp. 634–654.

Buck, G. "Figures of speech: A psychological study." In *Contribution to rhetorical theory,* edited by F. N. Scott. Ann Arbor: University of Michigan, 1895. Pp. 1–27.

Buckingham, L. H. "The development of social attitudes through literature." [*School and Society* 52 (1940): 446–454.] *Psychological Abstracts* 15 (1941) #1489.

Bugental, J. F. T., ed. *Challenges of humanistic psychology.* New York: McGraw-Hill, 1967.

Bühler, C. "Basic theoretical concepts of humanistic psychology." *American Psychologist* 26 (1971): 378–386.

Buirski, P. & Kramer, E. "Literature as a projection of the author's personality." *Journal of Projective Tests and Personality Assessment* 34 (1970): 27–30.

Burnshaw, S. "The body makes the minde." *American Scholar* 38 (1968–69): 25–39.

Bush, D. "Science and literature." In *Seventeenth century science and the arts,* edited by H. H. Rhys. Princeton, N. J.: Princeton University, 1961. Pp. 29–58.

Butler, R. N. "Age: The life review." *Psychology Today* 5 (1971): 49–51, 89.

Bychowski, G. "Marcel Proust as author using psychological analysis." *Psychological Abstracts* 7 (1933) #1450.

Cantril, H. & Bunstead, C. H. *Reflections on the human venture.* New York: New York University, 1960.

Carey, J. T. "The ideology of autonomy in popular lyrics: A content analysis." *Psychiatry* 32 (1969): 150–164.

Carmichael, D. Review of *The dynamics of literary response* by N. N. Holland. *Contemporary Psychology* 15 (1970): 242–244.

Carroll, H. A. *Prose appreciation test.* Minneapolis: Educational Test Bureau, 1935.

Carroll, J. B. "Vectors of prose style." In *Semantic differential technique,* edited by J. G. Snider & C. E. Osgood. Chicago: Aldine, 1969. Pp. 593–602.

Carter, H. " 'Sociology' in the new literature." *Sociological Review* 20 (1928): 250–255.

Cartwright, D. P. "Analysis of qualitative material." In *Research methods in the behavioral sciences,* edited by L. Festinger & D. Katz. New York: Dryden, 1953.

Carver, R. P. "Pupil dilation and its relationship to information processing during reading and listening." *Journal of Applied Psychology* 55 (1971): 126–134.

Chandler, A. R. *Beauty and human nature: Elements of psychological and experimental aesthetics.* New York: Appleton-Century, 1935. Chap. 13, pp. 238–276.

Chandler, A. R. & Barnhart, E. N. *A bibliography of psychological and experimental aesthetics 1864–1937.* Berkeley, Calif.: University of California, 1938.

Charvat, W. "Literary economics and literary history." *English Institute Essays,* 1949, 73–91.

Child, I. L. "Personality correlates of aesthetic judgment in college students." *Journal of Personality* 33 (1965): 476–511.

————. "Aesthetics." In *International encyclopedia of the social sciences,* edited by D. L. Sills. New York: Macmillan & Free Press, 1968. Vol. 1, pp. 116–121.

————. "Esthetics." In *The handbook of social psychology,* by Gardner Lindzey & E. Aronson. 2nd ed. Reading, Mass.: Addison-Wesley, 1969. Pp. 853–916.

————. "Esthetics." *Annual Review of Psychology* 23 (1972): 669–694.

Clark, C. *Shakespeare and psychology.* [London: Williams & Norgate, 1936.] *Psychological Abstracts* 12 (1938) #379.

Clay, R. "Literary allusions in selected newspaper editorials." *Journalism Quarterly* 37 (1960): 231–240.

Cohen, J. *Humanistic psychology.* New York: Collier, 1962. Chap. 10.

————. *Psychological time in health and disease.* Springfield, Ill.: C. C. Thomas, 1967.

Colby, B. N. "The analysis of culture content and the patterning of narrative concerns in tests." *American Anthropologist* 68 (1966): 374–388.

————. "Cultural patterns in narrative." *Science* 151 (1966): 793–798.

Colby, B. N., Collier, G. A., & Postal, S. K. "Comparison of themes in folktales by the general inquirer system." *Journal of American Folklore* 76 (1963): 318–323.

Coser, L. A., ed. *Sociology through literature.* Englewood Cliffs, N. J.: Prentice-Hall, 1963.

Cousins, N. "The computer and the poet." In *Perspectives on the computer revolution,* edited by Z. Pylyshyn. Englewood Cliffs, N. J.: Prentice-Hall, 1970. Pp. 499–500.

Cox, C. M. *The early mental traits of three hundred geniuses.* Vol. 2. *Genetic studies of genius.* Stanford, Calif.: Stanford University, 1926.

Creelman, M. B. Review of *Worlds in consciousness: Methopoetic thought in the novels of Virginia Woolf,* by J. O. Love. *Contemporary Psychology* 16 (1971): 232–233.

Crews, F. C. "Literature and psychology." In *Relations of literary study: Essays on interdisciplinary contributions,* edited by J. Thorpe. New York: Modern Language Association. 1967. Pp. 73–87.

――――. "Anaesthetic criticism." In *Psychoanalysis and literary process,* edited by F. Crews, Cambridge, Mass.: Winthrop, 1970. Pp. 1–24.

――――, ed. *Psychoanalysis and literary process.* Cambridge, Mass: Winthrop, 1970.

Crouse, J. H. "Retroactive interference in reading prose materials." *Journal of Educational Psychology* 62 (1971): 39–41.

Csikszentmihalyi, M. & Getzels, J. W. "Concern for discovery: An attitudinal component of creative production." *Journal of Personality* 38 (1970): 91–105.

Dale, E. & Chall, J. S. "A formula for predicting readability." *Educational Research Bulletin* 27–28 (1948): 11–20, 37–54.

Das, J. P., Rath, R., & Das, R. S. "Understanding versus suggestion in the judgment of literary passages." *Journal of Abnormal and Social Psychology* 51 (1955): 624–628.

David-Schwarz, H. "The psychology and pathology of Gerhardt Hauptmann's character *Crampton.*" *Psychological Abstracts* 4 (1930) #3962.

――――. "Hesse's *Narziss* and *Goldenmund* in two different settings." *Psychological Abstracts* 5 (1931) #3828.

Davidson, P. O. & Costello, C. G. $N = 1$: *Experimental studies of single cases.* New York: Van Nostrand, 1969.

Davies, J. C. "Political fiction." In *International encyclopedia of the social sciences,* edited by D. L. Sills. Vol. 9. New York: Macmillan & Free Press, 1968.

Day, W. F. "Humanistic psychology and contemporary behaviorism." *The Humanist* 31 (1971): 13–16.

Dearborn, W. F. "The psychology of reading." *Archives of Philosophy, Psychology, and Scientific Methods, Columbia University Contributions to Philosophy and Psychology,* 14 (1906) #1.

Decharms, R. & Moeller, G. H. "Values expressed in children's readers: 1800–1950." *Journal of Abnormal and Social Psychology* 64 (1962): 136–142.

Deese, J. *Psychology as science and art.* New York: Harcourt Brace Jovanovich, 1972.

Dellas, M. & Gaier, E. L. "Identification of creativity." *Psychological Bulletin* 73 (1970): 55–73.

Dennis, W. "Creative productivity between the ages of 20 and 80 years." *Journal of Gerontology* 21 (1966): 1–8.

Deutsch, D. "Music recognition." *Psychological Review* 76 (1969): 300–307.

Dewey, J. *Art as experience.* New York: Minton, Balch, 1934.

Dibble, V. K. "Four types of inference from documents to events." *History and Theory* 3 (1963): 203–221.

Diener, G. "Relation of the delusionary process in Goethe's *Lila* to analytic psychology and to psychodrama." *Group Psychotherapy and Psychodrama* 24 (1971): 5–13.

Dilthey, W. "Experience and poetry." *Psychological Abstracts* 13 (1939) #393.

Dollard, J. & Mowrer, O. H. "A method of measuring tension in written documents." *Journal of Abnormal and Social Psychology* 42 (1947): 3–32.

Dooling, D. J. & Lachman, R. "Effects of comprehension on retention of prose." *Journal of Experimental Psychology* 88 (1971): 216–222.

Dornbusch, S. M. "Content and method in the study of the higher arts." In *The arts in society,* edited by R. N. Wilson. Englewood Cliffs, N. J.: Prentice-Hall, 1964. Pp. 363–372.

Downey, J. E. "Literary self-projections." *Psychological Review* 19 (1912): 299–311.

———. "Literary synesthesia." *Journal of Philosophy* 9 (1912): 490–498.

———. "Emotional poetry and the preference judgment." *Psychological Review* 22 (1915): 259–278.

———. "A program for a psychology of literature." *Journal of Applied Psychology* 2 (1918): 366–377.

———. "The psychology of figures of speech." *American Journal of Psychology* 30 (1919): 103–115.

Drake, P. F. "Affective reactions to poetry." Paper present ed at Fourth International Colloquium in Experimental Aesthetics, Glasgow, Scotland, 1970.

Dreistadt, R. "An analysis of the use of analogies and metaphors in science." *Journal of Psychology* 68 (1968): 97–116.

——. "An analysis of how dreams are used in creative behavior." *Psychology* 8 (1971): 24–50.

——. "The prophetic achievements of geniuses and types of extrasensory perception." *Psychology* 8 (1971): 27–40.

Dudek, S. Z. "Portrait of the artist as a Rorschach reader." *Psychology Today* 4 (1971): 47–84.

Dudley, L. *The study of literature.* Cambridge, Mass.: Riverside, 1928.

Duffy, G. G. "The construction and validation of an instrument to measure poetry writing performance." *Educational and Psychological Measurement* 28 (1968): 1233–1236.

Dufort, R. H. "A suggested approach for the psychologist to the study of utopian writings." *Journal of Psychology* 60 (1965): 25–30.

Duncan, H. D. *Language and literature in society.* Chicago: University of Chicago, 1953.

Durr, R. A. *Poetic vision and the psychedelic experience.* Syracuse, N. Y.: Syracuse University, 1970.

Edel, L. *The modern psychological novel.* New York: Grove, 1959.

——. "Psychoanalysis and the creative arts." In *Modern psychoanalysis: New directions and perspectives,* edited by J. Marmor. New York: Basic Books, 1968. Pp. 626–641.

——. "Literature and biography." In *Relations of literary study: Essays on interdisciplinary contributions,* edited by J. Thorpe. New York: Modern Language Association, 1967. Pp. 57–72.

Ehrenzweig, A. *The psychoanalysis of artistic vision and hearing.* 2nd ed. New York: Braziller, 1965.

Eissler, K. R. "The relation of explaining and understanding in psychoanalysis: Demonstrated by one aspect of Freud's approach to literature." *Psychoanalytic Study of the Child* 23 (1968): 141–177.

Ellegard, A. "Estimating vocabulary size." *Word* 16 (1960): 219–244.

Erdelyi, M. "The relation between radio plugs and sheet sales of popular music." *Journal of Applied Psychology* 24 (1940): 696–702.

Escarpit, R. "The sociology of literature." In *International encyclopedia of the social sciences,* edited by D. L. Sills. Vol. 9. New York: Macmillan & Free Press, 1968.

Evans, D. R. "Paragraph complexity, arousal, and subjective evaluations of attractiveness." *Psychonomic Science* 23 (1971): 303–304.

Evans, R. I. *Psychology and Arthur Miller.* New York: Dutton, 1969.

Exline, R. V., Gottheil, E., Paredes, A., & Winklemeier, D. "Gaze direction as a factor in the accurate judgment of nonverbal expressions of affect." *Proceedings of the 76th Annual APA Convention* 3 (1968): 415.

Eysenck, H. J. *Sense and nonsense in psychology.* Rev. ed. Baltimore: Pelican, 1958. Pp. 308–339.

Farnsworth, P. R. "Psychology of aesthetics." In *Encyclopedia of psychology.* New York: Philosophical Library, 1946.

Fearing, F. "Psychological studies of historical personalities." *Psychological Bulletin* 24 (1927): 521–539.

Fellner, C. H. "Paperback psychiatry." *Journal of Medical Education* 44 (1969): 585–588.

Fernandez, R. "Dostoyevsky, traditional domination, and cognitive dissonance." *Social Forces* 49 (1970): 299–303.

———, ed. *Social psychology through literature.* New York: Wiley, 1972.

Fischer, J. L. "Art styles as cultural cognitive maps." *American Anthropologist* 63 (1961): 79–93.

Flesch, R. "A new readability yardstick." *Journal of Applied Psychology* 32 (1948): 221–233.

Flora, C. B. "The passive female: Her comparative image by class and culture in woman's magazine fiction." *Journal of Marriage and the Family* 33 (1971): 435–444.

Foster, S. "The *gestalt* configurations of Wallace Stevens." *Modern Language Quarterly* 28 (1967): 60–76.

Fraiberg, L. Review of *Hidden patterns: Studies in psychoanalytical literary criticism,* by L. Manheim & E. Manheim. *Contemporary Psychology* 13 (1968): 280–281.

Freud, S. "Dostoevski and parricide." Translated by D. F. Taut. In *Collected papers.* London: Hogarth, 1952. Vol. 5, pp. 222–242. Also in *Partisan Review* 14 (1945): 530–544.

_____. *A general introduction to psychoanalysis.* New York: Permabooks, 1953, Pp. 384–385. (Original 1920.)

_____. "The relation of the poet to daydreaming." In *Collected papers,* edited by E. Jones. London: Hogarth Press & Institute of Psychoanalysis, 1956. Vol. 4, pp. 173–183.

_____. *On creativity and the unconscious: Papers on the psychology of art, literature, love, religion.* New York: Harper, 1958. (Original 1925.)

Friedman, S. "Imagery: From sensation to symbol." *Journal of Aesthetics and Art Criticism* 12 (1953): 25–37.

Galton, F. *Hereditary genius: An inquiry into its laws and consequences.* London: Macmillan, 1869.

Gardner, H. "From mode to symbol: Thoughts on the genesis of the arts." *British Journal of Aesthetics* 10 (1970): 359–375.

_____. "The development of sensitivity to artistic styles." *Journal of Aesthetics and Art Criticism* 29 (1971): 515–527.

_____. "Problem-solving in the arts and sciences." *Journal of Art Education* 5 (1971): 93–113.

Gardner, H. & Gardner, J. "Children's literary skills." *Journal of Experimental Education* 39 (1971): 42–46.

Gardner, L. W. "A content analysis of Japanese and American television." *Journal of Broadcasting* 2 (1962): 45–52.

Gardner, R., Holtzman, P. S., Klein, G. S., Linton, H., & Spence, D. P. "Cognitive control." *Psychological Issues* 1 (1959) #4.

Gardner, R. W., Jackson, D. N., & Messick, S. J. "Personality and organization in cognitive controls and intellectual activities." *Psychological Issues* 2 (1960) #8.

Garratz, J. A. "The interrelations of psychology and biography." *Psychological Bulletin* 51 (1954): 569–582.

Gerbner, G., Holsti, O. R., Krippendorf, K., Paisley, W. J., & Stone, P. J., eds. *The analysis of communication content.* New York: Wiley, 1969.

Getzels, J. W. & Csikszentmihalyi, M. "The value-orientations of art students as determinants of artistic specialization and creative performance." *Studies in Art Education* 10 (1968): 5–16.

_____. "Aesthetic opinion: An empirical study." *Public Opinion Quarterly* 33 (1969): 34–35.

Getzels, J. W. & Jackson, P. W. *Creativity and intelligence: Explorations with gifted children.* New York: Wiley, 1962.

Ghiselin, B., ed. *The creative process.* New York: Mentor, 1952.

Gibson, J. J. *The senses considered as perceptual systems.* New York: Houghton Mifflin, 1966. Chap. 11.

Gilman, A. & Brown, R. "Personality and style in Concord." In *Transcendentalism and its legacy,* edited by M. Simon & T. H. Parsons. Ann Arbor: University of Michigan, 1967. Pp. 87–122.

Ginglinger, G. "Basic values in *Reader's Digest, Selection* and *Constellation.*" *Journalism Quarterly* 32 (1955): 56–61.

Giorgi, A. *Psychology as a human science: A phenomenologically based approach.* New York: Harper & Row, 1970.

Glasgow, G. M. "The effects of manner of speech on appreciation of spoken literature." *Journal of Educational Psychology* 52 (1961): 322–329.

Gleser, G. C., Gottschalk, L. A., & Springer, K. J. "An anxiety scale applicable to verbal samples." *Archives of General Psychiatry* 5 (1961): 593–605.

Golann, S. E. "Psychological studies of creativity." *Psychological Bulletin* 60 (1963): 548–565.

Goldstein, M. "Literature and psychology, 1948–1968: A commentary." *Literature and Psychology* 17 (1967): 159–176.

Gombrich, E. H. *Art and illusion.* 2nd ed. Princeton, N. J.: Princeton University, 1969.

Gordon, K. "A dissected-story test." *Psychological Bulletin* 14 (1913): 66.

_____. "George Meredith as psychologist." *Psychological Bulletin* 35 (1938): 522–523.

Gorham, D. R. "A proverb test for clinical and experimental use." *Psychological Reports, Monograph Supplement 1,* 2 (1956): 1–12.

_____. "Verbal abstraction in psychiatric illness." *Journal of Mental Science* 107 #446, (1961): 52–59.

Gossman, N. J. "Political and social themes in the English popular novel—1815–1832." *Public Opinion Quarterly* 20 (1956): 531–541.

Gottschalk, L. A. & Gleser, G. C. *The measurement of psychological states through the content analysis of verbal behavior.* Berkeley, Calif.: University of California Press, 1965.

Greenstein, F. I. *Personality and politics: Problems of evidence, inference, and conceptualization.* Chicago: Markham, 1969.

Greenstein, F. I. & Lerner, M., eds. *A source book for the study of personality and politics.* Chicago: Markham, 1971.

Greenwood, E. B. "Literature and philosophy." *Essays in Criticism* 20 (1970): 5–18.

Gruber, H. E., Terrell, G., & Wertheimer, M., eds. *Contemporary approaches to creative thinking.* Englewood Cliffs, N. J.: Prentice-Hall, 1962.

Guilford, J. P. "Creative abilities in the arts." *Psychological Review* 44 (1957): 110–118.

_____. "Traits of creativity." In *Creativity and its cultivation,* edited by H. H. Anderson. New York: Harper, 1959. Pp. 142–161.

_____. "Creativity: Retrospect and prospect." *Journal of Creative Behavior* 4 (1970): 149–168.

Haimovici, J. "Amiel, or morbid introspection in literature." *Psychological Abstracts* 3 (1929) #4128.

Hall, C. S. "Slang and dream symbols." *Psychoanalytic Review* 51 (1964): 38–48.

_____. "Attitudes toward life and death in poetry." *Psychoanalytic Review* 52 (1965): 67–83.

Hall, C. S. & Lind, R. E. *Dreams, life, and literature: A study of*

Franz Kafka. Chapel Hill, N. C.: University of North
Carolina Press, 1970.

Hall, C. S. & Lindzey, G. *Theories of personality.* New York:
Wiley, 1957.

Hall, C. S. & Van de Castle, R. L. *The content analysis of dreams.*
New York: Appleton-Century-Crofts, 1966.

Hall, E. "Hebb on hocus-pocus: A conversation." *Psychology
Today* 3 (1969): 21–28.

Hall, E. T. *The hidden dimension.* Garden City, N. Y.: Anchor,
1969.

Hall, M. H. "A conversation with Henry A. Murray." *Psychology Today* 2 (1968): 56–63.

Hannett, F. "The haunting lyric: The personal and social
significance of American popular songs." *Psychoanalytic
Quarterly* 33 (1964): 226–269.

Hargreaves, H. L. "The 'faculty' of imagination." *British
Journal of Psychology Monograph Supplements* 3 (1927): 1–165.

Harmes, E. "Psychology: Yesterday, today, and tomor-
row." Paper presented at the New York Academy of
Sciences Conference on Various Approaches to the Study
of Perception, New York City, 1969.

Harrower, M. "Poems emerging from the therapeutic experience." *Journal of Nervous and Mental Disease* 149 (1969):
213–233.

Harvey, J. "The content characteristics of best-selling novels." *Public Opinion Quarterly* 17 (1953): 91–114.

Haskins, C. P. "The humanities and the natural sciences."
American Scientist 58 (1970): 23–33.

Haskins, J. B. "Validation of the abstraction index as a tool
for content-effects analysis and content analysis." *Journal
of Applied Psychology* 44 (1960): 102–106.

Hatch, L. & Hatch, M. A. "Criteria of social status as
derived from marriage announcements in the *New York
Times.*" *American Sociological Review* 12 (1947): 396–403.

Head, S. W. "Content analysis of television drama programs." *Quarterly of Film, Radio, and Television* 9 (1954): 175–
194.

Heider, F. "The description of the psychological environment in the work of Marcel Proust." *Character and Personality* 9 (1941): 295–314.

Helson, R. "Sex-specific patterns in creative literary fantasy." *Journal of Personality* 38 (1970): 344–363.

Henderson, A. & Lindauer, M. S. "Autobiographical statements on creativity by artists, musicians, and writers." Unpublished study, State College at Brockport, 1971.

Henley, N. M. "Achievement and affiliation imagery in American fiction, 1901–1961." *Journal of Personality and Social Psychology* 7 (1967): 208–210.

Herzog, H. "What do we really know about day-time serial listeners?" In *Reader in public opinion and communication,* edited by B. Berelson & M. Janowitz. Glencoe, Ill.: Free Press, 1953.

Hevner, K. "An experimental study of the affective value of sounds in poetry." *American Journal of Psychology* 49 (1937): 419–434.

Hilgard, E. R. "Creativity and problem-solving." In *Creativity and its cultivation,* edited by H. H. Anderson. New York: Harper, 1959. Pp. 162–180.

Hilgard, E. R. & Atkinson, R. C. *Introduction to psychology.* 4th ed. New York: Harcourt, Brace & World, 1967.

Hill, J. C. "Poetry and the unconscious." *British Journal of Medical Psychology* 4 (1924): 125–133.

Hirsch, P. *The structure of the popular music industry.* Ann Arbor, Mich.: Institute for Social Research, 1969.

Hirsch, W. "Image of the scientist in science fiction: A content analysis." *American Journal of Sociology* 63 (1958): 506–512.

Hoffman, M. J. "Gertrude Stein in the psychology laboratory." *American Quarterly* 17 (1965): 127–132.

Hoggart, R. *The uses of literacy: Changing patterns in English mass culture.* Boston: Beacon, 1957.

_____. "Humanistic studies and mass culture." *Daedalus* 99 (1970): 451–472.

Holland, N. N. *Psychoanalysis and Shakespeare.* New York: McGraw-Hill, 1966.

_____. *The dynamics of literary response.* New York: Oxford, 1968.

Hollander, E. P. "Popular literature in the undergraduate social psychology course." *American Psychologist* 11 (1956): 95–96.

Holsti, O. R. *Content analysis for the social sciences and humanities.* Reading, Mass.: Addison-Wesley, 1969.

Honkavaara, S. "The psychology of expression." *British Journal of Psychology Monograph Supplements,* 1961, #32.

Horton, D. "The dialogue of courtship in popular songs." *American Journal of Sociology* 62 (1957): 569–578.

Hovland, C. I. "Psychology of the communication process." In *Communication in modern society,* edited by W. Schramm. Urbana, Ill.: University of Illinois, 1948. Pp. 59–65.

_____. "Social communication." In *Reader in public opinion and communication,* edited by B. Berelson & M. Janowitz. Glencoe, Ill,: Free Press, 1953. Pp. 181–189.

Hovland, C. I., Lunsdaine, A. A., & Sheffield, F. D. "Short-time and long-time effects of an orientation film." In *Reader in public opinion and communication,* edited by B. Berelson & M. Janowitz. Glencoe, Ill.: Free Press, 1953. Pp. 438–447.

Hudson, L. *Contrary imaginations.* New York: Schocken, 1966.

_____. "The question of creativity." In *Creativity,* edited by P. E. Vernon. Baltimore: Penguin, 1970. Pp. 217–234.

Hyman, R. "Creativity and the prepared mind: The role of information and induced attitudes." In *Widening horizons in creativity,* edited by C. W. Taylor. New York: Wiley, 1964. Pp. 69–106.

Hynes. S. Review of *Joseph Conrad and the fiction of autobiography,* edited by E. W. Said. *Novel* 2 (1969): 179–183.

Inglis, R. A. "An objective approach to the relationship between fiction and society." *American Sociological Review* 3 (1938): 526–533.

Jacob, C. F. "The psychology of poetic talent." *Journal of Abnormal and Social Psychology* 17 (1922): 231–253.

Jakobovits, L. A. "Evaluative reactions to exotic literature." *Psychological Reports* 16 (1965): 985–994.

_____. "Studies of fads; I. The 'hit parade.' " *Psychological Reports* 18 (1966): 443–450.

James, W. *The principles of psychology.* New York: Dover, 1950. Chap. 7.

Jastrow, J. "The antecedents of the study of character and temperament." *Popular Science Monthly* 86 (1915): 590–613.

Jennings, E. M., ed. *Science and literature: New lenses for criticism.* New York: Anchor, 1970.

Johns-Heine, P. & Gerth, H. H. "Values in mass periodical fiction." *Public Opinion Quarterly* 13 (1949): 105–113.

Johnson, D. M. "Psychology vs. literature." *Harper Books and Authors* 12 (1961): 1–4.

Johnson, E. "William James and the art of fiction." *Journal of Aesthetics and Art Criticism* 30 (1972): 285–296.

Jones, D. B. "Quantitative analysis of motion picture content." *Public Opinion Quarterly* 6 (1942): 411–428.

Jones, E. *Hamlet and Oedipus.* Garden City, N. Y.: Doubleday, 1955.

Jones, E. S. "Effect of letters and syllables in publicity." *Journal of Applied Psychology* 6 (1922): 198–204.

Jung, C. G. "On the relation of analytic psychology to poetic art." In *Contributions to analytical psychology,* by C. G. Jung. Translated by H. G. Baynes & C. F. Baynes. London: Kegan Paul, Trench, Trubner, 1928. Pp. 225–249.

_____. "The spirit in man, art, and literature." In *The collected works.* Vol. 15. New York: Bollingen Series XX, Pantheon Books, 1966.

Kadushin, C., Lovett, J., & Merriman, J. D. Reviews of *The general inquirer: A computer approach to content analysis,* by P. J. Stone et al. *Computers and the Humanities* 2 (1968): 177–202.

Kahn, S. J. "Psychology in Coleridge's poetry." *Journal of Aesthetics and Art Criticism* 9 (1951): 208–226.

Kammann, R. "Verbal complexity and preferences in poetry." *Journal of Verbal Learning and Verbal Behavior* 5 (1966): 536–540.

Kappel, J. W. "Book clubs and the evaluation of books." *Public Opinion Quarterly* 12 (1948): 243–252.

Kavolis, V. *Artistic expression: A sociological analysis.* Ithaca, N. Y.: Cornell University, 1968.

Kearl, B. "A closer look at readability formulas." *Journalism Quarterly* 25 (1948): 344–348.

Keeney, B. C. "The bridge of values." *Science* 169 (1970): 26–28.

Keith, A. L. "Vergil as a master of psychology." *Psycholanalytic Review* 9 (1922): 436–439.

Kelly, G. A. "Humanistic methodology in psychological research." *Journal of Humanistic Psychology* 9 (1969): 53–65.

Kern, A. "The sociology of knowledge in the study of literature." *Sewanee Review* 50 (1942): 505–515.

Kiell, N., ed. *Psychoanalysis, psychology, and literature: A bibliography.* Madison: University of Wisconsin, 1963.

King, D. J. "Initial observations on the learning of connected discourse to complete mastery." *Psychonomic Science* 20 (1970): 329–330.

Klapp, O. W. "The fool as a social type." *American Journal of Sociology* 55 (1950): 157–162.

Klein, S. P. & Skager, R. W. "Spontaneity vs. deliberateness as a dimension of esthetic judgment." *Perceptual & Motor Skills* 25 (1967): 161–168.

Klineberg, O. "Emotional expression in Chinese literature." *Journal of Abnormal and Social Psychology* 33 (1938): 517–520.

Knapp, R. H. "A study of the metaphor." *Journal of Projective Techniques* 24 (1960): 389–395.

Knapp, R. H. & Garbutt, J. T. "Time imagery and the achievement motive." *Journal of Personality* 26 (1958): 426–434.

Kneller, G. F. *The art and science of creativity.* New York: Holt, Rinehart & Winston, 1965.

Koch, S. "Psychological science versus the science-humanism antimony: Intimations of a significant science of man." *American Psychologist* 16 (1961): 629–639.

_____. "Psychology cannot be a coherent science." *Psychology Today* 3 (1969): 14–68.

_____, ed. *Psychology: A study of a science.* 6 vols. New York: McGraw-Hill, 1959–1963.

Koestler, A. *The act of creation.* New York: Macmillan, 1964.

_____. "The three domains of creativity." In *Challenges of humanistic psychology,* edited by J. F. T. Bugental. New York: McGraw-Hill, 1967. Pp. 31–40.

Koffka, K. "The art of the actor as a psychological problem." *American Scholar* 11 (1942): 315–326.

Korten, D. C. "The life game: Survival strategies in Ethiopian folktales." *Journal of Cross-Cultural Psychology* 2 (1971): 209–224.

Kracauer, S. "The challenge of qualitative content analysis." *Public Opinion Quarterly* 16 (1952): 631–642.

Kris, E. *Psychoanalytic explorations in art.* New York: Schocken, 1964.

Kris, E. & Leites, N. "Trends in twentieth century propaganda." In *Reader in public opinion and communication,* edited by B. Berelson & M. Janowitz. Glencoe, Ill.: Free Press, 1953. Pp. 278–288.

Krutch, J. W. *The modern temper.* New York: Harcourt, Brace, 1929.

_____. *The measure of man.* New York: Grosset & Dunlap, 1953.

Lana, R. E. *Assumptions of social psychology.* New York: Appleton-Century-Crofts, 1969.

Langfeld, H. S. "Experimental aesthetics." In *Encyclopedia Britannica.* 14th ed. Pp. 272–273.

Lasswell, H. D. "Why be quantitative?" In *Reader in public opinion and communication,* edited by B. Berelson & M. Janowitz. Glencoe, Ill.: Free Press, 1953. Pp. 265–277.

_____. "The social setting of creativity." In *Creativity and its cultivation,* edited by H. H. Anderson. New York: Harper, 1959. Pp. 203–221.

Lasswell, H. D., Leites, N., & Associates. *Language of politics.* Cambridge, Mass.: M.I.T. Press, 1965.

Lay, W. "Mental imagery." *Psychological Monographs 2,* no. 7 (1897–99): 1–59.

Lazarsfeld, P. F. "Audience research." In *Reader in public opinion and communication,* edited by B. Berelson & M. Janowitz. Glencoe, Ill.: Free Press, 1953. Pp. 337–346.

———. "The use of panels in social research." In *Reader in public opinion and communication,* edited by B. Berelson & M. Janowitz. Glencoe, Ill.: Free Press, 1953. Pp. 511–519.

Lazarsfeld, P. F. & Stanton, F. N., eds. *Radio research: 1942–1943.* New York: Duell, Sloan, & Pearce, 1944.

Leckart, B. T. & Faw, T. T. "Looking time: A bibliography." *Perceptual and Motor Skills* 27 (1968): 91–95.

Lee, V. "Studies in literary psychology. I. The syntax of De Quincey." *Contemporary Review* 84 (1903): 713–723.

———. "Studies in literary psychology: III. Carlyle and the present tense." *Contemporary Review* 85 (1904): 386–392.

Leedy, J. J., ed. *Poetry therapy: The use of poetry in the treatment of emotional disorders.* Philadelphia: Lippincott, 1969.

Leenhart, H. "The sociology of literature: Some stages in its history." *International Social Science Journal* 19 (1967): 517–533.

Lehman, H. C. "The creative years: Best books." *Scientific Monthly* 85 (1937): 65–76.

———. *Age and achievement.* Princeton, N. J.: Princeton University, 1953.

Lerner, M. & Mims, E., Jr. "Literature." In *Encyclopedia of the social sciences,* edited by E. R. A. Seligman. New York: Macmillan, 1935. Vol. 9, pp. 523–543.

Levine, J. M. & Murphy, G. "Learning and forgetting of controversial material." *Journal of Abnormal and Social Psychology* 38 (1943): 507–515.

Levitas, G. B., ed. *The world of psychology.* 2 vols. New York: Braziller, 1963.

Lewin, H. S. "Hitler Youth and the Boy Scouts of America: A comparison of aims." *Human Relations* 1 (1947): 206–227.

Leytham, G. W. H. "Literary statistics." *British Psychological Society Bulletin* 47 (1959): 14–17.

Librachowa, M. "The fiction from between the two world wars as a source of scientific material for the psychologist." *Psychological Abstracts* 22 (1948) #2808.

Lindauer, M. S. "The role of attitude and need in the learning and retention of relevant meaningful prose." Unpublished manuscript, State College at Brockport, 1960.

———. "The nature and use of the cliché." *Journal of General Psychology* 78 (1968): 133–143.

———. "Pleasant and unpleasant emotions in literature: A comparison with the affective tone of psychology." *Journal of Psychology* 70 (1968): 55–67.

———. "Duration aspects of time related words." *Perceptual and Motor Skills* 9 (1969): 100–101.

———. "Historical and contemporary attitudes toward numbers." *Journal of Psychology* 71 (1969): 41–43.

———. "A quantitative analysis of psychoanalytic studies of Shakespeare." *Journal of Psychology* 72 (1969): 3–9.

———. "Psychological aspects of form perception in abstract art." Paper presented at the Fourth International Colloquium on Experimental Aesthetics, Glasgow, Scotland, 1970. Also in *Science de l'Art* 7 (1970): 19–24.

———. "Toward a liberalization of experimental aesthetics." *Journal of Aesthetics and Art Criticism* 31 (1973): 459–465.

———. "The sensory attributes and functions of imagery and imagery evoking stimuli." In *The function and nature of imagery,* edited by P. W. Sheehan. New York: Academic Press, 1972.

Lindquist, E. F., ed. & Peterson, J. *Iowa tests of educational development: Examiner manual for test 7—Ability to interpret literary materials.* Chicago: Science Research Associates, 1951.

Lindzey, G. & Aronson, E., eds. *The handbook of social psychology.* Reading, Mass.: Addison-Wesley, 1969.

Lipsky, A. "Rhythm as a distinguishing characteristic of prose style." *Archives of Psychology* 24, no. 4 (1907): 1–44.

Little, L. K. "Psychology in recent historical thought." *Journal of the History of the Behavioral Sciences* 5 (1969): 152–172.

Lomax, A. "Special features of the sung communication."

In *Essays on the verbal and visual arts,* edited by J. Helm. Seattle: University of Washington, 1967. Pp. 109–127.

Louttit, C. M. "An historical note on the application of psychology." *Journal of Applied Psychology* 18 (1934): 304–305.

Lowenthal, L. "The sociology of literature." In *Communication in modern society,* edited by W. Schramm. Urbana, Ill.: University of Illinois, 1948. Pp. 83–100.

_____. "Biographies in popular magazines." In *Reader in public opinion and communication,* edited by B. Berelson & M. Janowitz. Glencoe, Ill.: Free Press, 1953. Pp. 289–298.

_____. *Literature, popular culture, and society.* Englewood Cliffs, N. J.: Spectrum, 1961.

_____. "The reception of Dostoevski's work in Germany: 1880–1920." In *The arts in society,* edited by R. N. Wilson. Englewood Cliffs, N. J.: Prentice-Hall, 1964. Pp. 122–147.

_____. "Literature and sociology." In *Relations of literary study: Essays on interdisciplinary contributions,* edited by J. Thorpe. New York: Modern Language Association, 1967. Pp. 89–110.

Lucas, F. L. *Literature and psychology.* 2nd ed. Ann Arbor: University of Michigan, 1957.

Lynch, J. J. "The tonality of lyric poetry: An experiment in method." *Word* 9 (1953): 211–224.

McClelland, D. C. *The achieving society.* Princeton, N. J.: Van Nostrand, 1961.

_____. *The roots of consciousness.* Princeton, N. J.: Van Nostrand, 1964.

McClelland, D. C., Davis, W., Wanner, E. & Kalin, R. "A cross-cultural study of folk-tale content and drinking." *Sociometry* 29 (1966): 308–333.

McClelland, D. C. & Friedman, G. A. "A cross-cultural study of the relationship between child-training practices and achievement motivation appearing in folk tales." In *Readings in social psychology,* edited by G. E. Swanson, T. M. Newcomb, & E. L. Hartley. Rev. ed. New York: Holt, 1952. Pp. 243–249.

Maccoby, N. Review of *The analysis of communication content*, by G. Gerbner et al. *Contemporary Psychology* 15 (1970): 598–599.

McCollom, I. N. "Psychological thrillers: Psychology books students read when given freedom of choice." *American Psychologist* 26 (1971): 921–937.

MacCormac, E. R. "Metaphor revisited." *Journal of Aesthetics and Art Criticism* 30 (1971): 239–250.

MacCorquodale, K. "Behaviorism is a humanism." *The Humanist* 31 (1971): 12–13.

McCurdy, H. G. "Literature and personality." *Character and Personality* 7 (1939): 300–308.

———. "Literature and personality: Analysis of the novels of D. H. Lawrence. Part I." *Character and Personality* 8 (1940): 181–203.

———. "Literature and personality: Analysis of the novels of D. H. Lawrence. Part II." *Character and Personality* 8 (1940): 311–322.

———. "La belle dame sans merci." *Character and Personality* 13 (1944): 166–177.

———. "A study of the novels of Charlotte and Emily Brontë as an expression of their personalities." *Journal of Personality* 16 (1947): 109–152.

———. "A mathematical aspect of fictional literature pertinent to McDougall's theory of a hierarchy of sentiments." *Journal of Personality* 17 (1948): 75–82.

———. "Literature as a resource in personality study: Theory and methods." *Journal of Aesthetics and Art Criticism* 8 (1949): 42–46.

———. *The personality of Shakespeare: A venture in psychological method.* New Haven: Yale, 1953.

———. *The personal world.* New York: Harcourt, Brace & World, 1961.

———. *Personality and science.* Princeton, N. J.: Van Nostrand, 1965.

———. "Shakespeare: King of infinite space." *Psychology Today* 1 (1968): 39–68.

_____. "The psychology of literature." *International encyclopedia of the social sciences,* edited by D. L. Sills. Vol. 9. New York: Macmillan and Free Press, 1968.

_____. Review of *The design within: Psychoanalytic approaches to Shakespeare,* edited by M. D. Faber. *Contemporary Psychology* 16 (1971): 115–117.

MacDougall, R. "The 'colored words' of art." *Psychological Review* 20 (1913): 505–516.

Mace, C. A. "Psychology and aesthetics." *British Journal of Aesthetics* 2 (1962): 3–16.

McGranahan, D. V. "The psychology of language." *Psychological Bulletin* 33 (1936): 178–216.

McGranahan, D. V. & Wayne, I. "German and American traits reflected in popular drama." *Human Relations* 1 (1948): 429–455.

McGuigan, F. J. *Experimental psychology: A methodological approach.* 2nd ed. Englewood Cliffs, N. J.: Prentice-Hall, 1968.

Machotka, P. "Visual aesthetics and learning." *Journal of Art Education* 4 (1970): 117–130.

McKellar, P. *Imagination and thinking.* New York: Basic Books, 1957.

McKenzie, G. "Critical responsiveness: A study of the psychological current in later eighteenth-century criticism." [Berkeley, Calif.: University of California, 1959.] *Psychological Abstracts* 24 (1950) #5125.

McKinney, F. "Psychology in relation to literature." In *Psychology in action: Basic readings,* edited by F. McKinney. New York: Macmillan, 1967. P. 348.

MacKinnon, D. W. "The structure of personality." In *Personality and the behavior disorders,* edited by J. McV. Hunt. Vol. 1. New York: Ronald, 1944.

_____. "The nature and nurture of creative talent." *American Psychologist* 17 (1962): 484–495.

_____. "The personality correlates of creativity: A study of American architects." In *Creativity,* edited by P. E. Vernon. Baltimore: Penguin, 1970. Pp. 289–311.

Mackler, B. & Shontz, F. C. "Creativity: Theoretical and methodological considerations." *Psychological Record* 15 (1965): 217–238.

Mackworth, N. H. & Morandi, A. J. "The gaze selects informative details within pictures." *Perception and Psychophysics* 2 (1967): 547–552.

MacLeod, R. Review of *Experience and behavior,* by P. McKellar. *Contemporary Psychology* 15 (1970): 332–333.

McMorris, M. N. "Aesthetic elements in scientific theories." *Main Currents in Modern Thought* 26 (1970): 82–91.

McWhinnie, H. J. "A review of selected aspects of empirical aesthetics III." *Journal of Aesthetic Education* 5 (1971): 115–126.

Maier, N. R. & Reninger, H. W. *A psychological approach to literary criticism.* New York: Appleton, 1933.

Malmud, R. S. "Poetry and the emotions (1) A dilemma for critics, (2) Experimental verification." *Journal of Abnormal and Social Psychology* 22 (1928): 443–472.

Manfredi, J. F. "The relationship of class-structured pathologies to the contents of popular periodical fiction 1936–1940." Ph.D. dissertation, Harvard University, 1950.

Manheim, L. & Manheim, E. *Hidden patterns: Studies in psychoanalytic literary criticism.* New York: Macmillan, 1966.

Maranda, R. "Computers in the bush: Tools for the automatic analysis of myths." In *Essays on the verbal and visual arts,* edited by J. Helm. Seattle: University of Washington Press & American Ethnological Society, 1967.

Mardershtein, I. G. "The reflection of physiological theory of the brain in literary writings." *Psychological Abstracts* 39 (1965) #75.

Marett, R. R. *Psychology and folk-lore.* London: Methuen, 1920.

Martel, M. U. & McCall, G. J. "Reality-orientation and the pleasure principle: A study of American mass-periodical fiction (1890–1955)." In *People, society, and mass communications,* edited by L. A. Dexter & D. M. White. Glencoe, Ill,: Free Press, 1964. Pp. 283–334.

Martin, F. D. "The imperatives of stylistic development: Psychological and formal." *Bucknell Review* 11 (1963): 53–70.

Martindale, C. "Degeneration, disinhibition, and genius." *Journal of the History of the Behavioral Sciences* 7 (1971): 177–182.

_____. "An experimental simulation of literary change." Unpublished manuscript, 1971.

_____. "Incongruity, stylistic elaboration, and regressive imagery in two poetic traditions." Unpublished manuscript, 1971.

_____. *The romantic progression: On the psychology of literary change.* Philadelphia: Temple University, forthcoming.

Marx, M. H. & Hillix, W. A. *Systems and theories in psychology.* New York: McGraw-Hill, 1963.

Maslow, A. H. "Toward a humanistic biology." *American Psychologist* 24 (1969): 724–735.

Matson, F. W. "Humanistic theory: The third revolution in psychology." *The Humanist* 31 (1971): 7–11, 18–19.

Mazlish, B. "Onward from Freud?" *Encounter* 29 (1967): 93–94.

Mead, M. "Creativity in crosscultural perspective." In *Creativity and its cultivation,* edited by H. H. Anderson. New York: Harper, 1959. Pp. 222–235.

Mednick, S. A. & Mednick, M. T. "An associative interpretation of the creative process." In *Widening horizons in creativity,* edited by C. W. Taylor. New York: Wiley, 1964. Pp. 54–68.

Meier, N. C. *Art in human affairs.* New York: Whittlesey House, 1942.

Merriam, C. E. "The significance of psychology for the study of politics." *American Political Science Review* 18 (1924): 469–488.

Metcalf, J. T. "Psychological studies of literary form." *Psychological Bulletin* 35 (1938): 337–357.

Meyerson, I. "Psychological functions and the works." *Psychological Abstracts* 22 (1948) #2530.

———. "Some aspects of the human being in romantic writings." *Psychological Abstracts* 26 (1952) #6131.

Michael, W. B., Rosenthal, B. G., & De Camp, M. A. "An experimental investigation of prestige-suggestion for two types of literary material." *Journal of Psychology* 28 (1949): 303–323.

Miller, G. A. *Language and communication.* New York: McGraw-Hill, 1951.

———. *Psychology: The science of mental life.* New York: Harper & Row, 1962.

Miller, G. R. & Coleman, E. B. "A set of thirty-six prose passages calibrated for complexity." *Journal of Verbal Learning and Verbal Behavior* 6 (1967): 851–854.

Milner, M. *The hands of the living god.* London: Hogarth, 1969.

Mindess, H. Review of *Psychology and Arthur Miller*, by R. I. Evans. *Contemporary Psychology* 15 (1970): 428–429.

Moles, A. *Information theory and esthetic perception.* Translated by J. E. Cohen. Urbana, Ill.: University of Illinois, 1968.

Moreno, J. L. "Comments on Goethe and psychodrama." *Group Psychotherapy and Psychodrama* 24 (1971): 14–16.

Mosteller, F. & Wallace, D. L. "Inference in an authorship problem." *Journal of the American Statistics Association* 58 (1963): 275–309.

Mullen, F. G., Jr. "Estimation of the universality of Freudian and Jungian sexual symbols." *Perceptual and Motor Skills* 26 (1968): 1041–1042.

Munro, T. "Aesthetics as science: Its development in America." *Journal of Aesthetics and Art Criticism* 9 (1951): 161–207.

———. *Toward science in aesthetics.* New York: Liberal Arts, 1956.

Munsterberg, E. & Mussen, P. H. "The personality structures of art students." *Journal of Personality* 21 (1953): 457–466.

Murphy, G. "An experimental study of literary vs. scientific types." *American Journal of Psychology* 28 (1917): 238–262.

Murray, E. "Some uses and misuses of the term 'aesthetic.'" *American Journal of Psychology* 42 (1930): 640–644.

Murray, H. A. *Explorations in personality: A clinical and experimental study.* New York: Oxford, 1938.

Myden, W. "Interpretation and evaluation of certain personality characteristics involved in creative production." *Perceptual and Motor Skills, Monograph Supplement no. 3,* 9 (1959): 139–158.

Nafziger, R. O. "The reading audience." In *Communication in modern society,* edited by W. Schramm. Urbana, Ill.: University of Illinois, 1948. Pp. 102–115.

Newman, E. B. & Gerstman, L. J. "A new method for analyzing printed English." *Journal of Experimental Psychology* 44 (1952): 114–125.

Newman, E. B. & Waugh, N. "The redundancy of texts in three languages." *Information and Control* 3 (1960): 141–153.

Nixon, H. K. *Psychology for the writer.* New York: Harper, 1928.

Ogden, C. K. & Richards, I. A. *The meaning of meaning.* New York: Harcourt, Brace, & World, 1923.

Ogilvie, D. M. "Individual and cultural patterns of fantasized flight." In *The analysis of communication content,* edited by G. Gerbner et al. New York: Wiley, 1969. Pp. 243–259.

Osgood, C. E. "Psycholinguistics." In *Psychology: A study of a science,* edited by S. Koch. New York: McGraw-Hill, 1963. Vol. 6, pp. 244–316.

Osgood, C. E., Suci, G. J. & Tannenbaum, P. H. *The measurement of meaning.* Urbana, Ill.: University of Illinois, 1967. Chap. 7.

Osgood, C. E. & Tannenbaum, P. H. "The principle of congruity in the prediction of attitude change." *Psychological Review* 62 (1955): 52–55.

Paisley, W. J. "Identifying the unknown communicator in painting, literature, and music: The significance of minor encoding habits." *Journal of Communications* 14 (1964): 219–237.

_____. "The effect of authorship, topic, structure, and time of composition on letter redundancy in English texts." *Journal of Verbal Learning and Verbal Behavior* 5 (1966): 28–34.

Panda, K. C., Das, J. K., & Kanungo, R. N. "A cross-cultural study on film preference on an Indian student population." *Journal of Social Psychology* 57 (1962): 93–104.

Panda, K. C. & Kanungo, R. N. "A study of Indian students' attitudes towards motion pictures." *Journal of Social Psychology* 57 (1962): 23–31.

Patel, A. S. "Attitudes of adolescent pupils toward cinema films: A study." *Journal of Education and Psychology* (Baroda) 9 (1952): 225–230.

Patrick, C. "Creative thought in poets." *Archives of Psychology* 26 (1935) #178.

———. "Creative thought in artists." *Journal of Psychology* 4 (1937): 35–73.

Paul, S. "Toward a general semantics literary theory." Etc. 4 (1947): 31–37.

Peckham, M. *Man's rage for chaos: Biology, behavior, and the arts.* Philadelphia: Chilton, 1965.

Peel, A. "On identifying aesthetic types." *British Journal of Psychology* 35 (1944): 61–69.

Peers, E. A. "Imagery in imaginative literature." *Journal of Experimental Pedagogy and Training College Record* 11 (1914): 174–187.

Pereboom, A. C. "Some fundamental problems in experimental psychology: An overview." *Psychological Reports Monograph, Supplements* 2-V28, 28 (1971): 439–455.

Peters, R. S., ed. *Brett's history of psychology.* London: George Allen & Unwin, 1962.

Philip, B. R. "The effect of general and of specific labelling on judgmental scales." *Canadian Journal of Psychology* 5 (1951): 18–28.

Pierson, G. W. & others. *Computers for the humanities?* New Haven: Yale, 1965.

Plank, R. *The emotional significance of imaginary beings: A study of the interaction between psychopathology, literature, and reality in the modern word.* Springfield, Ill.: C. C. Thomas, 1968.

Platt, J. R. "Beauty: Pattern and change." In *Functions of varied experience,* edited by D. W. Fiske & S. R. Maddi. Homewood, Ill.: Dorsey, 1961. Pp. 402–430.

Pratt, C. C. "Aesthetics." *Annual Review of Psychology* 12 (1961): 71–92.

_____. Introduction to *The task of Gestalt psychology*, by W. Kohler. Princeton, N. J.: Princeton University Press, 1969. Pp. 3–29.

Raben, J. "Content analysis and the study of poetry." In *The analysis of communication content*, edited by G. Gerbner et al. New York: Wiley, 1969. Pp. 175–186.

Rabkin, L. Y., ed. *Psychopathology and literature.* San Francisco, Calif.: Chandler, 1966.

Rands, A. C. "Thomas Brown's theories of associationism and perception as they relate to his theories of poetry." *Journal of Aesthetics and Art Criticism* 28 (1970): 473–483.

Ransom, J. C. "Freud and literature." *Saturday Review of Literature* 1 (1924): 161–162.

Ranta, J. "Counting and formal analysis." *Journal of Aesthetics and Art Criticism* 29 (1971): 453–466.

Rapaport, D., ed. *Organization and pathology of thought.* New York: Columbia, 1951.

Raskin, E. "Comparison of scientific and literary ability: A biographical study of eminent scientists and men of letters of the nineteenth century." *Journal of Abnormal and Social Psychology* 32 (1936): 20–35.

Razik, T. A. "Psychometric measurement of creativity." In *Explorations in creativity*, edited by R. L. Mooney & T. A. Razik. New York: Harper & Row, 1967, Pp. 301–309.

Read, H. *Icon and idea: The function of art in the development of human consciousness.* New York: Schocken, 1965.

Reeves, J. W. *Thinking about thinking.* New York: Delta, 1965. Pp. 216–265.

Reichardt, J., ed. *Cybernetic serendipity: The computer and the arts.* London: Studio International, 1968.

Rhys, H. H., ed. *Seventeenth century science and the arts.* Princeton, N. J.: Princeton University Press, 1961.

Richards, I. A. *Principles of literary criticism.* New York: Harcourt, Brace, 1925.

_____. *Science and poetry.* London: Kegan Paul, Trench, Trubner, 1926.

_____. *Practical criticism.* New York: Harcourt, Brace, 1950.

Roback. A. A. *A bibliography of character and personality.* Cambridge, Mass.: Sci-Art, 1927.

_____. "The psychology of literature." In *Present-day psychology,* edited by A. A. Roback. New York: Greenwood, 1968. Pp. 867–896.

_____. *The psychology of character.* 3rd ed. London: Routledge & Kegan Paul, 1952.

Roback, A. A. & Baskin, W. "Psychology of post-Freudian literature." In *New outlooks in psychology,* edited by G. P. Powers & W. Baskin. New York: Philosophical Library, 1968. Pp. 405–437.

Roblee, L. & Washburn, M. F. "The affective values of articulate sounds." *American Journal of Psychology* 23 (1912): 579–583.

Rockland, L. H. " 'What kind of fool am I?' A study of popular songs in the analysis of a male hysteric." *Psychiatry* 33 (1970): 516–525.

Roe, A. "Artists and their work." *Journal of Personality* 15 (1946): 1–40.

Rogers, C. R. "Toward a theory of creativity." *Etc.* II (1954): 249–260.

Rosen, J. C. "The Barron-Welsh Art Scale as a predictor of originality and level of ability among artists." *Journal of Applied Psychology* 39 (1955): 366–367.

Rosenberg, S. & Jones, R. "A method for investigating and representing a person's implicit theory of personality: Theodore Dreiser's view of people." Unpublished manuscript, undated.

Rosengren, K. E. *Sociological aspects of the literary system.* Stockholm: Natur och Kultur, 1968.

Rosenzweig, S. "The ghost of Henry James: A study of thematic appreciation." *Character and Personality* 12 (1943): 79–100.

Rosner, S. & Abt, L. E., eds. *The creative experience.* New York: Grossman, 1970.

Ross, S. D. *Literature and philosophy: An analysis of the philosophical novel.* New York: Appleton-Century-Crofts, 1969.

Rothenberg, A. Review of *The sins of the fathers: Hawthorne's psychological themes,* by F. Crews. *Transaction* 6 (1969): 674–677.

_____. "The iceman changeth: Toward an empirical approach to creativity." *Journal of the American Psychoanalytic Association* 17 (1969): 549–597.

_____. "Inspiration, insight, and the creative process in poetry." *College English* 31 (1970): 172–183.

_____. "The process of Janusian thinking in creativity." *Archives of General Psychiatry* 24 (1971): 195–205.

Royce, J. R. "Metaphoric knowledge and humanistic psychology." In *Challenges of humanistic psychology,* edited by J. F. T. Bugental. New York: McGraw-Hill, 1967. Pp. 21–28.

Rubinow, O. "The course of man's life—A psychological problem." *Journal of Abnormal and Social Psychology* 28 (1933): 207–215.

Rudin, S. A. "National motives predict psychogenic death rates 25 years later." *Science* 160 (1968): 901–903.

Ruesch, J. & Kees, W. "Function and meaning in the physical environment." In *Environmental psychology: Man and his physical setting,* edited by M. Proshansky, W. H. Ittelson, & L. G. Rivlin. New York: Holt, Rinehart & Winston, 1969. Pp. 141–153.

Runquist, W. N. "Verbal behavior." In *Experimental methods and instrumentation in psychology,* edited by J. B. Sidowski. New York: McGraw-Hill, 1966. Pp. 487–540.

Russell, D. H. "Psychology and literature." *College English* 25 (1964): 551–553.

Russell, F. T. "A poet's portrayal of emotion." *Psychological Review* 28 (1921): 222–238.

Sanford, F. H. "Speech and personality." *Psychological Bulletin* 39 (1942): 811–845.

Sardello, R. J. "Toward a reorganization of the psychology curriculum." *American Psychologist* 26 (1971): 1037–1038.

Sartre, J. P. *What is literature?* New York: Philosophical Library, 1949. Also in *Aesthetic theories,* edited by K. Aschenbrenner & A. Isenberg. Englewood Cliffs, N. J.: Prentice-Hall, 1965. Pp. 477–491.

Schapiro, M. "Style." In *Anthropology today,* edited by A. L. Kroeber. Chicago: University of Chicago, 1953. Pp. 287–312.

Schiff, W. "Perceived and remembered duration of films." *Perceptual and Motor Skills* 30 (1970): 903–906.

Schloss, G. A. & Grundy, D. E. Review of *Poetic therapy: The use of poetry in the treatment of emotional disorders,* edited by J. J. Leedy. *Literature and Psychology* 21 (1971): 51–55.

Schneider, L. & Dornbusch, S. M. *Popular religion: Inspirational books in America.* Chicago: University of Chicago, 1958.

Schoeck. R. J. "Mathematics and the languages of literary criticism." *Journal of Aesthetics and Art Criticism* 26 (1968): 367–376.

Schorer, M. "Fiction and the 'matrix of analogy.'" *Kenyon Review* 11 (1949): 539–560.

Schramm, W. L. *Approaches to a science of English verse.* University of Iowa Studies: Series of Aims and Programs of Research, no. 46. Iowa City, Iowa: University of Iowa, 1935.

———, **ed.** *Communication in modern society.* Urbana, Ill.: University of Illinois, 1948.

Schutz, W. C. "Reliability, ambiguity, and content analysis." *Psychological Review* 59 (1952): 119–129.

Schwadron, A. A. "On words and music: Toward an aesthetic consideration." *Journal of Aesthetic Education* 5 (1971): 91–108.

Scripture, E. W. "The nature of verse." *British Journal of Psychology* 11 (1921): 225–235.

Seashore, C. E. *In search of beauty in music.* New York: Ronald, 1947. Chap. 30.

Sebald, D. "Studying national character through comparative content analysis." *Social Forces* 40 (1962): 318–322.

Sebeok, T. A. & Zeps, V. J. "Computer research in psy-

cholinguistics: Towards an analysis of poetic language."
Behavior Science 6 (1961): 365–369.

Sedelow, S. Y. & Sedelow, W. A., Jr. "Categories and
procedures for content analysis in the humanities." In *The
analysis of communication content,* edited by G. Gerbner et al.
New York: Wiley, 1969. Pp. 487–499.

Segall, M. H., Campbell, D. T., & Herskovits, M. J. *The
influence of culture on visual perception.* Indianapolis: Bobbs-
Merrill, 1966. Pp. 37–41.

Seligman, E. R. A., ed. *Encyclopedia of social sciences.* New York:
Macmillan, 1935.

Severin, F. T., ed. *Humanistic viewpoints in psychology: A book of
readings.* New York: McGraw-Hill, 1965.

Sewter, A. C. "The possibilities of a sociology of art."
Sociological Review (London) 27 (1935): 441–453.

Shapiro, R. J. "The criterion problem." In *Creativity,* edited
by P. E. Vernon. Baltimore: Penguin, 1970. Pp. 257–269.

Sherwin, J. S. "Social and psychological assumptions about
human behavior in selected literary works." Ph.D. dissertation, New York University, 1954. Abstract: *Dissertation
Abstracts* 15 (1955): 245–246.

Shils, E. A. & Janowitz, M. "Cohesion and disintegration
in the Wehrmacht in World War II." In *Reader in opinion and
communication,* edited by B. Berelson & M. Janowitz.
Glencoe, Ill.: Free Press, 1953. Pp. 407–422.

Shoben, E. J. "Psychological theory construction and the
psychologist." *Journal of General Psychology* 52 (1955): 181–
188.

Shrodes, C., Gundy, J. V., & Husband, R. W., eds. *Psychology through literature: An anthology.* New York: Oxford, 1964.

Siegel, C. "Figures and similes in Schopenhauer; a contribution to the psychology of philosophical and literary
form." *Psychological Abstracts* 2 (1928) #1022

Sills, D. L., ed. *International encyclopedia of the social sciences.* New
York: Macmillan & Free Press, 1968.

Simonov, P. "Dostoevsky as a social scientist." *Psychology
Today* 5 (1971): 59–61, 102–106.

Singer, D. G. "Piglet, Pooh, & Piaget." *Psychology Today* 6 (1972): 71–74, 96.

Sinnott, E. W. "The creativeness of life." In *Creativity and its cultivation,* edited by H. H. Anderson. New York: Harper, 1959.

Skager, R. W., Schultz, C. B., & Klein, S. P. "Points of view about preference as tools in the analysis of creative products." *Perceptual and Motor Skills* 22 (1966): 83–94.

Skaggs, E. B. "The limitations of scientific psychology as an applied or practical science." *Psychological Review* 41 (1934): 572–576.

Skard, S. "The use of color in literature: A survey of research." *Proceedings of the American Philosophical Society* 90 (1946): 163–249.

Skinner, B. F. "The alliteration in Shakespeare's sonnets: A study in literary behavior." *Psychological Record* 3 (1939): 186–192.

_____. "A quantitative estimate of certain types of sound patterning in poetry." *American Journal of Psychology* 54 (1941): 64–79.

_____. "Has Gertrude Stein a secret?" In *Cumulative record,* by B. F. Skinner. Rev. ed. New York: Appleton-Century-Crofts, 1959. Pp. 261–271.

_____. *Walden two.* New York: Macmillan, 1966. (Original 1948.)

Slochower, H. "The psychoanalytic approach to literature: Some pitfalls and promises." *Literature and Psychology* 21 (1971): 107–110.

Smith, B. H. "Literature as performance, fiction, and art." *Journal of Philosophy* 67 (1970): 553–563.

Smith, R. A., ed. *Aesthetics and criticism in art education: Problems in defining, examining, and evaluating art.* Chicago: Rand McNally, 1966.

Smith, S. Review of *Psychoanalysis and literary process,* edited by F. Crews. *Contemporary Psychology* 16 (1971): 207–210.

Snow, C. P. *The two cultures and the scientific revolution.* New York: Cambridge, 1959.

Sorensen, R. C. & Sorensen, T. C. "A proposal for the use of content analysis in literary infringement cases." *Social Forces* 33 (1955): 262–267.

Sparshott, F. E. *The structure of aesthetics.* Toronto: University of Toronto, 1963.

Sperber, M. A. "Sensory deprivation in autoscopic illusion, and Joseph Conrad's 'The secret sharer.' " *Psychiatric Quarterly* 43 (1969): 711–718.

Spurgeon, C. F. E. *Shakespeare's imagery and what it tells us.* London: Cambridge, 1952. (Original 1935.)

Squires, P. C. "The creative psychology of César Franck." *Character and Personality* 7 (1938): 41–49.

Starch, D. "The 100 greatest books selected by 100 qualified persons." *Journal of Applied Psychology* 26 (1942): 257–267.

Stegner, W. "One way to spell man." *Saturday Review* 41 (1958): 8–44.

Stephenson, W. "Critique of content analysis." *Psychological Record* 13 (1963): 155–162.

Stoetzer, C. *Postage stamps as propaganda.* Washington, D. C.: Public Affairs Press, 1953.

Stone, A. A. & Stone, S. S., eds. *The abnormal personality through literature.* Englewood Cliffs, N. J.: Prentice-Hall, 1966.

Stuwart, I. R. "Personality dynamics and objectionable art: Attitudes, opinions, and experimental evidence." *Journal of Art Education* 4 (1970): 101–116.

Sutich, A. J. & Vich, M. A., eds. *Readings in humanistic psychology.* New York: Free Press, 1969.

Swartz, P. "Perspectives in psychology. VII. The criteria of validity in observational analysis." *Psychological Record* 8 (1958): 77–85.

_____. "Perspectives in psychology. IX. Literature as art and as knowledge." *Psychological Record* 9 (1959): 7–10.

_____. "A rose for behaviorism." *Psychological Reports* 27 (1970): 364.

Taviss, I. "Changes in the form of alienation: The 1900's vs. the 1950's." *American Sociological Review* 34 (1969): 46–57.

Taylor, C. W., ed. *Widening horizons in creativity.* New York: Wiley, 1964.

Taylor, G. O. *The passages of thought: Psychological representation in the American novel 1870–1900.* New York: Oxford, 1969.

Taylor, R. G., Jr. "Qualitative vs. quantitative methods in scientific research." *Human Potential* 1 (1968): 85–87.

Taylor, W. L. " 'Cloze procedure': A new tool for measuring readability." *Journalism Quarterly* 30 (1953): 415–433.

————. "Recent developments in the use of 'Cloze procedure.' " *Journalism Quarterly* 33 (1956): 42–48.

Teagarten, F. M. "Some psychological trends in modern literature." *Kadelpian Review* 9 (1930): 309–322.

Terman, L. M. "Psychological approaches to the study of genius." *Papers on Eugenics* 4 (1947): 3–20. Also reprinted in *Creativity,* edited by P. E. Vernon. Baltimore: Penguin, 1972.

Thompson, S. "Advances in folklore studies." In *Anthropology today,* edited by A. L. Kroeber. Chicago: University of Chicago, 1953. Pp. 587–596.

Thurstone, L. L. "A scale of measuring attitudes toward the movies." *Journal of Educational Research* 22 (1930): 93–94.

Toffler, A. "The art of measuring the arts." *Journal of Art Education* 4 (1970): 53–72.

Toulmin, S. "Seventeenth century science and the arts." In *Seventeenth century science and the arts,* edited by H. H. Rhys. Princeton, N. J.: Princeton University, 1961. Pp. 3–28.

Trevor-Roper, P. *The world through blunted sight: An inquiry into the influence of defective vision on art and character.* Indianapolis: Bobbs-Merrill, 1970.

Truzzi, M. & Morris, S. "Sherlock Holmes as a social scientist." *Psychology Today* 5 (1971): 62–64, 85–87.

Tsanoff, R. A. "On the psychology of poetic imagination." *American Journal of Psychology* 25 (1914): 528–537.

Tufte, E. R., ed. *The quantitative analysis of social problems.* Reading, Mass.: Addison-Wesley, 1970.

Tyler, F. B. "Knowledgeable respondents: Private club or public service?" *American Psychologist* 27 (1972): 191–196.

Underwood, B. J. *Psychological research.* New York: Appleton-Century-Crofts, 1957.

Valentine, C. W. "The function of images in the appreciation of poetry." *British Journal of Psychology* 14 (1923): 164–191.

_____. *The experimental psychology of beauty.* London: Methuen, 1962.

Van De Castle, R. L. *The psychology of dreaming.* New York: General Learning Press, 1971.

Vernon, P. E., ed. *Creativity: Selected readings.* Baltimore: Penguin, 1970.

Vinacke, W. E. *The psychology of thinking.* New York: McGraw-Hill, 1952.

Voss, G. A. de & Hippler, A. A. "Cultural psychology: Comparative studies of human behavior." In *Handbook of Social Psychology,* edited by G. Lindzey & A. Aronson. 2nd ed. Reading, Mass.: Addison-Wesley, 1969. Vol. 4, pp. 323–359.

Vygotsky, L. S. *The psychology of art.* Cambridge, Mass.: M.I.T., 1971. (Original 1925.)

Wakefield, D. F. "Art historians and art critics—VIII: Proust and the visual arts." *Burlington Magazine* 112 (1970): 291–296.

Walk, R. D. "Concept formation and art: Basic experiment and controls." *Psychonomic Science* 9 (1967): 237–238.

Wallach, M. A. "Art, science, and representation: Toward an experimental psychology of aesthetics." *Journal of Aesthetics and Art Criticism* 18 (1959): 159–173.

Wallach, M. A. & Kogan, N. *Modes of thinking in young children: A study of the creativity-intelligence distinction.* New York: Holt, Rinehart & Winston, 1965. Chap. 8.

Wallas, G. "The art of thought." In *Creativity,* edited by P. E. Vernon. Baltimore: Penguin, 1970. Pp. 91–97.

Waples, D. "The relation of subject interest to actual reading." In *Reader in opinion and communication,* edited by B. Berelson & M. Janowitz. Glencoe, Ill.: Free Press, 1953. Pp. 347–351.

Waples, D., Berelson, B., & Bradshaw, F. R. *What reading does to people.* Chicago: University of Chicago, 1940.

Warner, W. L. & Henry, W. E. "The radio day-time serial: A symbolic analysis." In *Reader in opinion and communication,* edited by B. Berelson & M. Janowitz. Glencoe, Ill.: Free Press, 1953. Pp. 423–437.

Washburn, M. F., Hatt, E., & Holt, E. B. "Affective sensitiveness in poets and in scientific students." *American Journal of Psychology* 34 (1923): 105–106.

Watt, I. "Literature and society." In *The arts in society,* edited by R. N. Wilson. Englewood Cliffs, N. J.: Prentice-Hall, 1964. Pp. 299–314.

_____. "Robinson Crusoe as a myth." In *The arts in society,* edited by R. N. Wilson, Englewood Cliffs, N. J.: Prentice-Hall, 1964. Pp. 148–174.

Wayne, I. "American and Soviet themes and values: A content analysis of pictures in popular magazines." *Public Opinion Quarterly* 20 (1956): 314–320.

Webb, E. & Roberts, K. H. "Unconventional uses of content analysis in social science." In *The analysis of communication content,* edited by G. Gerbner et al. New York: Wiley, 1969. Pp. 319–332.

Webb, E. J., Campbell, D. T., Schwartz, R. D., & Sechrest, L. *Unobtrusive measures: Nonreactive research in the social sciences.* Chicago: Rand McNally, 1966.

Weisgerber, C. A. "Accuracy in judging emotional expressions as related to understanding of literature." *Journal of Social Psychology* 46 (1957): 253–258.

Weiss, W. "Effects of the mass media on communication." In *The handbook of social psychology,* edited by G. Lindzey & E. Aronson. Vol. 5. Reading, Mass.: Addison-Wesley, 1969.

Weitz, M. *Hamlet and the philosophy of literary criticism.* Chicago: University of Chicago, 1964.

_____, **ed.** *Problems in aesthetics: An introductory book of readings.* New York: Macmillan, 1959.

Wellek, R. & Warren A. *Theory of literature.* New York: Harcourt, Brace, 1942.

Wells, F. L. "A statistical study of literary merit." *Archives of Psychology* 17 (1907) #7.

Werner, H. "On physiognomic perception." In *The new landscape in art and science,* edited by G. Kepes. Chicago: Paul Theobald, 1956. Pp. 280–282.

———, **ed.** *On expressive behavior.* Worcester, Mass.: Clark University, 1955.

Wescott, M. R. "Empirical studies of intuition." In *Widening horizons in creativity,* edited by C. W. Taylor. New York: Wiley, 1964. Pp. 34–53.

Whipple, L. "Sat Eve Post." *Journalism Quarterly* 5 (1928): 20–30.

White, R. K. "The versatility of genius." *Journal of Social Psychology* 2 (1931): 460–489.

———. "Black boy: A value-analysis." *American Psychologist* 2 (1947): 269.

———. "Black boy: A value-analysis." *Journal of Abnormal and Social Psychology* 42 (1947): 440–461.

———. *Value-analysis: The nature and use of the method.* N.p.: Society for the Psychological Study of Social Issues, 1951.

Wickens, D. D. "Encoding categories of words: An empirical approach to meaning." *Psychological Review* 77 (1970): 1–16.

Wiebe, G. "The effects of radio plugging on students' opinion of popular songs." *Journal of Applied Psychology* 24 (1940): 721–727.

Wilding, J. M. & Ferrell, J. M. "Selective attention: Superior detection of word targets with sound targets in a prose passage while shadowing another passage." *Psychonomic Science* 9 (1970): 123–124.

Willems, E. P. & Raush, H. L., eds. *Naturalistic viewpoints in psychological research.* New York: Holt, Rinehart, Winston, 1969.

Williams, C. B. "A note on the statistical analysis of sentence-length as a criterion of literary style." *Biometrika* 31 (1940): 356–361.

_____. "Statistics as an aid to literary studies." *Science News* 24 (1952): 99–106.

Williams, J. H. "Attitudes of college students toward motion pictures." *School and Society* 38 (1939): 222–224.

Wilson, B. "Relationships among art teachers', art critics', and historians', and non-art trained individuals' statements about *Guernica.*" *Studies in Art Education* 12 (1970): 31–39.

Wilson, E. C. "The listening audience." In *Communication in modern society,* edited by W. Schramm. Urbana, Ill.: University of Illinois, 1948. Pp. 117–125.

Wilson, R. N. "Literature, society, and personality." *Journal of Aesthetics and Art Criticism* 10 (1952): 297–309.

_____. "Poetic creativity: Process and personality." *Psychiatry* 17 (1954): 163–176.

_____. "Literary experience and personality." *Journal of Aesthetics and Art Criticism* 14 (1956): 47–57.

_____. "F. Scott Fitzgerald: Personality and culture." In *The arts in society,* edited by R. N. Wilson. Englewood Cliffs, N. J.: Prentice-Hall, 1964. Pp. 271–298.

_____. "The poet in American society." In *The arts in society,* edited by R. N. Wilson. Englewood Cliffs, N. J.: Prentice-Hall, 1964. Pp. 1–34.

_____. "Samuel Beckett: The social psychology of emptiness." *Journal of Social Issues* 20 (1964): 62–70.

_____. Review of *Dreams, life, and literature: A study of Franz Kafka,* by C. S. Hall & R. E. Lind. *Contemporary Psychology* 15 (1970): 596–597.

_____, ed. *The arts in society.* Englewood Cliffs, N. J.: Prentice-Hall, 1964.

Winick, C. "Trends in the occupations of celebrities: A study of news-magazine profiles and television interviews." *Journal of Social Psychology* 60 (1963): 301–310.

Withim, P. "The psychodynamics of literature." *Psychoanalytic Review* 56 (1969/1970): 556–585.

Witkin, H. A., Lewis, H. B., Herrtzman, M., Machover, K., Meissner, P. B., & Wapner, S. *Personality through perception.* New York: Harper, 1954.

Witte, W. "The sociological approach to literature." *Modern Language Review* 36 (1941): 86–94.

Wolfenstein, M. & Leites, N. *Movies—A psychological study.* Glencoe, Ill.: Free Press, 1950.

Wolman, B. B. *Contemporary theories and systems in psychology.* New York: Harper, 1960.

———. "Poetry and psychotherapy." *Voices* 6 (1970): 56–59.

Wood, A. B. "Psychodynamics through literature." *American Psychologist* 10 (1955): 32–33.

Woodrow, H. "The effect of type of training upon transference." *Journal of Educational Psychology* 18 (1927): 159–172.

Wyatt, B. N. "John Updike: The psychological novel in search of structure." *Twentieth Century Literature* 13 (1967): 89–96.

Wyatt, F. "A psychologist looks at history." *Journal of Social Issues* 7 (1961): 66–77.

———. "Psychology and the humanities: A case of no-relationship." In *Challenges of humanistic psychology,* edited by J. F. T. Bugental. New York: McGraw-Hill, 1961. Pp. 291–301.

Wyschogrod, M. "Art and life in art therapy." In *Aisthesis and aesthetics,* edited by E. W. Strauss & R. M. Griffith. Pittsburgh: Duquesne, 1970. Pp. 342–348.

Yarbus, A. L. *Eye movements and vision.* New York: Plenum, 1967.

Yule, G. U. *The statistical study of literary vocabulary.* London: Cambridge, 1944.

———. "Brainwash: Familiarity breeds comfort." *Psychology Today* 3 (1970): 33–62.

Zajonc, R. B. "Attitudinal effects of mere exposure." *Journal of Personality and Social Psychology Monograph Supplements* 9, no. 2, part 2 (1968): 1–27.

Zbaracki, R. J. "A curriculum design based on cognitive psychology for teaching narrative and dramatic literature in the secondary school." Ph.D. dissertation, University of Nebraska, 1970. Abstract: *Dissertation Abstract* 31 (1970) #1700-A.

Zener, K. & Gaffron, M. "Perceptual experience: An analysis of its relations to the external world through internal processing." In *Psychology: A study of a science,* edited by S. Koch. New York: McGraw-Hill, 1962. Vol. 4. Pp. 516–618.

Zoellner, R. "Talk-write: A behavioral pedagogy for composition." *College English* 30 (1969): 267–320.

Additional References

General discussions of science, art, and methodology (chapter 4)
Borroff, M. "Creativity, poetic language, and the computer." *Yale Review* 60 (1972): 481–513.
Child, I. L. *Humanistic psychology and the research tradition: Their several virtues.* New York: Wiley, 1973.
Jones, W. P. *The rhetoric of science: A study of scientific ideas and imagery in eighteenth-century English poetry.* Berkeley, Calif.: University of California, 1966.
Kuhns, R. *Structure and experience: Essays on the affinity between philosophy and literature.* New York: Basic Books, 1971.
Lyons, J. *Experience: An introduction to a personal psychology.* New York: Harper & Row, 1973.
Richardson, J. A. *Modern art and scientific thought.* Urbana, Ill.: University of Illinois, 1971.
Salm, P. *The poem as a plant: A biological view of Goethe's Faust.* Cleveland: Case Western Reserve, 1971.
Walsh, D. "The question of relevance in literature." *Journal of Aesthetics and Education* 10 (1972): 29–38.

Discussions relating psychology and literature (chapters 3 and 5)
Brooks, G. P. "The behaviorally abnormal in early Irish folklore." *Papers in Psychology* 5 (1971): 5–11.

Chanover, E. P. "Marcel Proust: A medical and psychoanalytical bibliography." *Psychoanalytic Review* 56 (1969 –70): 638–641.

Doederlein, S. W. "A compendium of wit: The psychological vocabulary of John Dryden's literary criticism." Ph.D. dissertation. Northwestern University, 1970. Abstract: *Dissertation Abstracts International* 31 (1972): 779–783.

Jung, J. "Autobiographies of college students as a teaching and research tool in the study of personality development." *American Psychologist* 27 (1972): 779–783.

Kirchner, J. H. "Psychology of the scientist: XXIX. Consider this: A psycholiterary study of *Walden two.*" *Psychological Reports* 26 (1970): 403–412.

McLaughlin, J. J. & Ansbocher, R. R. "Sane Ben Franklin: An Adlerian view of his autobiography." *Journal of Individual Psychology* 27 (1971): 189–207.

Michael, L. "The genesis of the American psychological novel." Ph.D. dissertation. University of Maryland, 1969. Abstract: *Dissertation Abstracts International* 31 (1970): 352.

Nadel, B. S. & Altrocchi, J. "Attribution of hostile content in literature." *Psychological Reports* 25 (1969): 747–763.

Stark, S. "Toward a psychology of knowledge: VI. The sublime, the mystical, and inner creative." *Perceptual and Motor Skills* 27 (1968): 767–786.

_____. "Suggestion regarding drama, inner creation, and role-taking (empathy): I. Dramatic arts and dramatic dreaming." *Perceptual and Motor Skills* 26 (1968): 1319–1346.

Stern, A. "Further considerations on Alfred Adler and Ortega y Gasset." *Journal of Individual Psychology* 27 (1971): 139–143.

Stites, R. S. "Alfred Adler on Leonardo Da Vinci." *Journal of Individual Psychology* 27 (1971): 208–212.

Waldman, R. D. "Convergence of concepts of Adler and Ortega y Gasset." *Journal of Individual Psychology* 27 (1971): 135–138.

Empirical studies:
A. Sociological (chapter 6)

Goodchilds, J. D. "On being witty: Causes, correlates, and consequences." In *The psychology of humor,* edited by J. D. Goldstein & P. E. McGhee. New York: Academic Press, 1972. Pp. 173–193.

Goodlad, J. S. R. *A sociology of popular drama.* Totowa, N. J.: Rowman & Littlefield, 1971.

Korten, David C. & Korten, Francis F. *Planned change in a traditional society: Psychological problems of modernization in Ethiopia.* New York: Praeger, 1972.

Pollio, H. R., Mers, R. & Lucchesi, W. "Humor, laughter, and smiling: Some preliminary observation of funny behavior." In *The psychology of humor,* edited by J. D. Goldstein & P. E. McGhee. New York: Academic Press, 1972. Pp. 211–239.

B. The author (chapter 7)

Koch, K. *Wishes, lies, and dreams: Teaching children to write poetry.* New York: Chelsea, 1970.

Maier, N. R. F., Julius, M. & Thurber, J. "Studies in creativity: Individual differences in the storing and utilization of information." *American Journal of Psychology* 80 (1967): 492–519.

Pine, F. "Thematic drive content and creativity." *Journal of Personality* 27 (1959): 136–151.

Smith, M. "The mobility of eminent men." *Sociology and Social Research* 22 (1938): 452–461.

C. The literary work (chapter 8)

Agnew, M. "The auditory imagery of great composers." *Psychological Monographs* 31 (1922): 279–287.

Beshai, James. "Content analysis of Egyptian stories." *Journal of Social Psychology* 87 (1972): 197–203.

Kreitler, H. & Kreitler, S. *Psychology and the arts.* Durham, N. C.: Duke, 1972. Chap. 11.

Lorge, J. "Estimating structure in prose." In *Testing problems* *in perspective,* edited by A. Anastasi. Washington, D. C.: American Council on Education, 1966.

Stephenson, W. "Applications of communication theory: Interpretation of Keats' 'Ode on a Grecian urn.' " *Psychological Record* 22 (1972): 177–192.

Tedford, W. H., Jr. & Synnott, C. S. "Use of the semantic differential with poetic forms." *Psychological Record* 22 (1972): 369–373.

D. The reader (chapter 8)

Ausubel, D. P. & Schwartz, F. G. "The effects of a generalizing-particularizing dimension of cognitive style on the retention of prose material." *Journal of General Psychology* 87 (1972): 55–58.

French, J. W. "Schools of thought in judging excellence of English themes." In *Testing problems in perspective,* edited by A. Anastasi. Washington, D. C.: American Council on Education, 1966.

Rothkopf, E. Z. "Incidental memory for location of information in text." *Journal of Verbal Learning and Verbal Behavior* 10 (1971): 608–613.

Wheeler, O. A. "An analysis of literary appreciation." *British Journal of Psychology* 13 (1923): 229–242.

Subject Index

Actor, 15, 38; personality changes in, 160

Aesthetics, 1, 7, 8–11, 36, 53; beauty and, 1, 9–10; criteria of, 10; and education, 10, 13; experimental, 10; formula for, 151; goals of, 171; liberalization of experimental, 181; in nature, 44; reviews of, 10–11; as structural response, 151; value of, 78. *See also* Science, and aesthetics

Age, and literary productivity, 116. *See also* Birth order

Aging, descriptions of, 67

Analogies. *See* Metaphor

Appreciation. *See* Preferences

Architects, 120

Art, 10–11, 13, 16, 25, 30, 182, 184; goals of, 43; studies of, relevant to literature, 186

Artist, the, 11, 46, 79; studies of, 144–146

Arts, the, 1, 8, 10

Associationism. *See* British empiricism and associationism

Attention, 15, 68; and structure of prose, 161. *See also* Perception; Thinking

Attitudes, 37, 91; toward life and death, in quotes, 143–144; toward quantitative concepts, in quotes, 142. *See also* Social psychology

Audience, the, 19, 36, 58, 89, 99. *See also* Reader, the

Author, the. *See* Writer, the

Authorship, 58; disputes of, 154–155

Autobiography. *See* Biography

Beauty. *See* Aesthetics, beauty and

Behavior, study of, 6

Behaviorism. *See* Theories; Behaviorism

Best sellers, 91, 95, 163–164; age at which produced, 117; vs. classics, 90,

180–181. *See also* Fiction; Novel, the

Bible, 71, 153–155, 163

Biography, 22, 38, 58, 69, 73, 76, 90, 102, 116; of creative people, 69, 124–126; and historical-political context, 90; and novels, 130–131; and personality, 113–114; psychoanalytic use of, 113–114; psychological use of, 113–114; and reader characteristics, 163–164; and talented people, 112–114. *See also* Creativity, and biography

Birth order, scientists, writers, and poets, 118. *See also* Age, and literary productions

Book clubs, 163; and marketing, 57. *See also* Book publishing industry

Book publishing industry, 93. *See also* Book clubs

British empiricism and associationism, 3–4, 36

Cartoon characters, 91

Children, 72; gifted, 111; literature for, 67; need for achievement of, in primers, 141; story writing of, 135–136

Cliché, the, 30, 147, 181

Cognition. *See* Thinking

Complexity. *See* Preference, and complexity

Computer, 54, 56, 58–59. *See also* Statistics

Consciousness. *See* Experience

Content analysis, 11, 57–60, 94, 132; critiques of, 58–62; of films, 100–101; social science use of, 102. *See also* Methodology

Correlational data, 57, 132, 179; linear or curvilinear, 162. *See also* Experimental psychology, vs. descriptive and correlational data; Methodology

Creative people, 124–125; artistic vs. nonartistic types of, 134–135; artistic

Name Index